Clinical Aspects of Sexual Harassment and Gender Discrimination

Clinical Aspects of Sexual Harassment and Gender Discrimination

Psychological Consequences
and Treatment Interventions

SHARYN ANN LENHART, M.D.

Brunner-Routledge
Taylor & Francis Group

NEW YORK AND HOVE

Published in 2004 by
Brunner-Routledge
29 West 35th Street
New York, NY 10001
www.brunner-routledge.com

Published in Great Britain by
Brunner-Routledge
27 Church Road
Hove, East Sussex
BN3 2FA
www.brunner-routledge.co.uk

Brunner-Routledge is an imprint of the Taylor & Francis Group.
Printed in the United States of America on acid-free paper.

10 9 8 7 6 5 4 3 2 1

Library of Congress Cataloging-in-Publication Data

*To my father, C. Laird Lenhart, who taught me to love the workplace
and to call a spade a spade.*

*To my premed adviser, Herbert S. Rhinesmith, PhD, who supported
women as physicians before it was politically correct
or legally mandated.*

*To my friend, Michael Babchuck, who committed himself to gender
equity as a labor consultant and a teacher.*

*To my husband, Lloyd Franklin Price, MD, who has provided
a consistent sense of caring and respect for me and for this project.*

*To my daughters, Allison and Heather Price, who represent the talent,
energy, and commitment of the next generation of working women.*

Contents

Acknowledgments

Warm appreciation and respect are extended to Rosanne LaBree, Lyn Dietrick, Pam Hastings, Elaine Martin, Peg Spinner, and Jeff Long for their research assistance; to George Zimmar, PhD, and Shannon Vargo for their editorial expertise; and to Patti Brown, Karen Adams, and especially Elaine Baril, for their assistance in the preparation of this manuscript. Thanks to colleagues Freda Klein, PhD; Diane Schrier, MD; Jess McCutchen, PhD; Cathy Ragovin, MD; and attorney Dahlia Rudavsky for contributing clinical and theoretical expertise. Greatest appreciation is extended to my daughters, Allison and Heather Price, and to my husband, Dr. Lloyd Price, who generously supported me through this lengthy project.

CHAPTER 1

Introduction and Overview

A Clinical Perspective of Sexual Harassment and Gender
     Discrimination
Political and Historical Perspectives
Definitions
Scope and Purpose
Structure and Content

A CLINICAL PERSPECTIVE
OF SEXUAL HARASSMENT
AND GENDER DISCRIMINATION

A clinically oriented book focusing on the diagnostic understanding and treatment of the mental and physical health consequences of sexual harassment and other significant forms of gender discrimination in work and educational settings is both ahead of schedule and woefully late. It is ahead in the sense that the psychiatric symptomatology, the psychological sequelae, and the treatment interventions that will be described are aimed at a serious mental health problem, one that has been both incompletely defined and underrecognized as a health problem. As a result, the solid body of empirical research that should be available as a framework for discussion is relatively new, relatively scarce, and limited almost entirely to sexual harassment, which constitutes only one of the many forms of psychologically damaging gender-based discrimination. It is woefully late in the sense that little has been written about treatment interventions for gender discrimination, even though women have been entering the workplace in large numbers that have been documented since the 1970s; exposing themselves to various forms of gender discrimination, whose prevalence has been well documented since the 1980s; and experiencing negative psychological consequences that have been well documented since the early 1990s.

POLITICAL AND HISTORICAL PERSPECTIVES

The origins of this dilemma lie in the political history of these issues. Sexual harassment and other forms of gender-based employment and academic discrimination are not new phenomena. Historical accounts of discriminatory behaviors toward working women date back to colonial times. Foner (1947) cites a notice published in the *New York Weekly Journal* in 1734 by a group of female domestic servants protesting their employment conditions. Bularzik (1978) and Fitzgerald (1993) cite many examples from the Industrial Revolution. A popular account of what now would be termed sexual harassment even appeared in *Harper's Bazaar* in 1908 (Bratton, 1987).

Despite such long-standing evidence of discriminatory behaviors, these phenomena remained unidentified elements of the work and academic environments that were deeply embedded into the culture but at the same time obscured from view (Wood, 1992). Both Miller (1976) and Wood (1992) have observed that those in power have the prerogative to define the world from their own perspective and thus both consciously and unconsciously exclude the experience of their subordinates. Because those in power seldom suffer the adverse effects of gender-based discrimination, it is not surprising that these phenomena remained unnamed and unexamined aspects of the work and academic environments. It required the political force of the Civil Rights Movement of the 1960s to provide a meaningful definition of gender discrimination. At that time sex discrimination was defined as an illegal act, along with discrimination related to race, color, religion, and national origin, as stated in the Civil Rights Act of 1964. Ironically, but perhaps prophetically, sex discrimination was not included initially because it was not considered a serious problem. Instead, a southern congressman opposing the bill included sex discrimination in it, hoping that the "ludicrousness" of such an addition would help defeat the bill (Roth, 1993).

In a similar manner, sexual harassment as a specific form of gender discrimination was defined during the 1970s Women's Movement, which focused attention on various forms of sexual violence against women. Once these phenomena were identified as political inequities requiring legal redress, a group of seminal legal and social science scholars began academic exploration of them, developing a theoretical framework within which current scholars continue to work. Widespread public knowledge of these issues remained obscure, however, until the highly publicized Clarence Thomas Supreme Court Confirmation Hearings, during which Anita Hill provided national televised testimony that included graphic descriptions of sexual harassment. Shortly thereafter, a proliferation of complex specialized prevalence studies focusing primarily on sexual harassment emerged from a broad spectrum of employment and academic settings (e.g., law, medicine, business, nursing, library science, and law enforcement), as well as from a broad spectrum of people who were victimized (e.g., university faculty and students, government employees, union workers, middle and high school students, health-care professionals, and lawyers). Although the studies varied greatly with regard to both methodology and behaviors studied, outcomes consistently documented that sexual harassment as a particular form of sex discrimination is prevalent, underreported, and associated with adverse outcomes to both individuals and institutions (Stockdale, 1996). Unfortunately, similar studies focusing on other forms of sex discrimination or on the interaction of sexual harassment and other forms of gender discrimination are currently in scarce supply.

Legal activity proliferated in parallel to social science and management research. An impressive body of case law further documented: (1) the nature of discriminatory actions, and (2) the extent of liability and damages (see Chapter 3 for legal history). Studies in the last decade have become more sophisticated with regard to delineating characteristics of harasser-victim interactions and documenting negative psychological sequelae, but again primarily with regard to sexual harassment. Nonetheless, the public in general, as well as most clinicians, still regard sex discrimination as a legal, rather than a health, issue. Physicians and mental health professionals often neglect to take work histories on women patients or clients. Large-scale well-designed studies focused on sexual harassment and other forms of gender discrimination are lacking. Specific studies on physical and mental health consequences are even more rare but are emerging. Research has typically been unfunded and pragmatically opportunistic, focusing on specific issues that were easily isolated. The dilemma presented by the lack of response by large funding organizations is well illustrated by the following vignette.

CASE VIGNETTE 1-1

Funding Organization's Bias Regarding Sex Discrimination Research

A faculty member at a prestigious university was approached with a proposal by a research team working for a national funding organization. She had just published a small sexual harassment study dealing with a specialized group of employees. The research team had inadvertently discovered similar results embedded in a large-scale study of employee attitudes and experiences in the workplace. The team encouraged the faculty member to submit a grant proposal to its organization for a large-scale sexual harassment study focusing on prevalence, health, and attitudinal outcomes. In collaboration with the research team, she submitted the proposal 3 months later but received no formal response from the research funding organization. Eight months later, she telephoned a member of the research team to inquire about the proposal. The researcher explained with embarrassment that the board had dismissed the proposal as insignificant, against the recommendations of its own research team and without the customary review process. He commented, "Our board just didn't want to see this as a legitimate issue worthy of research."

DEFINITIONS

For people to understand the mental health consequences of sexual harassment and gender discrimination, appropriate definitions must be provided.

Individuals victimized by gender discrimination need terminology to validate and process their experiences, to communicate their experiences to significant others, to obtain support and redress, and to cope with their experiences and stabilize their psychological equilibrium. Professionals and others wishing to understand the psychological consequences of gender discrimination need terminology in order to communicate effectively with victimized individuals, as well as other colleagues; to pursue studies and other scholarly pursuits; and to process the significance of these events in the broader organizational, legal and social, psychological, and ethical arenas. For this purpose, the terms (1) *gender* and *sex,* (2) *gender bias,* (3) *gender/sex discrimination,* and

(4) *sexual harassment* are defined both succinctly with regard to their use in this text and broadly with regard to their evolving meaning in relation to psychological consequences.

GENDER AND SEX: *Sex* refers to biological distinctions between males and females, based on differences in anatomy and physiology. *Gender* refers to the personal characteristics, abilities, and interests that are culturally assigned and socially constructed differently between the two sexes. Although conceptually distinct, sex and gender are intricately intertwined because gender characteristics are assigned based on whether one is born male or female. Scientists continue to argue regarding which characteristics are biologically innate and which are socially constructed. Burrell and Hearn (1989) provide a framework for these interrelations by conceptualizing sexuality and gender as follows: (1) biological essences, (2) outcomes of social roles, (3) fundamental political categories, and (4) communication practices and discourses of power. This broader definition is more relevant to understanding some of the psychological consequences of discrimination. Because of the current inherent difficulties in making distinctions between the terms of *gender* and *sex* and because they are often used interchangeably in the literature, they will be used interchangeably in this text.

GENDER BIAS: This is a term referring to situations in which some aspects of the work or educational experience differ based on the sex of the worker or student. The impact of this difference may be positive, negative, or neutral. Example 1—Neutral Impact: Waiters at a restaurant are required to wear black bow ties and trousers. Waitresses are required to wear red bow ties and trousers. Example 2—Negative Impact: Waiters and waitresses are both required to wear white T-shirts and black shorts, but female waitresses are required to wear T-shirts one size too small in order to emphasize their figures. Example 3— Positive Impact: Male and female waitstaff are assigned to different sections of a hotel restaurant. The female staff ends up working the bar restaurant, which is frequented by business clients who tend to leave significantly larger tips than other clients.

GENDER OR SEX DISCRIMINATION: This term refers to the types of gender bias that have a negative impact. The term has legal, as well as theoretical and psychological, definitions. Psychological consequences can be more readily inferred from the latter, but both definitions are of significance. Theoretically, gender discrimination has been described as (1) the unequal rewards that men and women receive in the workplace or academic environment because of their gender or sex differences (DiThomaso, 1989); (2) a process occurring in work or educational settings in which an individual is overtly or covertly limited access to an opportunity or a resource because of sex or is given the opportunity or the resource reluctantly and may face harassment for picking it (Roeske & Pleck, 1983); or (3) both. This latter definition includes the social forces that inhibit individuals from fully seeking appropriate lawful and educational work experiences outside those that are culturally defined as appropriate for their sex. Roeske and Pleck contend that this constitutes discrimination because these individuals are banned from opportunities and resources as effectively as if they had applied for and then been declined in the employment or the academic market. Theoretically, both men and women can experience sex discrimination; however, most in-house complaints, legal cases, and documented psychological consequences have reportedly involved women who were victimized. For this reason we will be dealing with the psychological consequences of victimized women in this text, unless otherwise specified.

The legal definition of sex discrimination is more limited than the theoretical concepts discussed thus far. Legally, sex discrimination can be proved if pervasive patterns of disparate treatment or disparate impact or the creation of a hostile environment can be documented to impact negatively upon a student or an employee of one sex as compared to the other. Sexual harassment, wage discrimination, and pregnancy discrimination are some of the most common forms of sexual discrimination brought to court (Women's Legal Defense Fund, 1988).

Disparate treatment refers to situations where men and women are treated differently in the workplace or in academia, based upon their sex. For example, two employees with the same educational credentials apply for a job. The man is routed to management training and the woman to the support staff pool. A man and a woman with comparable credentials apply for a position, and the woman is denied the job under the assumption that she does not need to support a family. A man and a woman assert themselves for a promotion, but the man's behavior is perceived positively as assertive and ambitious, whereas the woman's behavior is perceived negatively as pushy and unattractive.

Disparate impact refers to behaviors, policies, procedures, and so on, that appear neutral on the surface in the workplace but that have a differentially negative impact on one sex over the other. For example, if an academic or a business institution has a limited parental leave policy or a limited personal day policy, this will have a differentially negative impact on female workers as long as they continue to assume primary responsibility for household and child-rearing responsibilities. If an academic institution's tenure requirements place emphasis on a high output of publications and research during the first decade after graduate school, this will have a differentially negative impact on females who may need to reduce workloads for child-bearing purposes during this period but who have the capacity to increase productivity later in their professional work cycle, if given the opportunity.

A hostile environment refers to behaviors or other aspects of the work environment that make it hostile, offensive, intimidating, or abusive differentially to one sex or that occur as frequently or repetitively so as to alter the actual terms or conditions of employment, or both. A hostile environment does not require a power differential between the victimized person and the perpetrator. For example: (1) No private toilet facilities are provided on an offshore oil rig, so that the single female employee is forced to urinate in front of male coworkers in a way that is publicly humiliating; (2) Female medical students receive handouts during lectures that include crude anatomical drawings and devaluing comments about women; (3) Female students eating lunch in the school cafeteria are rated on attractiveness on scales of 1–10 by male students, and devaluing comments are made publicly regarding their bodies.

It is crucial to note that there are many forms of sex discrimination, as defined theoretically, that do not meet the criteria for sex discrimination, as defined legally. Serious psychological consequences can and do occur, independent of whether the legal criteria are met. For this reason, in this text the more expanded definition of gender discrimination, offered by Roeske and Pleck (1983), will be utilized, except in instances where specific references are made to the legal definition of sex discrimination.

SEXUAL HARASSMENT: Sexual harassment is the most widely studied and publicized form of sex discrimination, but ironically, it is a phenomenon with an evolving definition yet no universally agreed-upon operational terminology. Much of the complexity arises from the issue of differentiating the experience of sexual harassment from the perception of sexual harassment. Research has shown that people have different interpretations of the same experience (Stockdale, 1996). What follows, then, is a discussion of various concepts of harassment, with an emphasis both on the complexity of the issue and the psychological consequences that follow harassing experiences. Fitzgerald (1990) and Fitzgerald and Schullman (1993) divide definitions of sexual harassment into two broad categories: a priori and empirical. A priori definitions are derived from theoretical constructs and contain either a general statement regarding the nature of sexually harassing behaviors or specific lists of behaviors that constitute sexual harassment. Empirical definitions consist of lists of behaviors derived from databases developed through empirical investigations regarding what various groups of individuals perceive to be sexual harassment. The commonly accepted a priori definition of sexual harassment is contained in the Equal Employment Opportunity Commission (EEOC) guidelines, which provide the standard for legal and institutional definitions of sexual harassment in the United States. These guidelines state

> Unwelcome sexual advances, requests for sexual favors, and other verbal or physical conduct of a sexual nature constitute sexual harassment when (1) submission to such conduct is made either explicitly or implicitly a term or condition of an individual's employment, (2) submission to or rejection of such conduct by an individual is used as a basis for employment decisions affecting such individual, or (3) such conduct has the purpose or effect of substantially interfering with an individual's work performance or creating an intimidating, hostile, or offensive working environment. (Equal Employment Opportunity Commission, 1980)

The first two situations that are referred to in these guidelines relate to what MacKinnon (1979) refers to as "quid pro quo" harassment—harassment in which employment or academic opportunities or services are exchanged for sexual compliance. The exchange is coercive, in that the refusal to comply brings reprisal. The third section of the guidelines refers to situations where damage is created by a hostile environment, a term previously described.

Some well-known examples of empirical definitions of harassment were developed by Till (1980) and Fitzgerald et al. (1988). The psychometrically standardized definition reported by Fitzgerald et al. is similar to Till's definition and correlates well with the legal definition of harassment. It is composed of five levels of harassing behavior, defined as follows:

1. Gender harassment—generalized sexist remarks and behaviors not necessarily designed to elicit sexual cooperation but to communicate insulting, degrading, or sexist attitudes about women. (2) Seductive behaviors—inappropriate and offensive sexual advances. Although such behavior is unwanted and offensive there is no penalty explicitly attached to the woman's negative responses nor does this category include sexual bribery. (3) Sexual bribery—solicitation of sexual activities or other sexual behavior such as dating by promise of reward. (4) Sexual coercion—coercion of sexual activity or other sexual behavior by threat of punishment. (5) Sexual imposition—sexual imposition such as attempts to touch, kiss or grab, or actual sexual assault. (Fitzgerald, 1990, p. 34)

Empirical definitions such as these emphasize the importance of perception in defining harassment. Situational factors such as the severity of the conduct, the power differential between the person being victimized and the perpetrator, and the nature of prior interactions between the victimized person and the perpetrator consistently affect what is perceived as harassment (Stockdale, 1996). Individual characteristics of the perceiver also affect perception, with the gender of the perceiver being the single most important variable (Charney & Russell, 1994). Women consistently report perceived behaviors as harassing when men do not. This has led to the development of the reasonable woman or victim standard considered in some courtrooms and to the notion that liability is defined via the target's perspective. Forell (1993) discusses the evolution of this legal standard, and Paetzold and O'Leary-Kelly (1996) summarize the ambiguity and its current usage. Gutek (1993) discusses the perception of harassment in terms of the different rights and responsibilities perceived by groups of people representing different roles and viewpoints. For example, feminists, managers, and legal experts all emphasize different aspects of the harassing experience. Often the individual perceptions and reactions of the person who experienced harassment become lost in the conflicting viewpoints of others. The psychological consequences to the victimized individual are similarly obscured in these instances.

Both a priori and empirical definitions of harassment have limitations and may not correlate directly to psychological consequences. Fitzgerald (1990) offers the following solution in the form of a definition of harassment based on a combination of empirical and theoretical perspectives:

Sexual harassment consists of the sexualization of an instrumental relationship through the introduction or imposition of sexist or sexual remarks, requests or requirements, in the context of a formal power differential. Harassment can also occur where no such power differential exists, if the behavior is unwanted by or offensive to a woman. Instances of harassment can be classified into the following general categories: gender harassment, seductive behavior, and solicitation of sexual activity by promise of reward or threat of punishment, and sexual imposition or assault. (Fitzgerald, 1990, p. 39)

These five categories are often condensed to three: gender harassment, unwanted sexual attention, and sexual coercion (Fitzgerald, Gelfard & Drasgow, 1994).

This definition emphasizes the importance of the power differential and the victimized individual's response. These principles correlate better with psychological consequences and allow for the possibility of experiences that do not qualify as legal harassment but are psychologically damaging. This definition also implies that sexual harassment is a process, rather than an event, which is consistent with most research findings (Fitzgerald, 1990; Fitzgerald & Schullman, 1993). For these reasons, this more broad-based definition will be used within this text. More recently, Fitzgerald, Swan, and Mugley (1997) defined sexual harassment psychologically as "unwanted sex-related behavior at work that is appraised by the recipient as offensive, exceeding her resources, or threatening her well being" (p. 15). This definition will be utilized in addition in sections discussing mental health consequences and treatment. In chapters dealing specifically with the legal aspects of sexual harassment, the EEOC guidelines will be utilized.

The following case vignettes illustrate the clinical importance of properly defining these experiences in treatment.

CASE VIGNETTE 1-2

Defining Sexual Harassment Helps the Victimized Person to Cope

Jane Hood was a 55-year-old department store sales clerk who entered treatment for "extreme jitteriness." Her anxiety symptoms included sleeplessness, irritability, poor concentration, palpitations, tremulousness, cold extremities, and pervasive feelings of impending death. She had no sense of the source of her anxiety, noting only that the symptoms had appeared precipitously over the past month. Six weeks into treatment, she realized that her symptoms occurred while she was watching a TV biography of Anita Hill. This insight led to the recollection that when she was age 18, a department store manager attempted to seduce her during an evening work shift. Her refusal of his overtures resulted in his threatening to fire her and later to his refusal to support her goal to train as a buyer. Shamed and intimidated, she told no one and recognized only in retrospect the impact of the experience in terms of her lack of self-assertion in the workplace and her constricted view of her work role. Although she was now too old to train as a buyer, she was able to utilize her new insight to assert herself appropriately and obtain a long overdue promotion. Her anxiety symptoms subsided in this context. In terminating her therapy, she remarked, "Finding a name for that experience after all these years really helped me to feel less anxious and to fight back. I only wish it could have been sooner. Maybe I could have done something with my career."

SCOPE AND PURPOSE

This book is designed to assist clinicians, such as physicians, psychiatrists, psychologists, social workers, counselors, and EAP (Employee Assistance Program) professionals, in the diagnostic understanding and treatment of people victimized by sexual harassment and other significant forms of gender discrimination in the workplace and academia. It can also be helpful to other associated professionals, such as attorneys, administrators, managers, EEO (Equal Employment Opportunity) personnel, and others interested in the psychological aspects of these phenomena.

Extensive background information is included from a variety of nonclinical disciplines, but the book is not intended to be either an extensive legal review or a summary of current research. Instead, relevant information is provided to allow clinicians who traditionally focus on intrapsychic issues to become acquainted with the complex external environmental factors associated with individual discriminatory experiences. This is a necessary prerequisite for conceptualization and implementation of effective treatment plans. The psychiatric treatment of sex discrimination requires an active, flexible, eclectic treatment that focuses on both internal and external needs and that transcends traditional treatment. This cannot be accomplished without an understanding of the workplace and the legal environment.

Gender discrimination is usually perceived as a woman's mental health issue. This is because the overwhelming majority of legal cases, formal complaints, and survey results involves male perpetrators and victimized women. This book will therefore deal primarily with the experiences of women, although information regarding victimized men and other special populations will be offered when available.

Sexual harassment and gender discrimination appear together in the title of this book and are deliberately discussed together throughout the text. Although sexual harassment is the more widely publicized of the two problems, they most frequently appear together and produce negative psychological consequences jointly. Depending on the individual and her circumstances, the psychological consequences of sex discrimination can, in fact, be more significant than the impact of sexual harassment. DiTomaso (1989) argues that women who transcend traditional support roles in the workplace or otherwise challenge male authority are most likely to become conscious of sexual harassment and sex discrimination. Those who reproduce subordinate roles in the workplace or who work in isolation from men are less likely to be conscious of these phenomena. Gutek and Koss (1993a, p. 809) report, "Sexual harassment and sex discrimination appear to go together. Women who report a lot of sexual harassment in their organization also tend to believe that the organization is discriminatory in its treatment of women." DiTomaso (1989) and Ragins and Scandura (1992) concur. A Finnish study showed that women who had encountered sexual harassment in their workgroups were more likely than were other women to experience sex discrimination, and that harassment and discrimination are not related for men (Hogbacka, Kandolin, Haavio-Mannila, & Kauppinen-Toropainen, 1987). The following case vignette illustrates how other forms of gender discrimination can be as psychologically damaging as sexual harassment.

CASE VIGNETTE 1-3

*Gender-Based Wage Discrimination More Psychologically
Damaging Than Sexual Harassment*

Dr. Susan Heines was a 35-year-old assistant professor of surgery at an urban academic institution. She entered treatment for depression, the onset of which she attributed to inadvertently learning that her salary was approximately $8,000 less than those of her three male colleagues. In the context of giving her history, Susan described 5 years of what her therapist considered serious sexual harassment, including colleagues blowing into her ear and pinching her buttocks during surgical procedures, colleagues telling crude sexual jokes in front of her in the operating room, colleagues calling her "she man" and "supercrotch," and a senior attending physician attempting to seduce her. These experiences had occurred consistently over the last 5 years, but Susan described her morale and energy level as fine during this period of time. When her therapist found it surprising that her depression did not occur earlier in her career, Susan unhesitatingly explained. She stated that she had been the youngest of five children, and her four older siblings were all male. She stated that her brothers continuously harassed her physically and verbally as expressions of both their affection and their competitive issues with her. She said that she had become quite adept at managing their harassing behavior; they had never been problematic to her, because her father had explained the importance of holding her own with her brothers and consistently expressed his respect for her and her abilities. Susan interpreted her department chair's deliberate assignment of a lower salary to her as a demoralizing devaluation to which she was unaccustomed. She stated that she viewed the sexually harassing behaviors as either fun or as necessary components of learning to get along with her "colleague" brothers. However, the salary differential disturbed her greatly and precipitated her depression when she felt helpless in overcoming it.

STRUCTURE AND CONTENT

The chapters in this book are organized in an order that will help readers first understand the complexity of environmental components of gender discrimination and then move on to identifying and treating the negative psychological sequelae.

Chapter 2 discusses current and future gender trends in the workplace and summarizes the etiologic theories of discrimination that identify key contributing components of the work environment.

In Chapter 3, the legal environment is then explored, in the context of those issues most relevant to clinicians: (1) an introduction to discrimination law, (2) an outline of the process of filing a discrimination lawsuit, (3) the clinician's role as expert witness versus the clinician's role as treater, and (4) the impact of the legal environment on patients or clients and clinicians.

Chapter 4 reviews recent research on the dynamics of victim-perpetrator interactions. Topics include: (1) characteristics of victimized people, (2) response patterns of victimized people, (3) perpetrator characteristics, (4) perpetrator styles of interaction, (5) contextual and environmental factors affecting the victim-perpetrator interaction, (6) dynamics involving significant others, (7) dynamics involving special populations of victimized individuals, and (8) secondary victims of gender discrimination.

Chapter 5 summarizes the psychological sequelae in terms of (1) physical and emotional symptoms and psychiatric disorders, (2) maladaptive coping responses, (3) disruptions in work and interpersonal relationships, and (4) psychological grief reactions related to internal and external losses.

Chapter 6 introduces a nine-step treatment approach and describes the initial phases of treatment in terms of (1) clarifying the therapist's role and forming an alliance, (2) assessing the severity of the immediate crisis, and (3) identifying and treating the immediate symptoms and forming a therapeutic contract for the collaborative ongoing monitoring of symptoms.

Chapter 7 outlines the intermediate stages of treatment, which involve (1) ventilation of feelings and exploration of negative internal perceptions, (2) formulating an appropriate plan of action, and (3) proactively anticipating negative reactions and developing measures to protect against retaliatory behaviors and associated losses.

Chapter 8 summarizes the concluding stages of treatment, which include (1) identification and mourning of inevitable losses, (2) reinvestment in previous or newly formulated life goals and activities, and (3) attention to long-term or other significant treatment issues.

Case vignettes are presented throughout the text. They are composites of real cases known to the author and are included to illustrate the clinical relevance of the theoretical material being presented.

CHAPTER 2

Relevant Aspects of the Work and Educational Environments

*The Clinical Psychological Implications of Sex
    Discrimination Theories
Reduction of Unconscious Internalization of Blame
    and Responsibility
Assistance in Formulation and Enactment of Adaptive
    Coping Strategies
Correction of Therapist Bias*

U nderstanding the employment and academic environments in
    which individuals work is essential for understanding not only
    the negative psychological consequences of sex discrimination
but also how victimized people recover from these adverse experiences.
Appreciating how the structural and environmental conditions of an
individual's work or educational environment contribute to discriminatory events is clinically significant for several reasons. (1) It helps the
clinician avoid the negative therapeutic consequences of the classic psychoanalytic bias by allowing the clinician to focus on external, as well
as intrapsychic, factors in evaluating patients or clients with work-related complaints. (2) It helps the victimized person to avoid immobilization and internalization of guilt and shame. (3) It helps the therapist
and the patient/client in collaborating to formulate an effective and adaptive coping plan.

This chapter will provide an overview of the clinically relevant
aspects of the current employment and academic environments. Pragmatic information, theoretical concepts, and current trends will be discussed. Case examples will be provided to illustrate significant points.
More detailed use of this material in the specific treatment process will
be discussed in Chapters 6, 7, and 8.

RELEVANT TRENDS IN TODAY'S WORK
AND EDUCATIONAL ENVIRONMENTS

The impact of gender in the workplace and in academic settings has
increased dramatically in the last 50 years. There have been both significant gains and significant areas of stagnation in regard to gender
equity. In the early 1970s, women began to enter the employment market in significantly larger numbers, and since then their numbers have
continued to increase. In 1970 43% of adult women were either employed or seeking employment. In 1998 that number had increased to

60% (U.S. Department of Labor, 1998a, 1998b). During this same time period, the participation of men in the labor force decreased from 80% to 74%, resulting in an increased proportion of woman in the total labor force from 38% in 1970 to 46% in 1998. A similar gender equity has occurred in the distribution of men and women entering previously male-dominated professional schools, such as law and medicine. In addition, the proportion of woman managers has risen from 16% in 1970 to 44% in 1998 (Powell, 1999a). Among these increased numbers of employed women in general is an increase in the numbers of mothers of young children and single mothers. Along with shifts in numbers have come shifts in women's attitudes and expectations regarding work outside the home (Nadelson, 1989). As a result, career and salaried employment plays a more salient role in women's sense of themselves. In short, more women are impacted by the work environment, and this impact is of higher psychological significance.

Perceptions of men's and women's roles are also in great flux. Innumerable variations between traditional and egalitarian attitudes now exist between individuals, their families, and their workplace contacts. Thus two women with similar credentials, career attitudes, and goals may have very different experiences, depending on the attitudes of their colleagues, coworkers, mentors, bosses, and significant individuals in their personal lives. Of special importance is the lack of attitudinal change in CEOs and other high-level administrators. Current research indicates that these top policy and decision makers continue to demonstrate traditional gender stereotypes and stereotypical beliefs regarding men and women (Stroh & Reilly, 1997). These individuals may either resist promoting women altogether or only help women who are significantly junior or subordinate to them.

Paralleling these significant changes for women are significant areas of stagnation. The average full-time female worker continues to receive less pay than the average full-time male worker does. Female-dominated occupations still receive lower pay than male-dominated occupations do, and women are still paid less than men are for the same occupation. Furthermore, the gender gap in earnings appears to be increasing, after a period of decline (Powell, 1999b; Roos & Gatta, 1999). In addition, sex segregation, although declining, remains a defining element of occupational structure, affecting choices for both men and women and still confining women to lower-paying and female-dominated occupations and positions (Jacobs, 1999; Powell, 1999a).

Most significantly, the number of women in top management and administrative positions in work and educational organizations remains consistently and disproportionately low, around 10% (Powell, 1999a). Gary Powell (1999b) summarizes the recent research that documents the persistence of gender stereotyping that operates against women seeking top positions, despite changes in opportunity and attitudes for women at other levels. This makes it difficult for women to impact the policies and structures of their work and educational environments. In addition, support and resources for housework, child care, elder care, and other duties traditionally performed by women homemakers have not kept pace with the needs of the growing number of these women who are now employed or are students outside the home. Despite the increased involvement of men, women continue to carry out most domestic responsibilities, and many expect to continue to do so (Cooper & Lewis, 1999).

EMERGING TRENDS IN THE WORK ENVIRONMENT

Cooper and Lewis (1999, pp. 37–47) recently reviewed the gender implications of several new trends emerging in the workplace. Their discussion provides a framework for summarizing these trends. Beginning in the 1990s, globalization, recession, and advancements in information technology have resulted in (1) radical and continuous restructuring of work organizations, and (2) an information overload and accelerated work pace. The fundamental unspoken employer–employee contract promising long-term stable employment and advancement in the work hierarchy, in return for hard work, high performance, and loyalty, has been eroded. This has impacted morale, motivation, and employee loyalty but has also provided an opportunity for change. Work organizations, ranging from manufacturing companies to educational institutions, are relying more on a small core of permanent full-time employees working in-house, supplemented by a much larger pool of part-time and contract employees working on specific projects or tasks, oftentimes from their homes. Employees ranging from factory line workers to administrators, college professors, and physicians are having the experience of fewer people doing more work with less job security.

Several elements of this transition—namely, the flexible workplace, job insecurity, long work hours, and the existence of virtual organizations—have gender implications (Cooper & Lewis, 1999). Women have traditionally been part-time discontinuous workers with more flexible attitudes toward work. The question arises as to whether or not they will be more adaptable and therefore more preferred workers in this new environment. Women's career aspirations and management styles have traditionally focused on performance, achievement of expertise, and satisfaction within a job, rather than on promotion (Cooper & Lewis, 1999). Their management styles have included good communication and people skills, flexibility, a capacity to mentor others, and good transitional leadership skills (Cooper & Lewis, 1999). It remains to be seen whether careers of achievement in flat organizations in a culture of rapid change will be a better fit for women than men or whether for men will adapt more feminine styles (Cooper & Lewis, 1999).

Cooper and Lewis' (1998, pp. 37–47) discussion raised many questions with gender implications. Will career paths regress back to the traditional styles within these new organizations, with men still at the top of most organizations, or will men be willing to share or relinquish power in this time of change? Will job insecurity and the likelihood of unanticipated periods of unemployment force men and women to adapt more egalitarian roles in the home? Will the opportunity to partake in more flexible work structures lead to more sharing of gender roles in the home, or will this make it more likely that women will continue to shoulder the burdens of domestic responsibilities? If women at times are the sole providers for their families, will men become active at home, or will a woman's job be played down or be considered temporary? Will women continue the current norm of experiencing job stress not only for themselves but also on behalf of their spouses, or will men begin to be impacted by women's occupational stresses and share some of the emotional burden of family life? Will employees continue the trend toward working longer hours to guard against job loss, or will they rebel and become more assertive in moving from organization to organization in accordance with their needs? Will this create a new trend of horizontal, rather than vertical, movement? Will parents' working long hours to succeed create more stress at home, and will they then spend even more time at work to escape these tensions? Will families' stress spill into the workplace? Will couples have fewer children? Will men and women unite and adapt to the lack of work permanence by demanding a better balance between work and family, a higher quality of life? Will home-based work in virtual organizations allow more opportunities for caretakers to obtain employment and for egalitarian integration of work, or will gender inequities persist, with employers paying less to predominantly female home-based workers and more money to men maintaining the traditional boundaries between home and work? As work-home boundaries blur, will workers multitask successfully or will they become workaholics?

It is clear that the recent radical changes in the work and educational environments are challenging many of the fundamental tenets of gendered organizations, such as (1) the male model of work, (2) continuous full-time careers based on advancement, and (3) the physical and psychological separation of work and family. The possibility for shifts in gender roles and experiences at work certainly exists but is by no means certain. Women have been in the workplace in significantly large numbers for over 30 years, and they have made considerable gains. Many men have become increasingly involved in family life but not on parity with women. The glass ceiling, especially at the top of the work hierarchy, has remained firmly in place. Work and educational organizations continue to be led by men and structured according to male values. Women continue to take primary responsibility for home and family life and for home and family responsibilities. The evolving global economy will affect American jobs and introduce gender roles from other cultures. The impact of the recent terrorist attacks on the United States and the related world conflicts that are evolving and the potential repercussions for the economic and work climate remain to be seen. Cooper and Lewis (1999) note that it is unlikely that these emerging structural changes in the workplace alone can alter embedded gender elements that currently exist, unless the need to challenge gender role inequities is articulated and specifically pursued in the larger sociocultural arena.

The way in which women are pursuing this agenda will be discussed in the next chapter, which deals with the legal environment. I will first explore in this chapter the way in which the current work and educational environments contribute to discriminatory experiences for women.

HOW THE WORK AND EDUCATIONAL ENVIRONMENTS CREATE DISCRIMINATORY EXPERIENCES FOR WOMEN

In the last 20 years, researchers from a variety of disciplines have constructed a spectrum of theories to explain the current inequity between the sexes in the work and educational environments. Some were designed to explain sex discrimination in general, and others apply specifically to sexual harassment. Many of these etiologic theories overlap, and some lend themselves to psychological interpretation more than others do. In general, these models point to an interaction between (1) factors at the socioenvironmental level that impact on the workplace, such as sex role prescriptions or labor market conditions; (2) factors inherent in the structure of the workplace such as hierarchical and power differentials, interactions between workgroups and employees, and biases at the level of key decision makers; and (3) factors at the individual level, such as motivation, attitudes, personality, and coping strategies. An understanding of the etiologic factors of sexual discrimination can help both clinicians and patients/clients assess the external factors that contribute to the patient/client's situation. This not only provides an opportunity to analyze the problem and develop effective coping strategies but also prevents the likelihood of the victimized person's internalization of guilt, shame, and responsibility for the situation. This section will summarize the most important etiologic models of sexual harassment and gender discrimination. Clinical examples will be given to illustrate each model, and models can be compared by referring to Table 2.1, which lists conceptual focuses, strengths and weaknesses, and psychological implications for each model. Models of gender discrimination will be described first, followed by models specific to sexual harassment. (See Table 2.1 at the end of chapter.)

GENDER DISCRIMINATION MODELS

Model #1: The Individual Deficit Model

This perspective, defined by Nieva (1982, pp. 187–191), views gender discrimination in terms of men and women as individuals. The model focuses on differences in innate biology and early socialization, which presumably lead to fixed results in adulthood. Women are seen as more emotional, less logical, and more motivated by wishes for security and connection than are men. Men are perceived as logical, stable, and more comfortable with high-risk challenges and individual achievements. Women may have difficulty with leadership positions, due to fear of success or tendencies to achieve via indirect and vicarious routes. Women's subordinate status as workers or students is best explained in terms of deficits in motivation, in personality development, and in essential traits, such as a lack of assertiveness and sensitivity to organizational networks and political gains.

Although this model emphasizes female deficits, it can also be utilized to highlight the negative impact of male attitudes and perceptions about female workers or students. This impact is especially significant for women working at higher levels or at nontraditional jobs or educational tracts, where their presence is more unusual and where they are prone to be viewed as deficient by superiors. In addition, male deficits, such as insecurity regarding masculinity and defensiveness regarding healthy competition from women, can also be used to explain women's problems in the workplace.

This model has many significant shortcomings and is not substantiated by the bulk of empirical literature. It exaggerates biological difference and oversimplifies the complex factors leading to discrimination. From a psychological standpoint, it can also lead women to internalize blame and responsibility for situations created by organizational, cultural, and political factors well beyond the scope of their individual culpability and strengths. It is included in this text because it helps to explain the specific cases in which adverse early socialization significantly impacts a woman's employment or academic status. The following case example illustrates this point.

CASE VIGNETTE 2-1

Early Socialization Results in Deficits in Individuals' Work Functioning

Gretchen Young was a 45-year-old middle-management business executive who had worked in a series of public relations companies with moderate success. Although she received regular promotions and salary increases, her work history was punctuated by a series of love affairs with her immediate bosses, all of whom were married and none of whom could offer a gratifying personal relationship. One of her lover-mentors also discouraged her from pursuing her goal of developing her own small company, minimizing her ability and maximizing his displeasure at not having her accessible to him. The blurring of boundaries between her work and her personal relationships also undercut Gretchen's confidence in her work performance. She was uncertain as to whether or not her promotions were the result of her abilities or her sexual relationships with her bosses. Despite an awareness of the disadvantages of her behavior, she continued to respond to sexual overtures

in the workplace with no conscious understanding of her motivation. In the context of her therapy, she identified the origins of the
patterns in the context of her family of origin. Her father, a successful business executive, very much like herself, functioned well
at work but was a closeted alcoholic who physically and verbally
abused both Gretchen's mother and brother. They remained his
intimidated victims but expressed their own pent-up anger toward
Gretchen. Her father spared her his verbal and physical abuse but
fondled Gretchen's genitals for a brief period early in her childhood and explained his behavior as "special coddling for a special
girl." He constantly expressed his delight in Gretchen's physical
attractiveness and "cute behavior." He consistently responded
warmly toward her and with apparent favoritism. Gretchen's mother
exacerbated the problem by overemphasizing traditional sex roles,
especially the importance of attracting men who could provide for
her economic security. Gretchen was devastated when her father
emotionally abandoned her in the context of her first dating relationship. She ultimately identified her repetitive colluding in the
sexualizing of her work relationships with her bosses as an attempt to maintain the only emotional form of gratification that she
had experienced as a child. In addition, this replicated the only
form of economic and personal security that she had been socialized to achieve.

Model #2: The Structural Institutional Model
of Gender Discrimination

In this model, Nieva (1982, pp. 191–198) addresses the limitations that
Kanter (1977) and others have raised regarding the individual deficit
model's tendency to leave the work or educational environment
unexamined and unchanged. This model focuses specifically on the
impact that the work or educational organization has on individual men
and women and the ways in which people reflect their work or educational environment in their individual behaviors. Women's personalities and motivations are seen more as the consequences of work or
educational situations than as the causes. If low aspirations exist in
women, they are seen as adaptive adjustments to the reality of limited
opportunities. Women's difficulties with integrating into traditionally

male work or academic environments result from their low numbers, token positions in the organization, and the accompanying unconscious group dynamics that make these women extremely visible and subject to special pressures and stereotyping, yet at the same time excluding them from essential networks of information and alliances. Leadership problems are not the result of women's inappropriate styles but rather are the logical consequences of powerless and dead-end isolated positions to which they are assigned. Women's limitations thus are similar to the legitimacy and entitlement problems experienced by other newcomers and minority groups who do not control the operations of the environments in which they work. The following case vignette illustrates the difficulties of such a token woman attempting to integrate into a traditionally male work environment.

CASE VIGNETTE 2-2

Group Dynamics Impede Progress of Token Women

Mary Doe was a 32-year-old courier service driver and single mother of two who entered treatment with symptoms of anxiety and depression, following an episode in which her union representative had failed to support her in filing a discrimination claim. That same afternoon her tires were slashed at work. She suspected her angry coworkers. Mary's 4-year experience in the position had been highly unpleasant, but she had remained at the job due to the excellent pay, which was well above that of several other traditional female positions she had considered. The company employed only two women drivers out of 40, and each of the four regional supervisors was male. While on the job, her male colleagues usually talked around her, focusing on subjects related to sports or sexual exploits. Whenever Mary would try to enter a conversation, usually to discuss union matters, the other conversants would stop and walk away. The men nicknamed her "britches," after a dockloader began the habit of nudging her buttocks with a forklift whenever she entered the warehouse. On the few occasions she was called to the office to pick up a parcel she had erroneously delivered, the supervisor would announce the situation over the loudspeaker. Her coworkers would then clap and some would shout, "Way to go, britches!"

After being in the position for over 18 months, Mary applied to be certified to deliver biological specimens, a job that paid a significantly higher salary. Within the next year, she approached her supervisor on three separate occasions regarding her application. Each time she was turned down and told she did not qualify. Finally, she requested qualification information from her union rep and learned that she did indeed meet the prerequisites. When her supervisor learned that Mary had spoken to the union representative, he angrily advised her to get married if she wanted to bring in more money. He began assigning her deliveries in the slum areas of town. She approached her union representative regarding the possibility of filing a discrimination complaint. His response was critical, and he discouraged her from moving forward. He stated that he doubted that she had much of a case. Mary telephoned the other female worker for advice but was cautioned by her female colleague not to be a troublemaker. When she entered work the following morning, she heard several of her co-workers snickering at her. One of them whispered loudly, "Britches is getting too big for her britches." That afternoon she left work to find her tires slashed in the employee parking lot.

Model #3: The Sex Role Model

In this conceptual model of discrimination, Nieva (1982, pp. 48–207) focuses on societal behaviors and attitudes. Cultural definitions of male and female roles are stressed, including but not limited to, the work or academic aspects of life. The focus of this model is the amount of congruence between a woman's exhibited behaviors or attitudes and those prescribed by her sex role ideal or those appropriate to specific female roles exemplified by wife, mother, and sexual object. This model suggests that sex role prescriptions impose upon a wide range of work-related behaviors. Women will select or be pressured into jobs or academic situations that require traits that are seen as congruent with their sex roles or that allow for major commitment to their roles as wives and mothers, even if these jobs or educational situations offer a low level of reward. According to the sex role model, the problems of women workers stem from the inappropriate spillover of sex-related roles into the workplace. Independent of their capabilities or preferences, women are forced to perform or are perceived as performing functions similar to those they perform in their nonwork roles. Current perceptions and assessments, as well as future expectations, derive from traditional female role traits such as nurturer and supporter, even though these traits may be irrelevant or damaging to the performance of their specific work or academic roles. Women's job and academic descriptions involve functions that are typically auxiliary and satisfactions that are typically vicarious. Training and advancement opportunities are prescribed as appropriate for male colleagues only. Women must choose either to stagnate or to deviate from accepted norms and risk sanctions.

For women workers or students who are also wives and mothers, the problems are even more severe. These traditional expectations demand they accommodate their work or academic lives to the demands of their husbands, households, and children. The interrupted patterns and part-time employment or student characteristics of women adapting to these demands carry a multitude of career penalties, such as disproportionately low salaries, limited benefits, and truncated career or educational ladders.

Conversely, men are expected to alter their family responsibilities to suit their work roles so that men who attempt to help their working wives with family responsibilities may face their own sanctions. Women who choose to violate traditional sex role prescriptions of behavior in work or educational settings face entry and acceptance problems. They may be exposed to harassment, hostility, and ostracism. Such groundbreaking women must tolerate internal strain, resulting from role conflicts and the uncertainty and self-doubt that arise from nonsupportive work or academic environments. The following two case vignettes illustrate the multitude of problems exemplified by this model.

CASE VIGNETTE 2-3

Culturally Defined Sex Roles Negatively Impact Nontraditional Couple

Dr. Sandra Hughes was a third-year psychiatry resident, married happily to Dr. Arnold Young, who was a third-year resident in radiology. The couple were enjoying and excelling in their training programs. They had enjoyed a long-standing relationship that had resulted in their desire to begin a family. Sandra was delighted when she learned that she was pregnant. As she and her husband discussed their situation, they decided jointly that Sandra would take a short maternity leave, but Arnold would take a longer child-rearing leave because the nature of his training program compartmentalized rotations, allowing him to be more readily able to schedule a prolonged period of time at home. Both Sandra's and Arnold's department chairs sanctioned their plans. Arnold, who was being groomed by his department chair to join the junior faculty, was even told that he was especially respected for this position. The chair mentioned that he himself felt that he had taken too little time to be with his children.

The pregnancy and the delivery went well, and Sandra returned from her short maternity leave on schedule. Although she continued to do well in the program, she was somewhat dismayed by a variety of experiences with colleagues that negated the lip-service sanction she had received for her plan. On several occasions, colleagues worried out loud regarding her capacity to bond with her child. An administrator commented on her getting home early to make dinner for her husband. She was automatically left out of plans to attend professional meetings. When she spoke with her residency director about this, he apologized and said, "We assumed that you would want more at-home time now." She also was dismayed to learn that she was now assigned a half-time office, the underlying assumption being that she would see fewer outpatients now that she had a child.

Arnold, on the other hand, was having difficulty integrating into the predominantly female mothers' network active in their community. He found that the women were awkward regarding talking to him about the new baby he was caring for and seldom approached him in the park. One month prior to his scheduled return to his residency, Arnold checked in with his department chair, who told him brusquely that his research project had been given to another resident. Three months after Arnold returned to work, his department chair informed him that he would not be selected as a chief resident and that his leave had created great animosity among the residents. Arnold's chief also said that he would not be recommending Arnold for a postgraduate fellowship, because the chief had some concerns about Arnold's commitment to the workplace. Angered and dismayed, Arnold changed specialties and ultimately became quite depressed, precipitating anxiety and guilt in his wife and creating significant problems in their sexual relationship and in their adjustment to parenthood.

Model #4: The Intergroup Relationship Model

In the fourth model of discrimination, the intergroup relations model, Nieva (1982, pp. 206–222) focuses on the relationship between men and women as group members. This model expands upon the previously described dynamics associated with tokenism. The premise of this model is that men and women, as members of two fundamentally different groups, will interact according to the dynamic factors that typically develop in relationships between groups. When work and educational groups are formed based on dominant characteristics such as sex, both the differences between groups, as well as similarities within groups, are emphasized and exaggerated, resulting in stereotypes that supersede individual characteristics in actual job or academic performance. For example, all men are assertive and committed to their careers, or all women are nurturing and committed to child rearing and family life. Such stereotyping affects the interactions between members of the two different groups, creating more stress and discomfort when they are placed in an interactive situation. Their stereotyped roles and expectations of each other generate incompatible sets of behavior, resulting in further distancing, polarization, and exacerbation of the existing stereotypes.

Intergroup dynamics also result in the creation of a hierarchy, wherein one group is seen as superior to the other group. Traditionally, males have been viewed as the dominant "in-group" in the workplace and academia. Male characteristics are automatically used to set the norm for "goodness," regardless of what traits might in reality correlate best with performance of a designated work or academic task. Promotional and career track performance expectations are based on the male life cycle, with no allowances for child rearing. In addition to the assumed superiority of male traits is the assumption that male occupational and academic activities are automatically superior to female occupational and academic activities. This is demonstrated by Touhey's (1974) research, which showed that simply changing the composition of an occupation to include more females lowered the desirability and prestige of that occupation.

According to this intergroup model, individuals are treated in strict accordance to the status associated with their characteristic group membership. In work settings, when an individual's educational level or job title may not be immediately evident, that person's sex is always obvious. Women, as members of the lower-status group, may automatically be perceived to have less power, less prestige, and less potential for accomplishment, independent of their actual level of performance. In addition, as members of the subordinate status group, women themselves may

1. expect less
2. initiate less
3. overevaluate higher-status males
4. denigrate members of their own group
5. accept the dominant group's distorted definitions of them
6. attempt to identify with the dominant group members at their own expense or at the expense of their female colleagues

Numerous researchers (Blumberg, 1979; Hartmen, 1981) have correlated women's subordinate sex status with their lesser degrees of control over the resources valued by society, such as money, land, political influence, legal power, and intellectual and occupational resources, as compared to youth, beauty, and child-rearing potential. Although valued resources may differ from society to society, economic power is seen as the key variable in most cultures. Protection of the established system of reward allocation and resources controlled by the male-dominant groups remains a major obstacle for females entering the workplace. Multiple rationalizations, including the individual deficit model of females, are utilized to preserve the status quo.

A variation of the intergroup model originates from economic and labor relations theory and focuses on the concept of vulnerable workers. Some aspects of this theory can be applied to academic settings as well. Wilborn (1991) identified vulnerable workers through the analysis of three interacting variables. First, a group's level of vulnerability in the workplace depends on the ability of employers to distinguish at low cost between group members and non–group members. Women's gender meets this criterion. Second, a group's level of vulnerability depends on ideas or preoccupations about the group that might cause employers or coworkers to discriminate against the group. Sex role stereotypes and perceptual biases about women's competence meet this criterion. Finally, a group's level of vulnerability depends on structural aspects of the labor market that are disadvantageous to them. Some examples that apply to women are

1. tax laws that discriminate against secondary earners within families
2. proportionately low compensation packages for part-time workers
3. the unavailability of child care and elder care

The following example illustrates the issues addressed in the inter-group model.

CASE VIGNETTE 2-4

Stereotype Gender Issues Polarize Male-Female Interactions and Incapacitate a Work Group

The CEO of a small pharmaceutical company, wishing to intro-duce a new women's health product to the marketplace, appointed a six-person educational advisory panel, consisting of two male physicians, two female physicians, a female nurse, and a female president of a women's health consumer group. This team was to work collaboratively with one female marketing executive, two male marketing executives, and a male pharmacologist from the corporate headquarters. Although one male marketing executive assumed the role of leader of the group without discussion by the others, the team members nonetheless worked well together until it was time to travel to an international conference where they would supervise and coordinate a series of educational lectures to be given by an outside male physician, using educational materi-als that the group had designed. During the course of his lectures, the outside speaker made several sexist jokes that created some consternation among the advisory committee. The lecturer caused further consternation when at an informal dinner he showed a se-ries of slides with sexist portraits of women. The audience, which was largely male, clearly was not offended by the presentation, but the advisory group was split. A further bone of contention was the issue of an earlier presentation made by the nurse who repre-sented a strong women's health organization. Some members of the conference audience were offended that a nurse should open the presentation. The group was split as to how to handle the situ-ation. All of the women and one of the men found the male presenter's jokes and slide show offensive. This group also felt strongly that it had been appropriate to open the conference with the nurse's presentation, even though some members of the audi-ence had objected. As the discussion progressed, the female mar-keting executives and one of the female physicians shifted and ultimately took the position that the male physician and presenter was acceptable and that the nurse's presentation should be eliminated at future conferences. Although the objecting members reluctantly acquiesced to continuing the program, the group was not able to agree on either additional curriculum materials or future conference plans. It was ultimately disbanded by the CEO. Although the advisory group was composed of an equal number of men and women and displayed an initial ability to work effectively, it became polarized and incapacitated when stereotype gender issues were introduced at the conference.

BEHAVIORAL AND CONCEPTUAL MODELS OF SEXUAL HARASSMENT

In keeping with the current widespread publicity and legal activities surrounding the issue, theoretical models explaining the etiology of sexual harassment appear more frequently and in greater numbers in the research literature than do models of gender discrimination (Fitzgerald & Schullman, 1993; Lapointe, 1990; McKinney & Maroules, 1991; Paludi, Ed., 1990; Paludi & Barickman, 1991; Pryor, 1992; Pryer, LaVite & Stoller, 1993; Russell, 1984; Terpstra & Baker, 1991). There are, however, parallels between the two sets of models. The conceptual framework for the etiology of sexual harassment depends on the same three levels of factors as those addressed in discrimination, namely:

1. Factors at the macro or environmental level, such as socioeconomic inequities, sex role prescriptions, legal sanctions, and economic and labor market conditions;
2. Factors at the organizational level, such as hierarchical and power differentials, organizational climates, sex ratios, employee composition, and disparate compensation and benefit structures; and
3. Factors at the individual levels, such as motivation, attitudes, personality, communication, leadership styles, and strategies of workplace victims and offenders (Terpstra & Baker, 1986).

The bulk of the literature on sexual harassment focuses on four explanatory models, three of which were developed by Tangri, Burt, and Johnson (1982) and a fourth by Gutek and associates (Gutek, 1985; Gutek & Cohen, 1987; Gutek & Dunwoody, 1987; Gutek & Morasch, 1982). Based on their review of courtroom cases of sexual harassment,

Tangri et al. (1982) defined (1) the natural biological model, (2) the organizational model, and (3) the socioeconomic model. Gutek (1985) and associates (Gutek & Cohen, 1987; Gutek & Dunwoody, 1987; Gutek & Morasch,1982) defined (4) the sex role spillover model, based on their own extensive research. Table 2.1 provides a brief comparative description of each model, including its psychological implications.

Model #1: The Natural Biological Model of Sexual Harassment

The model explains the occurrence of sexual harassment as a personal issue, based on natural sexual interactions between men and women. Sexual harassment is simply an idiosyncratic outcome of the natural expression of men's stronger sex drive and not an intentional effort to harass. This model denies the negative consequences of sexual harassment on women's psychological health and upon their employment or educational status. Tangri et al. (1982) note that if this model were adequate in explaining harassment, given recipients should be similar to their male harassers in age, race, and occupational status. They should be unmarried, and their behavior should resemble courtship and should stop once the woman shows disinterest. Harassed women should report feeling flattered by the behavior. Testing of this model with data from the U.S. Merit Protection Board Study (Tangri et al., 1982) found that it was not supported. Saal (1996) provides an extensive discussion of why this model does not serve well in explaining the widespread phenomenon of sexual harassment. Included for completeness, however, is one example known to the author of a sexual harassing situation in which the primary motivation appeared to be misguided courtship behavior.

CASE VIGNETTE 2-5

Sexual Harassment Resulting from Misguided Courtship Behavior

Kathy Smith was a 23-year-old graduate student working in a lab with her preceptor, Dr. Jon Boonvell, who had 20 years of research experience. At age 44, Jon was undergoing a painful divorce. Having focused most of his time on lab work, Jon had few social skills and was not reacting well to the isolation he was experiencing since his wife left him. On several occasions while working in the lab, he approached his student protégé and clumsily asked her for a date. Kathy was courteous but firm, tactfully making it clear that she already had a boyfriend. Her preceptor persisted, becoming more and more desperate, pleading with her and offering to buy her a plane ticket to accompany him to an international meeting. He began collecting Kathy's papers and kept a photograph of her in his room. In the evenings, he would write her imaginary letters, which ultimately he began to send. Kathy consulted her dean and was advised to continue her firm denial of his request for dates. Ultimately, her professor appeared at Kathy's apartment one evening, claiming that he did not think he could live if she would not agree to date him. Kathy did not file a harassment complaint, but the administration intervened and assisted the preceptor in obtaining psychiatric treatment.

Model #2: The Organizational Model of Sexual Harassment

This model shifts the focus away from the individual and focuses on the organizational structures and situations in which men and women work and study. This model suggests that sexual harassment results from the opportunity presented by power and authority relationships derived from the hierarchical structure of organizations. It defines the problem as an abuse of power, based on

1. differential power positions within the organization,
2. numerical ratios of males to females within those positions,
3. the norms and the social climate of organizational life, and
4. the unavailability of effective formal and informal grievance and resolution procedures.

By focusing on the asymmetrical relations between supervisors, primarily male, and subordinates, primarily female, this model provides a better explanation for the studies by Tangri et al. (1982), showing the consistent negative reactions of women who are victimized and the tendency of individuals with greater degrees of personal vulnerability and dependence on their jobs to experience more harassment. The following example illustrates many of the issues delineated in the model:

CASE VIGNETTE 2-6

Sexual Harassment Involving Organizational Power Differentials and Ineffective Grievance Procedures

Susan Stone was a 26-year-old unmarried graduate student at a prestigious Ivy League school. She was honored to be working as a junior editor on an international journal edited by her professor Dr. Jon Smith, who was an international celebrity in this highly specialized area. Recognizing the unique opportunities for networking, as well as the special literary and editing expertise she could accomplish through this work, Susan willingly agreed to work late at the request of her professor. One evening when they were working alone, he approached her from behind and kissed her neck while stroking her hair. Startled, she jumped and firmly asked him to "Stop that." He responded in a highly offended manner, and Susan became concerned that she may have damaged their relationship. Her professor continued to make the same overtures every evening that they worked together alone. Susan attempted to discourage this by finding daytime hours in which to complete her work. Jon then persisted in his advances publicly during the day, prompting a male colleague to state, "I see how you are advancing in the field." Troubled, Susan consulted an administrative dean, who acquainted her with the institution's sexual harassment policy. Susan first tried to speak directly to Jon by solicitously asking him to allow their relationship to remain purely professional and reiterating her respect and gratitude for the opportunity to work on the journal. His response was curt and abrasive, as he reminded her that "There are twenty more where you came from." This prompted her to worry that her job was in jeopardy. She returned to the dean, who assisted her in filing a sexual harassment complaint. The committee investigating the claim found that it had merit but did not feel able to dislodge Jon from his position, given the revenue and prestige his reputation brought to the school. They instead offered Susan a transfer to another supervisor, acknowledging freely that there was no way to transfer her work on the journal. She became depressed and confused with regard to whether or not her actions were appropriate, given that she had lost a valuable opportunity by filing a complaint.

Model #3: The Sociocultural Model of Sexual Harassment

The sociocultural model, like the organizational model, focuses on the unequal distribution of power and status between men and women, but the sociocultural model takes the issue one step further. In this model, sexual harassment is seen as only one manifestation of a larger patriarchal system, in which men are the dominant group in society as a whole. Harassment, then, is a specific example of men asserting personal power based on their sex. According to this model, sex would be a better predictor of who harasses and who is victimized than would organizational position. Women would be more likely to be victimized, especially in male-dominated populations in the workplace. Using data from U.S. Merit System Protection Board Study, Tangri et al. (1982) reported stronger empirical support for the organizational and sociocultural models, which both view sexual harassment as arising from power and status disparities. Following is a case vignette that exemplifies the sociocultural model.

CASE VIGNETTE 2-7

*Sexual Harassment Involving Male Asserting Personal Power
Despite Equal Organizational Position*

Jenny Boyd was a 32-year-old married mother of two who was returning to the workforce for the first time since her graduation from college, concurrent with her children's return to school. Jenny was especially pleased to have obtained a job as a sales person and distributor for a regional telecommunications firm that permitted her to maintain a flexible and autonomous work schedule. Almost immediately, Jenny noticed a good deal of flirtatious behavior and exchange of sexual jokes between men and women in the central office. She remarked to a coworker, "Gee, I'm a little shocked at what goes on here. I've been an old married woman, so I must be out of step with the time." Her coworker responded "I'm sure you won't be left out." Things nonetheless went well, and Jenny was soon making significant commissions that greatly added to her family's economic stability.

Jenny was especially pleased to be selected to be one of the resource people to attend a 3-day company conference held 100 miles from her home. She found the didactic sessions stimulating but was greatly concerned when one of her coworkers persistently sat next to her and put his arm around her shoulder. When she tried to deter him in a joking manner, he replied, "Honey, you are just too cute. I can't help myself." The coworker seated himself at her dinner table and asked him to join her for a drink after dinner. Jenny made it quite clear that she would be returning to her room to study for the next day's seminar.

When her roommate, Sue, told Jenny that she would be joining some other sales people for a drink, Jenny wished her a good evening and told her she would be turning in early. She was awakened from a deep sleep at approximately 12:30 A.M. Her roommate, Sue, had returned. Jenny heard Sue's voice, along with a male voice. Before she could sit upright and turn on the light, her coworker Tom came into her bed. He slid on top of her and proceeded to push up her nightgown, massaging her body. Completely shocked and startled, she froze but then attempted to push him off. She screamed to her roommate when she realized that she was being raped. Her roommate was in a drunken state in the other bed and did not respond. Tom slid off and exited the room, leaving Jenny humiliated and in shock. She left the conference the following morning but was unable to tell her husband about this experience. Her work performance declined, and she ultimately entered treatment for depression. Four months after the incident, she was able to admit to her therapist that she had been raped and discuss her shame and guilt for not being more active in fending off the attack.

Model #4: The Sex Role Spillover Model of Sexual Harassment

None of the three previous models has received absolute empirical support in the literature. As an alternative, Gutek and Morasch (1982) proposed the sex role spillover model. Sex role spillover explains sexual harassment as a carryover of gender-based role expectations of behavior into the work and educational environments. When an occupation is dominated by one sex, the gender roles associated with that dominant sex group become incorporated into the work or academic role expectations of the occupation. Sex role spillover is exacerbated by skewed sex ratios, and it impacts women in two ways: (1) women employed or studying in nontraditional settings under a token status will be treated as role deviants because their sex does not correspond to the sex roles normally associated with their occupation. They are perceived and treated differently from their male colleagues and are more likely to report instances of sexual harassment. In this case, the role spillover is to the individual. (2) Women working or studying in traditionally female areas will experience a different type of sex role spillover, in which their sex role and their work role merge together. These women may be unaware that some of their treatment in the work or educational setting is based on their sex. These types of occupations tend to be devalued and underrewarded because of the sex typing associated with them. In this case, the role spillover is to the occupation as a whole. The sex role spillover model is compatible with the sociocultural model of harassment and gains support from research that demonstrates a greater incidence of sexual and gender harassment of women working in nontraditional areas (Shullman & Fitzgerald, 1985; Till, 1980). The following case example illustrates sex role spillover occurring in a traditional female occupation.

CASE VIGNETTE 2-8

Sex Role Spillover to a Traditional Female Occupation

Karen Cliff was a 25-year-old engaged dental assistant who had been happily employed by a small dental practice for approximately 5 years. Although friends had warned her that dental assistants were underpaid in this practice, Karen had always remained loyal. She appreciated the generous personal bonuses that her boss provided. Karen enjoyed her work, found the office atmosphere friendly, and respected her boss's expertise and professionalism. She was proud of the fact that he taught at a local dental school. She was therefore flattered when he offered her extra pay to work some additional hours to assist him on the weekends in upgrading the practice's sterilization techniques and equipment. The work was to take place over a 3-month period that involved nearly every Saturday. Karen enjoyed the time with her employer and found the work stimulating. An easy social rapport developed between them as they ate out for lunch and occasionally dinner on Saturdays. Her employer teased her that her fiancé might get jealous. In the context of what Karen perceived to be an innocent social relationship, her employer began to discuss his problems with the office and with his marriage, stressing how he appreciated her caring and concerned attitude toward him. He continued to confide important details of both the practice and his personal life to her in their times together. Karen felt confused, not sure whether to be flattered or uncomfortable with his overtures. As the period of overtime work drew to a close, Karen's boss presented her with a bonus envelope at one of their luncheons together. To her shock, he then invited her to a motel with him that evening, stating that he loved her for her kindness and understanding. Karen reminded him that she was engaged, declined the offer, and left work early that afternoon. She immediately spoke with her fiancé about the situation and was dismayed that he became angry with her, accusing her of being seductive toward her boss.

Model #5: The Terpstra and Baker Models

Terpstra and Baker (1991) have developed a lesser known but somewhat parallel set of sexual harassment models, defined as follows:

1. biological
2. sex role conditioning
3. intentional-instrumental
4. organizational

Each of their models focuses on the motivation of the perpetrator. A brief description will be included for completeness. The biological model is identical to the natural biological model previously described. It is based on the notion that men are biologically more aggressive than women and that men have stronger sex drives than women and that these behaviors present themselves in the work and educational settings. The sex role conditioning model is similar to the sex role spillover model previously described and centers on the role of learning or conditioning, noting that men and women, prior to entering work and academic environments, have been exposed to different socialization patterns and have learned behaviors consistent with existing sexual definitions. In these settings men will behave as dominant, aggressive, and forceful and will initiate sexual activity. Women will be submissive, passive, and receptive to the demands of men. Sexual harassment, then, is simply the exhibition of conditioned sex role behaviors. The intentional-instrumental model is similar to the sociocultural model. It focuses on the role of the conscious intentions of harassers, as opposed to the biological conditioning situations described in the previous two models. In this model, sexual harassment provides a means for men to maintain dominance over women in work or educational settings, as well as in society. Sexual harassment serves as an instrumental function for men, who intentionally harass women in order to maintain their own position of economic privilege, power, or high status. The organizational model is similar to the organizational model previously described by Tangei et al. (1982), which emphasizes the power differentials between men and women in work and educational organizations and the abuse of power by men in positions of authority toward women in subordinate positions.

Secondary Models of Sexual Harassment: The Dispute Model, the Role Model, and the Group Relations Model

Three additional models of sexual harassment are worth noting but are limited in scope and empirical support. Lach and Gwartney-Gibbs (1993) proposed a workplace dispute model of sexual harassment, that could also apply to academic settings. They propose that sexual harassment is a concrete example of a multitude of workplace disputes and resolution processes that systematically disadvantage women. Their model describes workplace disputes, including sexual harassment, as consisting of origins, processes, and outcomes. Unlike other models that view harassment as a unique and deviant workplace behavior with unique consequences, the workplace dispute model suggests that harassment is only one type of significant dispute in the workplace with gender implications.

Sexual harassment appears to be patterned by gender roles, occupational sex segregation, and social organization of work. Individual, occupational, and organizational level variables influence the origin of sexual harassment. The processes and outcomes of such disputes are best explained on the individual level. Due to their gender roles, women are more likely to experience workplace difficulties over leaves, absenteeism, and scheduling related to family responsibilities. They are also likely to be the passive recipients of sexual attention. Sex role spillover can result in unwanted sexual behavior for women working in both traditional and nontraditional positions. Because women are often socialized to avoid conflict and to doubt their own perceptions, they may attempt to resolve their disputes informally and not pursue formal complaint channels. This trend would be compounded for all women working in the skewed groups who might feel pressured not to voice difficulties to gain acceptance by the dominant group. Because women workers and students are often distributed differently across work and educational organizations, they may also lack access to formal channels of dispute resolution. In addition, they may lack access to informal networks for resolution or for information and support to facilitate pursuing complaints. Lacking appropriate resolution, workplace disputes for women may result in greater job turnover, lower job satisfaction, lower vocational functioning, and psychological sequelae, as compared to those of men, whose problems are heard in a safe setting and resolved. Although very limited in its scope, this model does help explain

1. The widely documented underreporting of sexual harassment experiences by women, and
2. The multiple reports documenting psychological trauma and difficulties with the complaint channels, written by professionals working with women who were involved in the complaint process.

Connecting Theories of Sexual Harassment and Gender Discrimination: The Social Psychology Model of Gender

The social-psychological or cognitive-behavioral model of gender provides a connecting link between all of the models of harassment and discrimination just reviewed. This model describes how gender is defined, created, and maintained through sociocultural influences in the context of social interactions. It provides a way of understanding how negative perceptual biases regarding women as workers and students creates and perpetrates workplace discrimination at individual, group, organizational, and cultural levels. Haslett, Geis, and Carter (1992) provide a comprehensive discussion of these phenomena. They outline a self-fulfilling prophecy of gender beliefs and behaviors consisting of two basic elements: (1) a mental element, consisting of knowledge, beliefs, expectations, feelings, attitudes, values, goals, and motivations; and (2) a behavioral component, including actions, words, pictures, body language, and facial expressions. The premise behind the self-fulfilling prophecy is that stereotypic beliefs about men and women cause biased perceptions and discriminatory behaviors, including discriminatory role and status assignments at work and school, and biased perceptions of performance, which then result in behaviors and achievement levels that seem to confirm the initial stereotypic expectations.

THE CLINICAL PSYCHOLOGICAL IMPLICATIONS OF SEX DISCRIMINATION THEORIES

This section has outlined the principal models of sexual harassment and gender discrimination with regard to theories of etiology. All of the theories imply a dynamic relationship between individual, interpersonal, organizational, and sociocultural factors. Many of the theories overlap. No one theory fully encompasses the complexity of the phenomena, yet each one contributes a layer of understanding with regard to the many external factors that contribute to the discriminatory experiences based on gender. They provide a compelling and empirically based illustration of how environmental factors operating in the workplace and academia transcend the importance of any individual characteristics of the victimized person in creating discriminatory events. Few clinicians are familiar with these theories, despite their relevance to the psychological treatment of victimized people. Well-intentioned treatment can in fact be harmful to clients/patients if the treating clinician is unfamiliar with the associated environmental factors. The following discussion highlights this relevance with regard to three key treatment issues.

Reduction of Unconscious Internalization of Blame and Responsibility

Theoretical models of discrimination consistently stress the high significance of conscious and unconscious cultural and organizational factors, as compared to the lower significance of individual characteristics, in contributing to discrimination. In addition, both harassment and discrimination models highlight the potential for perceptual fallibility, abuse of power among key decision makers in the work and educational settings, or both. Such theories counteract traditional forces operating in the educational and work environments, as well as in society, that automatically press women to internalize blame and responsibility for inequities. People victimized by harassment who are familiar with conceptual models are less likely to blame themselves for provocative behavior or lack of finesse in managing unwanted sexual attention. Difficulties with tenure, promotion, pay equity, and training opportunities will not be immediately interpreted as personal inadequacies, such as lack of talent, poor performance, insufficient expertise, or poor leadership abilities. More psychological energy may be available to direct toward changing work environments and discriminatory systems, as opposed to blaming oneself and becoming depressed, anxious, and immobilized.

Women who, in the course of their work, encounter discouragement, decreased self-confidence, and lowering of their career aspirations and motivations may consider their reactions in the light of the cycle of powerlessness models suggested by Ragins and Sundstrom (1989). They describe two separate paths for power—one for men and one for women—and they outline the special difficulties encountered by women. Instead of opting out of the workplace, thus decreasing their investment in their work, women may consider strategies based on a more realistic assessment of their situation. They may take into consideration the specific way in which men are socialized and tracked into powerful positions, which enables them to gain access to more powerful coalitions, networks, and mentors, which in turn enhances their confidence and career aspirations, whereas women, on the other hand, are socialized to accept primary responsibility for children and domestic duties and are not expected to pursue or are not tracked into high-power occupations or positions with accompanying positional resources. Women, therefore, do not gain as ready access to coalitions, mentors, or networks that would enable them to use their interpersonal or individual powers to compensate for a lack of positional power. Discouraged from trying to advance, they may turn to more domestic roles for reward and become less motivated, less confident, and less career-oriented. Women familiar with Ragins and Sundstrom's model may be less likely to consider their reactions as permanent and intransigent or intrinsically related to their abilities. They are less likely to develop psychological symptoms and disorders and more likely to seek other strategies in dealing with their reactions, as discussed in the next section.

CASE VIGNETTE 2-9

Internalization of Blame for Discriminatory Experience

Dr. Simone Barns was a 32-year-old female physician, a member of a bimonthly network group for professional women. She had two small children and was happily married to a businessman. Shortly after joining the group, she became pregnant with her third child. Her career had proceeded smoothly to this point. She currently held a staff position at a top-ranking hospital associated with an Ivy League medical school, to which she was also given a faculty appointment. She frequently expressed feelings of satisfaction in mastering her work. The network group especially appreciated her energy, good humor, honest enthusiasm, and pleasure in approaching her work and home life. Her input to group discussion focused on the challenges she encountered in raising her children and fostering her career and the joy that she experienced in meeting these challenges.

Simone's pregnancy proceeded smoothly; she delivered a healthy baby, and then began a 3-month prearranged maternity leave. During her leave, she continued to attend the group regularly, focusing her discussions on the new baby and on the reactions of her older children toward a new sibling. Although she missed her baby, she felt that her new family was settled and she was comfortable with her children's nanny when she returned to work. Shortly after resuming her job, she expressed great pleasure at being back, stating she was increasingly aware of how much she had missed the challenge.

During the next 6 months, she gradually became reticent in the group. When she did participate, she spoke more of her family and less of her job. When asked specifically about her work, she began to express some doubts about her ability, focusing on a variety of specific tasks, ranging from medical student teaching to publication requirements within her department. She responded to the group's supportive comments but clearly lacked enthusiasm. When she failed to take any pleasure in being a recipient of a highly coveted teaching award at her hospital, a group member asked her specifically, "Are you depressed?" Simone responded in the negative but began to miss meetings and was again confronted by a group member asking, "What has happened to you? You used to be our role model." Simone responded by crying and acknowledging that she had begun treatment for depression. She stated that she felt she might need to leave the group because she no longer felt competent and had a sense of letting down her co-members. With support, she was able to continue and she began to explore a series of problems related to her department head's negative comments regarding working mothers, criticism for lack of publications, unpleasant work assignments, and a punitive night-call schedule, arranged to "pay her back for all the time she missed." Although the group acknowledged that her situation was discriminatory, she quickly became identified as the "needy one," a position associated with some humiliation for her. She felt that she had lost her position of leadership and respect.

The climate changed when one member brought a newspaper article to the group describing gender discrimination as common in professional settings. Although Simone was initially targeted to be the recipient of the article, other members began to identify with the situations described. Over the next month, group members expressed dismay as individuals began to cite specific examples of work experiences that had been humiliating, devaluing, or detrimental to their careers. Following these disclosures, the group was temporarily immobilized but eventually shifted to a stance that acknowledged the reality of discrimination but focused on brainstorming strategies to address problems. In this context Simone become less depressed, and at the end of the second year of group meetings she was able to negotiate a new position that involved a promotion, a salary increase, and a relocation to a more hospitable work environment.

Assistance in Formulation and Enactment of Adaptive Strategies

For people victimized by harassment and discrimination, a critical step in recovery from psychological sequelae is the formulation and enactment of a strategy to deal with this situation. (See Chapters 6, 7, and 8.)

Reviewing a variety of options, choosing an option that best suits their needs and minimizes their losses, and proceeding with that plan at a pace reasonable for them as individuals is crucial in reestablishing a victimized individual's sense of control and confidence. The shift from a powerless stance associated with depression, anxiety, psychosomatic complaints, and traumatic reactions to a cognitive problem-solving stance is uniformly associated with a reduction in psychiatric symptomatology. Theoretical models of discrimination assist in this process by providing a cognitive explanation for complicated, emotionally laden employment situations. Models enable victimized people to isolate the etiology of their difficulties—a manager's bias, a tracking problem, and so on. They can then formulate effective strategies that focus on the specific problems they are encountering. Models also enable them to identify in advance which work situations will be most favorable to them or to readily locate more positive work environments, if their current situation is untenable.

Correction of Therapist Bias

Genovich-Richards (1992) and Bernstein and Lenhart (1993) have reported on the lack of information regarding sexual harassment and gender discrimination in the health-care and mental health literature. Clinicians are traditionally trained to focus on intrapsychic factors. Familiarity with conceptual models of discrimination leads to a heightened awareness of the importance of also assessing external sociocultural factors during the evaluation of women with work-related complaints. Beginning in this context allows the therapist to validate the serious reality of the patient's experience and to assist the patient in realistically assessing her situation and in mobilizing effective coping responses. This approach prevents her from internalizing blame and regressing to a devalued, depressed, and helpless state and essentially reexperiencing the work-place trauma within the treatment. Awareness of the complicated cultural and organizational climate in which women work also assists the clinician in appreciating the challenge and the special areas of stress to be addressed. Appreciating in advance the way the conflict between sex roles and work roles can create double binds for women at work can assist the therapist in avoiding two common pitfalls at the onset of employment-related therapy:

1. Devaluing the patient for initial inability to take definitive action in her work situation.
2. Failing to intervene when the patient is taking immediate actions that are impulsive and not in her best interests.

Finally, theoretical knowledge of discrimination can sensitize clinicians regarding the essential importance of work, not only for men but also for women. The value of taking initial work histories on both male and female patients, as well as of eliciting a more detailed work history from patients who present with psychological symptoms but make only vague references to work problems, is considerable.

CASE VIGNETTE 2-10

Exacerbation of Sexual Harassment Problems Secondary to Therapist Bias

Carmen Gonzales was a 28-year-old married mother of three who worked as a clerical supervisor for a shipping company. She was referred to therapy by her internist for a series of psychosomatic complaints that were unresponsive to treatment and that were causing frequent absences from work. In the course of eliciting a history, her therapist found that Carmen had had numerous arguments with her husband regarding her work status. Both Mr. and Mrs. Gonzales grew up in a Hispanic home, where traditional sex roles were emphasized and mothers stayed at home to raise large families. Carmen had consistently worked throughout her marriage because of her family's real economic needs and because of her own firm stance that she liked her job and wanted to work. In pursuing this conflict, the therapist learned that, recently, Carmen had begun to experience guilt regarding her decision to remain employed outside the home despite her husband and family's values. With her therapist's support, Carmen began to explore the possibility of staying at home full time. Six weeks later, she quit her job. She continued to meet with her therapist on a weekly basis for an additional month, during which time she focused on transition issues and noted the subsiding of her somatic complaints. Viewing her problem as resolved, she and her therapist agreed to a mutual termination of treatment. Three months later Carmen was hospitalized for depression. In the course of her inpatient evaluation, her new therapist learned that she had been sexually harassed by a trusted supervisor who was in the midst of a tumultuous divorce. Carmen had felt humiliated by the experience and too embarrassed to discuss it and had felt that her inability to prevent her supervisor from touching her breast had brought shame to her husband and family. Her guilt reactivated her unresolved ambivalence about resisting her spouse's wishes and her family's injunction that she not pursue a job that she enjoyed. Her therapist had pursued this traditional conflict without taking a complete work history. Her treatment inadvertently contributed to the escalation of her problem.

This chapter has summarized the clinically relevant aspects of the current employment and academic environments in which discrimination occurs. Emphasis has been placed on how the nature of this workplace contributes to the etiology of discriminatory events in a manner that transcends the characteristics of the victimized individual, as illustrated by the theoretical empirically based models presented. The clinical relevance of the models is discussed in terms of three key treatment issues. Relevant trends and emerging trends in regard to gender issues in the workplace and academia are also described. It is emphasized, however, that any emerging structural changes in the workplace are unlikely to alter the embedded discriminatory elements that currently exist, unless the need to challenge gender role inequities is articulated and specifically pursued in the larger sociocultural arena (Cooper & Lewis, 1999). The way in which this agenda is being pursued will be discussed in Chapter 3, in which the relevant aspects of the legal environment are addressed.

TABLE 2.1. Etiologic Models of Gender Discrimination and Sexual Harassment

	Gender Discrimination Models		
Name	Description	Strengths & Weaknesses	Psychological Implications
I. Individual Deficit Model	(1) Views discrimination in terms of men and women as individuals. (2) Discrimination is the result of innate differences in biology and early socialization.	(1) Has the least empirical support. (2) Limited scope underrepresents the impact of environment. (3) Is somewhat helpful in elaborating gender differences in attitudes and styles and ways in which individuals can contribute.	(1) May be misused to blame women. (2) Implies deficits in women's competence and men's attitudes. (3) Places too much emphasis on individual contributions but does help elaborate them.
II. Structural Institutional Model	(1) Views discrimination in terms of the impact of the work organization on individual behavior, personality, and motivation. (2) Introduces concepts of roles, hierarchy, and power differentials.	(1) Has better empirical support. (2) Has a better explanation of the scope of problem. (3) Does not address the impact of individual responses and coping styles. (4) Does not address the larger cultural impact.	(1) Helps individuals understand the strength of external factors operating on them. (2) Is less likely to cause self-blame in victims. (3) Encourages effective problem solving and coping mechanisms in victimized individuals. (4) Does not explain the impact of individual coping styles.
III. Sex Role Model	(1) Discrimination occurs when culturally defined sex role presumptions of women spill over into the workplace.	(1) Has the best empirical support. (2) Is the most comprehensive model (considers individual, organizational, and cultural factors).	(1) Exemplifies the complexity of discrimination. (2) Encourages an individual to reflect on how she views herself and how others view her.
IV. Intergroup Relations Model	Discrimination occurs due to naturally occurring intergroup dynamics.	(1) Emphasizes group processes over gender processes. (2) Has limited scope but helps explain some specific situations. (3) Has little empirical support.	(1) Depersonalizes issue. (2) Encourages exploration of group vs. gender dynamics.

Behavioral and Conceptual Models of Sexual Harassment

Name	Description	Strengths & Weaknesses	Psychological Implication
I. Natural Biological Model (similar to Individual Deficit Model of Discrimination and Terpstra & Baker's Biological Model of Sexual Harassment)	(1) Sexual harassment is a personal issue based on natural sexual interactions between men and women.	(1) Has poor empirical support. (2) Is extremely limited in scope. (3) Is not consistent with either literature or case reports. (4) Is largely discounted currently.	(1) Is applicable in a few cases where dysfunctional courtship behavior is the key issue.
II. Organizational Model (similar to Structural Institutional Model of Discrimination and Terpstra & Baker's Organizational Model of Sexual Harassment)	(1) Sexual harassment results from the opportunity presented by power and authority relationships derived from the hierarchical structures of organizations.	(1) Has some empirical support. (2) Introduces the importance of power differentials. (3) Does not address cultural factors.	(1) Depersonalizes issues. (2) Focuses women on addressing their subordinate status.
III. The Sociocultural Model (similar to Intentional Instrumental Model of Terpstra & Baker)	(1) Sexual harassment is the result of the ongoing struggle for power and status between men and women in the culture at large, not just within the work institution.	(1) Has stronger empirical support. (2) Introduces larger gender-related cultural issues to the workplace.	(1) Depersonalizes issues. (2) Focuses women on societal as well as work roles.
IV. The Sex Role Spillover Model (similar to Sex Role Conditioning Model of Terpstra & Baker)	(1) Sexual harassment is a carryover of gender-based role expectations of behavior into the workplace. (2) Gender role expectations carry over to occupations, as well as individuals.	(1) Has the best empirical support. (2) Is the most comprehensive discussion of individual, organizational, and cultural factors.	(1) Depersonalizes issues. (2) Focuses women on individual societal and work roles. (3) Emphasizes carryover of subordinate status to female-dominated professions.

(Continues)

TABLE 2.1. *Continued*

Name	Description	Strengths & Weaknesses	Psychological Implication
V. Dispute Model	(1) Sexual harassment is part of a continuum of workplace disputes based on gender.	(1) Has very limited scope. (2) Has little empirical data. (3) Helps explain difficulties with current complaint channels.	(1) Women require improved complaint channels.
VI. Role Model	(1) Sexual harassment is a role problem arising from role conflict and role ambiguity.	(1) Is an oversimplification. (2) Has no empirical data to support. (3) Is a weaker, limited model.	(1) Highlights the problem of ambiguous roles.
VII. Group Relations Model	(1) Sexual harassment is the result of unconscious intergroup processes in which women advocate for all those with limited power.	(1) Has a global role and political scope. (2) Has little empirical support. (3) Is not helpful in explaining case studies and much of literature.	(1) Emphasizes symbolic role. (2) Has few implications for individual women.

CHAPTER 3

Relevant Aspects
of the Legal Environment

Historical Background
Legal History: Federal Laws and Landmark Cases
Understanding the Legal Process Regarding Sex
 Discrimination
The Clinician as an Expert Witness
 Clinical Evaluation of the Plaintiff
 Postevaluation Conference with Attorney
 Expert Testimony
The Treating Clinician as a Material Witness
Clinical Implications of the Legal Environment

In one segment of the larger sociocultural environment, the gender irregularities embedded in the employment and educational environments have been articulated and pursued—namely, in the legal arena. Appreciation of the current legal environment regarding gender discrimination helps the clinician and the patient or client to (1) understand the significant reactions of employers and coworkers, (2) consider the legal options for redress, (3) evaluate the psychological costs and benefits of litigation, (4) avoid retraumatization of the client or patient during the litigation process, and (5) protect the therapeutic alliance by clarifying the role of expert witness versus the role of the therapist during litigation. This chapter will provide an overview of the clinically relevant aspects of the current legal environment. Pragmatic information, historical background, and current trends will be discussed. Case examples will be provided to illustrate significant points. More detailed use of this material in the specific treatment process will be discussed in Chapters 6, 7, and 8.

HISTORICAL BACKGROUND

In the 1960s, the political force of the Civil Rights Movement provided a meaningful legal definition of gender discrimination within the Civil Rights Act of 1964. In a similar manner, sexual harassment as a specific form of gender discrimination was defined during the Women's Movement in the 1970s, which focused attention on various forms of sexual violence against women. Once these were identified and defined as political inequities requiring legal redress, a group of legal and social science scholars began academic exploration of these phenomena. Concomitantly, a pioneering group of victimized individuals filed lawsuits, with mixed results. Widespread public knowledge of these issues remained obscured, however, until a series of highly publicized complaints focused public attention on the issues in the early 1990s. For example, the Clarence Thomas Supreme Court Confirmation Hearings provided nationally publicized testimony by Anita Hill that included graphic descriptions of sexual harassment and other forms of gender discrimination. Consequently, lawsuits regarding these issues burgeoned during the next decade. This legal evolution significantly impacted upon employers, employees, victimized people, and mental health professionals. This section will provide an introduction to the legal issues that clinicians and others interested in the treatment of victimized individuals should be aware of. Case examples will be given to illustrate key issues.

LEGAL HISTORY: FEDERAL LAWS AND LANDMARK CASES

Federal laws prohibiting sexual harassment and other forms of gender discrimination have significantly impacted the current employment and academic environments, making these problems a common ground for litigation. This has resulted in an increase in discrimination lawsuits and has provided a rich body of case law further clarifying (1) the nature of discrimination, (2) the extent of liability for the perpetrator and the employer, and (3) the type of damages available to those victimized. These federal cases have also been utilized as models for antidiscrimination legislation at the state level.

The Equal Pay Act of 1963 required employers to pay the same salaries to men and women for work requiring equal skill, effort, responsibility, and performance under similar working conditions. It included equity in benefits such as sick leave, overtime, and uniforms. The Equal Protection and Due Process Clauses of the 14th Amendment prohibit laws that treat men and women differently in unreasonable or arbitrary ways. Title VII of the Civil Rights Act of 1964 made discrimination based on sex illegal if pervasive patterns of disparate treatment, disparate impact, or the creation of a hostile environment could be documented to impact negatively upon one sex as compared to the other. Title III made the resources of the Equal Employment Opportunity Commission (EEOC) available to victimized people and provided monetary compensation for damages, back pay, lost benefits, and attorney's fees. It also allowed for the possibility of job reinstatement. In 1972 the Title IX Educational Amendment to the bill extended the law to educational institutions. It forbade discrimination by educational programs receiving federal funding. The Pregnancy Discrimination Act of 1978 prohibited employers from refusing to hire a pregnant woman, terminating her employment, or forcing her to take maternity leave. It guaranteed job reinstatement rights, including accumulated seniority. It also mandated that pregnancy must be treated like any other temporary disability.

In 1980 the EEOC recognized sexual harassment as a form of sex discrimination and published the following guidelines, which form the basis for the current legal definition.

> Unwelcome sexual advances, requests for sexual favors, and other verbal or physical conduct of a sexual nature constitute sexual harassment when (1) submission to such conduct is made either explicitly or implicitly a term or condition of an individual's employment, (2) submission to or rejection of such conduct by an individual is used as a basis for employment decisions affecting such individual, or (3) such conduct has the purpose or effect of substantially interfering with an individual's work performance or creating an intimidating, hostile, or offensive working environment. (Equal Employment Opportunity Commission, 1980)

Although these guidelines do not have the force of law, they provided victimized individuals with an official format for pursuing sexual harassment litigation via Title VII. Within a limited time after the incident, the claimant must file a claim with the EEOC Field Office for her state, which then provides the authority for her to proceed to federal court if her claim is deemed valid. In addition to codifying sexual harassment litigation at the federal level, these guidelines also expand the nature of harassment to include hostile environments (environmental harassment) and harassment resulting from coworkers, as well as superiors.

A series of landmark cases has upheld the EEOC guidelines, as well as expanded upon the definition and nature of liability. In *Meritor Savings Bank v. Vinson* (1986), the Supreme Court upheld the EEOC guidelines and also held that (1) voluntary conduct is not a defense, (2) the test is whether the advances were unwelcome, and (3) the cases should be judged according to the totality of the circumstances. In *Broderick v. Ruder* (1988), the court ruled that an environment that promotes those who provide sexual favors and fails to promote those who do not constitutes a hostile environment. In *Ellison v. Brady* (1991), a reasonable woman standard was promulgated on the basis that women are most commonly victimized and that conduct that men consider acceptable may offend women. This standard remains controversial in its acceptance. In *Robinson v. Jacksonville Shipyards* (1991), the court ruled that pornography in the workplace is a form of nonverbal sex discrimination. In *Jensen v. Evaleth Taconite* (1993), the court approved the first class action suit involving discrimination. In 1992, in *Franklin v. Gwinnett County School District*, the court afforded the right to students to pursue damages against schools for sex discrimination. In *Harris v. Forklift Systems* (1993), the court held (1) that to be actionable, conduct must meet a reasonable person's standard, (2) that the definition of totality of circumstances may include such things as the frequency and severity of the events, (3) that the victimized person must directly perceive the environment to be abusive, (4) that psychological harm is relevant to delineating that the work circumstance have been discriminatory but that psychological damage is not necessary in order to pursue a claim. (Psychological harm refers to adverse psychological effects occurring at the time of the event[s]. Psychological damage refers to more enduring adverse psychological effects that transcend the events and are often associated with a specific psychiatric diagnosis requiring treatment.) In *Oncale v. Sundowner Offshore Service* (1998), it was held (1) that same-sex harassment is actionable, (2) that harassing conduct need not be motivated by sexual desire, and (3) that offensive sexual connotations are insignificant if they do not meet the reasonable person's standard. In *Burlington Industries v. Ellerth* and *Faragher v. Boca Raton* (1998), the Courts found employers liable for discrimination caused by a supervisor, unless (1) the employer succeeded to a reasonable degree in taking care to prevent and promptly correct the conduct, (2) the plaintiff unreasonably failed to take advantage of the complaint process and the opportunities provided by the employer. Proof that the employer promulgated a sexual harassment and discrimination policy is not always necessary as a matter of law.

The Civil Rights Act of 1991 provided victimized individuals with the right to add punitive damages to the compensatory damages previously allowed. It also provided for the payment of related medical bills. The Family and Medical Leave Act of 1993 guarantees 12 weeks' unpaid leave to care for a new baby, a sick child, a parent, or a spouse. It prevents employers from terminating employees for these family-related absences, a practice that disparately impacted women. It does not, however, protect employees from other retaliatory behaviors and adverse work consequences, such as biased perceptions that such employees are less motivated, available, and committed to their work. These perceptions can lead to discriminatory limitations in opportunities, such as the "mommy track." The high incidence of reports by women of such negative consequences may partially explain why few men take advantage of these leaves.

UNDERSTANDING THE LEGAL PROCESS REGARDING SEX DISCRIMINATION

Despite increases in discrimination litigation and increased legislation aimed at further delineating the bounds of discriminatory behaviors, clients victimized by gender discrimination and their treaters seldom understand the litigation process well enough to appreciate the time and the psychological demands that litigation will place upon them. The following section will outline the process so that patients and their therapists can appropriately assess the challenges and rewards of litigation and work collaboratively and effectively in considering this as a possible means of redress.

People victimized by gender discrimination wishing to seek legal redress can take action via four major routes (Benedek, 1996).

1. Charges of sexual discrimination under Title VII of the Civil Rights Act of 1964 and its 1972 amendments and the Equal Rights Protection Clause of the 14th Amendment.
2. Civil actions based upon common law, such as negligence, assault and battery, infliction of emotional distress, interference with contractual relationships, and wrongful discharge.

3. Workers' Compensation. This is a form of federal government insurance designed to compensate workers who are injured on the job and unable to earn a living. Compensation rates are limited by standardized tables, yielding lower damages than for other types of legal action. They are less favored, therefore, by attorneys and clients than are other types of legal proceedings.
4. Criminal charges. Criminal charges are rare and usually involve rape in combination with sexual harassment or other forms of gender discrimination.

Schafran (1996, pp. 134–138) provides an excellent sequential description of the legal process. An adapted version of her discussion is presented here, along with additional information from other sources. Victimized people can initiate litigation (1) by themselves (appearing pro se), (2) via a private attorney, or (3) in some cases via government agencies. Most plaintiffs utilize private counsel and spend considerable time finding attorneys whom they can afford, whom they can trust, whom they feel comfortable with, and who have expert knowledge and experience in discrimination law. Therapists can be helpful in referring patients or clients to attorneys who have expertise and are sensitive to psychological issues. Occasionally, attorneys are willing to work for reduced fees or work on a contingency basis, meaning that they will not charge the client up front but instead will take a portion of the damages won in the lawsuit as their fee. If a victimized person wins a lawsuit, he or she can recover legal fees as part of the damages. Within a certain set time limit after the discriminatory event or events have occurred, the attorney for the victimized person files a complaint that cites the specific objectionable and illegal actions. After that, the defendant has a period of time to answer to the charges. Many complainants are not prepared for the defendant's refuting the charges and presenting a different version of the story that is detrimental to the complainant. The following case example exemplifies this difficulty.

CASE VIGNETTE 3-1

Litigant Immobilized by Defendant's Rebuttal of Charges

Ann Bates was a 23-year-old file clerk in a small municipal housing agency. She filed a hostile environment sexual harassment suit against her boss. In response to her complaint, her boss not only denied her allocations but also described her as a marginally effective employee with a poor performance rating, with regard to both the speed and accuracy of her work and her work attendance. Prior to her charges, Ann, a single mother, had always received high praise from her boss. He also gave her permission to leave work to pick up her son after school and drive to daycare on a regular basis, in return for working later hours. The Town Hall operated informally, and no performance records or documentation of Ann's approval for her 45-minute school pick-up was available. Realizing that she had no way to document her performance, she became anxious and depressed. She was referred to treatment by her attorney when she became ambivalent and immobilized in regard to pursuing her case.

After the initial complaint has been filed and the defendant has responded to the complaint, the process of discovery begins. During the discovery period, each side seeks all information deemed relevant to the case. The information is collected through submission of formal written questions (interrogatories) to the other side. Demands can be make for medical records, including therapy records, work records, and other relevant documents, or by each side formally questioning the other side's witnesses in sessions called depositions. During depositions, witnesses are orally questioned under oath by the opposing side's attorney, with a legal stenographer present to transcribe all questions and responses verbatim. Depositions are often lengthy and stressful for witnesses and for the complainant, who often audits the session.

In addition, the discovery process is often prolonged and distressing for the complainant. Defense attorneys may attempt to probe into sensitive areas of her private life, such as past psychiatric treatment, sexual assaults, divorces, love affairs, and so on. They may also investigate any aspect of the complainant's life that may bear on her credibility, such as credit records, court records, police records, school records, past employment records, medical and psychiatric records, bankruptcy records, and drug or alcohol use. In addition, the complainant may witness depositions given by previous friends, mentors, and colleagues that are false, invalidating, and protective of the perpetrator. She may be disappointed by friends and coworkers who refuse to testify on her behalf because they find the litigation process intimidating or fear that they will suffer retaliation from the work or academic organization. If the complainant is well prepared and well validated by both witnesses and supportive people in her private life, the traumatic effects are greatly mitigated, and the process may be experienced as an empowering opportunity to speak up and defend herself.

Attorneys may dispute any aspects of the discovery process, including what documents and materials are provided, what questions are answered, and whether the plaintiff must have a psychiatric or a medical evaluation. If this is the case, expert witnesses are usually retained by each side to perform the evaluation. Recently, there has been some movement toward protecting the litigant from scrutiny regarding past sexual abuse, similar to the prohibitions allowed for rape victims. This is a controversial issue and far from resolved. Discovery remains for many victimized individuals an intrusive and intimidating process. In addition, it is likely to be expensive, disruptive, and lengthy. Time is necessary to (1) schedule multiple witnesses, (2) resolve disputes between opposing attorneys, (3) gather materials for expert witnesses to review, and (4) allow experts to review materials, write reports, be deposed, or any combination of these.

The following case examples illustrate the complications of this phase of litigation.

CASE VIGNETTE 3-2

Psychologically Intrusive Discovery Process Inhibits Litigant from Pursuing Lawsuit

Dr. Delora Thomas was a 35-year-old divorced dentist who worked as a salaried professional employee of a large, highly successful dental practice with several practice locations. During her recent divorce, Delora had entered psychiatric treatment for depression and issues related to the breakup of her marriage. In the context of treatment, she explored her difficulties with self-assertion in regard to her husband's devaluing and abusive behavior. She also identified a related pattern of failing to address mistreatment by her employers, which included significant salary and benefit inequities. Feeling the need to act more assertively on her own behalf, she brought suit against her employers without reviewing either the decision or the potential process with her therapist. During the discovery process, her psychiatric records were subpoenaed and the defense attorneys learned that her ex-husband had engaged in sexual perversions. The psychiatric records also clarified Delora's distaste for her husband's perverse sexual wishes and her refusal to engage in perverse sexual acts. Delora had indeed cited sexual incompatibility as a primary cause for the divorce. During her deposition, the defense asked repeated questions regarding her sexual relationship with her husband and made repeated suggestions that she enjoyed "kinky sex." In addition, the only other female dentist employed by the group refused to testify regarding similar salary and benefit inequities and, in fact, testified on behalf of the defense stating that she felt well treated by the dental practice group. Feeling unsupported and fearing public embarrassment if the details of her marriage were made public during trial, Delora accepted a disproportionately small settlement and gave up a potentially successful lawsuit in return for confidentiality.

As the previous case suggests, many lawsuits settle prior to trial for a variety of reasons. Examples include (1) pressure from judges with backlogged case calendars, (2) wishes on the part of the plaintiff or the defendant for confidentiality, (3) attempts to shorten the procedure, (4) wishes to avoid publicity, (5) unwillingness to take the risk of a jury's unpredictability, (6) efforts to decrease costs, and (7) wishes for psychological closure. Some businesses require their employees to sign contracts prohibiting litigation for employment discrimination and agreeing to settle any such matters via arbitration, which, in some instances, can be equally stressful for victimized people. In the current litigious climate, defensive and often attacking stances by employers are the norm, and the victimized person's colleagues, coworkers, and mentors may be persuaded to testify against the complainant. Successful mediation in conflict-resolution techniques by managers or administrators within businesses is rare but potentially beneficial for both employees and employers. It allows for resolution of the issue and continuation of the work relationships and job assignment without the costs, stress, and polarizing effects of litigation. This relational, rather than adversarial, approach also appeals to many complainants, who simply want the discrimination to stop, without harm to their jobs and their relationships at work.

If a case is not settled or arbitrated, it can take years to come to trial, making it difficult for the complainant to get closure on the experiences and for the witnesses to remain clear on the details of the events.

The trial itself is a costly and potentially stressful event as well. During the proceedings, the victimized person and her witnesses testify regarding their account of the events. At the end of their testimony, each witness is cross-examined by the defense attorney. The defendants and their witnesses then give their testimony and are cross-examined by the plaintiff's attorney. Complainants frequently find it difficult to have their credibility subject to attack, to have their testimony curtailed by procedural rules, and to hear witnesses who discredit them or whom they perceive to be lying. If their treating clinician's records are subpoenaed or if their treating clinician is subpoenaed to testify, they may feel betrayed by the clinician's inability to keep confidential certain sensitive aspects of the patient's life when on the witness stand. They may be disappointed that their treater cannot save and protect them. This can disrupt the therapeutic alliance and leave the victimized individual with the loss of yet another supportive person.

After each side has presented its case, the jury will decide either for or against the victim (plaintiff). If the jury finds for the plaintiff, the judge may reduce the damages if these are perceived as too high. Whoever loses the case may appeal. Then the case must be presented anew in an Appellate Court of Appeals, again prolonging the process and delaying closure. If the appealing side loses its appeal in the Appellate Court, it may apply to the Supreme Court, creating an even further time delay. Few cases regarding discrimination reach the high court, however. If the plaintiff (victim) wins, the individual may still have difficulty collecting damages from a defendant who hides assets, goes bankrupt, or does not provide payments at the agreed-upon times. The stress, time delays, and expensive litigation are potentially traumatizing for many complainants. Others find the process validating and empowering, and they may find it helpful (1) to be able to tell their stories, and (2) to obtain justice in the form of damages or public validation and public assignment of guilt to the perpetrator. This can be especially true if multiple plaintiffs sue jointly and support each other through the process. Complainants who lose in court can be devastated by their inability to obtain "justice" or may be relieved at finally getting closure on the process and feeling they have done everything possible to remedy the situation. Specific therapeutic strategies for helping victimized people both decide upon the wisdom of litigation and deal with the litigation process will be outlined in Chapter 7. The following case example illustrates the complexities of the trial portion of the litigation process.

CASE VIGNETTE 3-3

Lawsuit Disrupts Ongoing Psychotherapy and
Exacerbates Psychiatric Symptoms

Dr. Beth Lipinsky was a 35-year-old single physician who filed a lawsuit against the chief of staff in her community hospital, following an incident in which he cornered her in an isolated office, tried to persuade her to accompany him to a motel, and attempted to rape her when she refused. Approximately 1 year prior to this event, Beth had entered weekly psychotherapy because of escalating difficulties with affective lability and global anxiety in her relationship with her lesbian partner.

In the course of her lawsuit, Beth's psychotherapy records were subpoenaed. Following this, she began to experience harassing comments at work for the first time regarding her gay identity. Connecting this harassment with her lawsuit, Beth became angry with her therapist for a perceived breach in confidentiality and for the therapist's working diagnosis, with which she did not agree. At the same time, her therapist began to express concerns regarding testifying in court and urged Beth to speak with her attorney regarding obtaining a forensic psychiatrist to assist her. Beth experienced this as additional betrayal and abandonment and terminated her therapy, with her therapist's mutual consent. Her attorney discussed concerns that the defense would further use her psychiatric records to discredit her and thus discouraged her from seeking consultation regarding the disruption of ongoing therapy. In this context, Beth's original affective symptoms were exacerbated. She also developed debilitating anxiety in the course of her extensive deposition. Her work functioning was disrupted for the first time, which depressed her even more.

At this point, Beth sought a psychiatric consultation. The consultant recommended (1) a forensic consultation to assist with the lawsuit, (2) time-limited meetings with her previous therapist to achieve a more reasonable termination, (3) further individual psychotherapy and psychopharmacological treatment, and (4) continued contact with the consultant to assist in carrying out the recommendations. Beth initially received the consultation well, but 1 week later called to say she was too ambivalent and mistrustful regarding mental health professionals to continue the consultation or to allow her attorney to speak with the consultant. Fortunately, Beth was able to manage her trial testimony in a calm and credible fashion. She was supported by an excellent attorney and several validating witnesses. She won a large settlement and then obtained a therapy referral from her consultant and resumed treatment.

THE CLINICIAN AS AN EXPERT WITNESS

In addition to having their records subpoenaed and potentially being required to testify in discrimination cases involving their patients, clinicians may also become involved in the process via a new route, that of the expert witness. The role of the expert witness is distinctly different from that of the treating clinician. Mental health professionals should not attempt to combine the two. Expert witnesses conduct clinical evaluations that address the pertinent legal issues involved in the case. The evaluations are not confidential. A doctor–patient or clinician–patient relationship does not exist, and no treatment is offered. The process usually involves (1) a pre-examination conferencing between the attorney and the clinician serving as the expert witness, (2) clinical evaluation of the plaintiff, (3) post evaluation conferencing with the attorney, (4) preparation of a formal written report, a verbal report, or both, of findings during deposition, and (5) courtroom testimony and cross-examination. Benedek (1996, pp. 113–133) outlined various aspects of this process, especially in regard to sexual harassment. An adapted version of her discussion is presented here, along with information from other sources. Pre-examination conferencing with the attorney should involve a dialogue between both the clinician and the attorney. The attorney asks the clinician to review materials, evaluate the plaintiff, and render various psychological opinions related to the case. The clinician should also discuss various issues with the attorney prior to agreeing to take the case. Patients calling directly to request the services of a clinician should be advised to have their attorneys contact the clinician. Any contact between the clinician and the plaintiff prior to the examination will diminish the expert's credibility. The fee for the clinician's work should be agreed upon in advance and can never be contingent upon the expert's opinion. Many experts ask attorneys to forward them a retainer (a set amount of money based on an estimation of how much work will need to be done), which they work against. The clinician then informs the attorney when additional retainer fees are necessary. This clarifies both the attorney's contractual responsibility for payment and the necessity that payment be unrelated to either the evaluation results or the case's successful outcome. The clinician should also discuss with the attorney which materials will be reviewed. The expert should feel free to request all materials he or she feels would be relevant, to assure an unbiased opinion. Medical records, employment records, school records, psychological testing, and past employment records, as well as depositions and interrogatories, are commonly reviewed. The scope of the clinician's role should also be clarified. Is the clinician going to provide a psychiatric or psychological evaluation of the plaintiff? Will the clinician provide general information regarding psychiatric or psychological treatment or particular psychiatric or psychological conditions? Will the clinician provide information regarding the nature of psychiatric or psychological reactions to abuse or the nature of harassment or gender discrimination? Will the clinician serve as a consultant to the attorney and provide scientific studies, case examples, and relevant materials? Will the clinician advise the attorney regarding case strategies, psychological issues related to jury selection, or the defendant's character?

Expert witnesses provide testimony regarding relevant issues in the area of their expertise. Forensic experts provide consultation to the attorney regarding relevant aspects of the case and strategies, expert witnessing, or both. Simon (1996) warns against clinicians who provide expert testimony and then join the counsel at the counsel's table, providing ongoing input as the trial progresses. This behavior can undermine the credibility of the expert's testimony. Any forensic consultation should take place privately between the attorney and the clinician, outside the courtroom. The clinician should ask the attorney to arrange for the clinical evaluation of the plaintiff and provide times in which he or she could be available, as well as a professional office location for the interview. Any arrangements regarding necessary psychological testing should also be made. The clinician should discuss whether a formal report will be required and, if so, whether a particular format is mandated by the court. Many attorneys will prefer to discuss the expert's findings regarding the plaintiff via a private conference prior to obtaining a written report. This provides the opportunity for the attorney to terminate further services if the opinion is unfavorable to the case. Clinicians should feel free to define areas where they do not feel they have expertise in which to testify and to limit the scope of their services in accordance with their areas of expertise and experience.

Clinical Evaluation of the Plaintiff

Clinical evaluation of the plaintiff must be done in person, in order to obtain an accurate mental status. If the court permits, it should preferably be conducted during two consecutive sessions to allow for corroboration, follow-up questions, and additional information the plaintiff may remember after the first interview. The interview should be conducted in a neutral professional space, and the plaintiff should be permitted breaks, as needed. The presence of third parties should be avoided, in the form of either attorneys or supportive individuals, so that the content of the interview is not distorted. At the onset the plaintiff should be informed (1) of the purpose of the evaluation; (2) who has retained the clinician; (3) that confidentiality cannot be promised, as the clinician may testify in court regarding the contents of the evaluation; (4) that no treatment relationship exists and no treatment will be offered; (5) that the impact of the interview on the plaintiff's case may be positive, negative, or neutral; (6) that the plaintiff will not be forced to answer questions, although refusals to answer will be noted; and (7) that the plaintiffs may take breaks at any time. All relevant collateral materials should be reviewed by the clinician, if possible, prior to the clinical interview.

In general, experts evaluating plaintiffs are asked for opinions regarding (1) general information about harassment and discrimination, (2) specific psychiatric conditions related to the case, (3) opinions regarding the plaintiff's credibility and any evidence of distortions, (4) factors related to work performance evaluations and termination, (5) the nature of the plaintiff's current psychiatric condition and its cause, (6) factors affecting the severity of the psychiatric condition, (7) other concomitant or preexisting possible causes of the plaintiff's psychiatric condition, (8) relevant medical conditions, and (9) the plaintiff's prognosis and treatment needs (Binder, 1992). Clinicians vary in how they collect this information. Some clinicians start with the most neutral information, such as the past psychiatric history and family history. This allows for some time to develop an interviewing relationship and allows the plaintiff to become more relaxed. Others prefer to start with the plaintiff's account of the events, feeling that the plaintiff may fear that the background information is intrusive and unrelated to what he or she wishes to say. A potentially useful guideline for conducting the evaluation is included in the chapter dealing with the psychiatric or psychological evaluation of new patients in Chapter 6.

In establishing credibility, the expert should avoid any opinions regarding whether or not the discrimination occurred, a question to be decided only by the judge or the jury. Statements regarding the consistency and the validation of the plaintiff's view of the events, the similarity of the plaintiff's reactions to those of others victimized by discrimination, and comments regarding whether or not the plaintiff's symptoms are consistent with his or her preexisting character may help establish credibility if such questions are permitted in the courtroom. Credibility testimony is often disallowed. Evidence of distortion and paranoia due to (1) Axis I or II diagnoses; (2) revenge motivations; or (3) monetary motivations, and so on, are also important to include. History of past sexual assaults and evidence of hypersensitivity, based on previous assaults, may be elicited but may also be inadmissible in court (Simon, 1996). The significance of the plaintiff adding additional details is also notable. This is common during the process of litigation because plaintiffs are often humiliated or traumatized by the events and therefore reluctant to reveal all of the details. If further details come out just prior to deposition, however, this would be more of an indication of attempts at embellishment (Binder, 1992; Simon, 1996). Poor performance evaluations or terminations from employment also need to be evaluated. Are they evidence of retaliation? Are plaintiff's lowered functions secondary to the stress of discrimination or evidence of preexisting difficulties and therefore alternative explanations for the plaintiff's complaint? For example, alcohol and drug use may be the cause of poor work performances or the result of the plaintiff's attempts to manage anxiety and depression caused by harassment and discrimination. Asking plaintiffs what they hope to gain from the litigation, what they feel they may have done to contribute to the situation, or what they would have liked to have done differently can be helpful in establishing honesty and credibility.

The expert witness will be asked to evaluate the plaintiff's current psychological condition and its cause. This may include any related medical conditions, such as stress-related ulcers, headaches, and so on. This requires a review of the medical and psychiatric records and a clinical interview of the plaintiff, including mental status evaluation. Psychological impact may range from (1) psychiatric and psychosomatic symptoms; (2) damaged interpersonal relationships; (3) damage to sense of self; (4) diagnosable psychiatric conditions, such as PTSD and major depression; and (5) grief reactions related to multiple losses in the workplace and beyond (see Chapter 5 for details). These reactions may be the result of the original harassment or discrimination or may be the result of retaliative measures against the victimized individual for complaining. It is important for the expert to avoid inappropriate or overuse of *DSM-IV* diagnoses. If indeed the plaintiff does not meet criteria for full diagnosis, such as PTSD, it is better to state the damages in terms of symptomatology and other psychological injuries, rather than to overdiagnose a condition such as PTSD.

Preexisting psychiatric conditions, preexisting life stressors, the presence or absence of supportive relationships, the trauma of the litigation process, and the severity, duration, and context of the original discriminatory events may all contribute to the severity of the reactions. If, in some cases, the adverse reactions to the litigation process cannot be claimed as damages, then the expert may be asked to differentiate between conditions related to the original events and conditions related to the stress of litigation (Binder, 1992).

The expert will also be asked to outline any possible non–employment related causes of the current psychological condition. Life stressors concomitant with or occurring after the discriminatory events, preexisting psychiatric illness, or related medical conditions with psychological symptoms will need to be documented—for example, hypothyroidism.

Finally, the expert will be asked to comment on the plaintiff's prognosis and treatment needs. This will depend upon many factors, such as the existence of preexisting psychiatric conditions and the presence or absence of current diagnosable illness. If no psychiatric illness is present, the severity and the degree of the damage to the self, relationships, and other related losses, as well as the difficulty the victimized person has obtaining closure regarding the discrimination and resuming her normal life will all play a role in assessing treatment needs.

During the evaluation, the clinician should also be on the alert for countertransference reactions. Involvement in sexual harassment and gender discrimination cases elicits strong feelings and can exaggerate personal biases. Experts need to remain aware of their own professional responsibility to remain objective, and there are many factors that may skew their judgment. Strong ideological biases for or against women's' rights and strong opinions regarding the significance of gender discrimination as a problem can interfere with judgment. Experts may be inadvertently pulled into the adversarial atmosphere of the litigation process and appear to be more of a "hired gun" than an impartial expert. The expert may confuse the role of forensic evaluator with the role of treating clinician and attempt to save the patient or align with her inappropriately (Simon, 1996).

Experts may make treatment recommendations but should not offer treatment or agree to be the treating clinician for the plaintiff or for any family members of the plaintiff after the case has closed. Positive or negative media attention toward the case may also skew the expert's judgment. If the experts have ever been victimized by abuse, they may overidentify with the plaintiff's damages or, conversely, minimize the plaintiff's distress if they themselves had very little reaction to their abuse. Analytically trained clinicians may view the allegations as fantasy or have a tendency to blame the victimized person. Clinicians overidentified with the "victim culture" may see the victimized person as always right (Simon, 1996).

Postevaluation Conference with Attorney

After the evaluation and the review of the materials are complete, the expert should report the findings to the attorney. The conclusions, as well as the reason for the conclusions, should be presented. If this verbal report is unfavorable, the attorney may wish to terminate the consultation at this point or ask the expert for advice regarding how to best present the unfavorable information. If the consultation is to continue, the attorney should inform the expert whether a formal report is needed and of any stipulations regarding the format. Written reports in general should include (1) a list of the materials reviewed; (2) a summary of the plaintiff's history and clinical evaluation, including the mental status; (3) any relevant past history; (4) diagnosis; (5) prognosis and treatment recommendations; (6) any conclusions regarding other relevant legal questions pertaining to the case; and (7) the reasons for the prognosis and the treatment recommended. Attorneys will discuss potential dates and times for testimony in court or for depositions, if this will be required. If a pretrial deposition is required, the attorney will request potential times that the expert could be available. The attorney is also responsible for making the deposition arrangements regarding time and place with the opposing attorney, who is responsible for paying the expert for the deposition time. It is prudent for experts to have a preagreement regarding the length of time for depositions, as well as in regard to prepayment. If no deposition is required, a similar discussion regarding potential trial dates, potential times the expert could be available for trial testimony, and payment of the expert's fee should be negotiated.

Expert Testimony

Prior to the deposition or the trial, the attorney and the expert need (1) to review any additional information that may have been accumulated since the time of the evaluation, (2) to discuss the legal issues of the case and the attorney's theory regarding the case, and (3) to plan the deposition or the trial strategy. The attorney may also anticipate the questions that will be posed by the opposing attorney and discuss these with the expert. If the expert is deposed, he or she will be asked to review and sign a typed transcript of the deposition prior to trial. Prior to trial, the attorney will plan the sequence of questions for the expert, review the deposition, and anticipate opposing attorney questions that are likely to occur during cross-examination. Some review of the expert's CV, qualifications, and special expertise may also be discussed prior to trial.

Clinicians unfamiliar with court proceedings may choose to visit a courtroom or practice their answers to proposed questions via a mock trial. This can help to reduce anxiety for people unused to providing testimony but should not be done to excess, as a practiced, pat answer will diminish the witness's credibility. Dressing neatly and conservatively for the courtroom appearance is also recommended; it commands respect, as well as demonstrates respect for the legal process (Benedek, 1996).

During the first portion of the courtroom testimony, the attorney will ask the expert witness a standard series of questions regarding the expert's education, training, and expertise, in order to establish the individual's credibility (voir dire) process. Relevant information regarding publications, and so on, should be obtained from the expert's CV, which should be made available to the attorney prior to trial. The opposing attorney will then continue the interrogation, focusing on any areas in which the expert may be weak. This testimony can provide the expert with the opportunity to accustom himself or herself to the courtroom, assess the attitudes of the jury and the opposing attorney, and prepare for direct testimony. After qualifying, the expert will be asked to describe the clinical examination, including any psychological testing or laboratory results. The expert may be asked to testify on opinions regarding the plaintiff's credibility, the plaintiff's current psychological conditions, factors contributing to the plaintiff's current conditions, other possible causes for the plaintiff's condition, general questions regarding common psychological reactions to harassment and discrimination, general questions regarding the nature of discrimination, and the types of psychological illnesses that are commonly associated with it. The treatment recommendations and prognosis, as well as the reasons for the recommendations, will be elicited. The opposing attorney may object to questions at any point during the testimony. The court will rule on the merits of any objections, after which testimony will resume. Experts should not take objections personally and should feel free to ask that questions posed to them be repeated or clarified.

After direct testimony has been completed, the opposing attorney will cross-examine the expert and attempt to discredit the expert or any opinions that are unfavorable to his or her case. Attorneys may clarify materials previously introduced via the redirect process. Opposing attorneys may then cross-examine regarding any redirect testimony, and the redirect process can be repeated. If the testimony is lengthy, the witness may ask for a break, and it is usually permissible. When testimony is concluded, the witness is excused by the judge and usually leaves the courtroom. If the expert is also serving as a forensic consultant to the attorney, he or she may remain in the courtroom to hear other testimony. Sitting at the counselor's table and providing direct assistance during the courtroom process, however, would undermine the expert's credibility as a witness. Preparing the attorney prior to the courtroom proceedings or conferencing with the attorney during recesses is advised.

Experts should ask the attorney to provide information regarding the outcome of the case and should feel free to contact the attorney if this is not provided. It is appropriate and ethical for experts to make clear to the plaintiff any treatment recommendations that are needed and to assist in making a referral, but it is not wise for the expert to actually provide the treatment, even after the case has been concluded.

THE TREATING CLINICIAN AS A MATERIAL WITNESS

Clinicians should avoid testifying for patients or clients they are treating and should insist on the use of expert witnesses. Treating clinicians who are subpoenaed as witnesses are often asked questions that cannot be answered because the nature of a forensic evaluation is different from the nature of a clinical evaluation process. They may also be asked to reveal clinical information regarding the patient's private life or other unrelated materials that are intrusive. They may be asked to answer questions that may undermine their alliance with the patient. Patients may harbor unrealistic wishes to be saved by their therapists and are often deeply disappointed that their confidentiality cannot be protected in the courtroom. Patient records can be subpoenaed, however, even when an expert witness has been obtained. It is best to discuss these possibilities with patients directly. (See Chapter 6, regarding establishing boundaries in treatment and a therapeutic alliance.) Treating clinicians are advised to keep records that are clear, concise, medically oriented, and devoid of fantasy material or extensive historical or speculative material that is not directly relevant.

CLINICAL IMPLICATIONS OF THE LEGAL ENVIRONMENT

The overall impact of the legal environment, which has just been described, is complicated for victimized individuals and their treaters. On the positive side, legal professionals have done much to heighten awareness of the significance and the psychological impact of discriminatory behaviors and have provided victimized people with a powerful means for redress. Laws clarifying the liability of employers for employees acting in discriminatory manners, combined with the increased amount of sex discrimination litigation, have led to the formulation of sexual harassment and discrimination policies within institutions, as well as to complaint channels that provide another means of redress. The legally mandated training of managers and administrators regarding the handling of sexual harassment and discrimination complaints has heightened their awareness of, and sensitivity to, the importance of these issues, which has also been useful. Although these policies and programs have no doubt been beneficial to victimized individuals, they have also spawned a defensive climate, in which employers may focus more on protection against liability and less on resolution of the issues that are often the major concern of the victimized people.

Sex discrimination litigation can polarize the workplace, isolate the person who was victimized, expose her to retaliatory behaviors, and create an adversarial win-lose environment. Litigation can also skew psychiatric treatment and psychiatric conditions in favor of establishing damages, as opposed to recovering psychologically. Litigation can be retraumatizing to patients and disruptive to their treatment. Many clinicians in fact are reluctant to treat patients or clients because they find the process of litigation intimidating. Many clinicians become overidentified with the legal process and concentrate more on determining whether the patient's situation constitutes harassment and discrimination from a legal standpoint, than on understanding the patient's symptomatology, appreciating the meaning of the event for the patient, and assisting him or her in recovering. The clinical treatment may be misused via (1) forced psychiatric evaluations; (2) forced psychiatric treatment; and (3) fitness for duty evaluations, in which the clinician is in conflict of interest with the client or patient. Confidentiality can be compromised in unethical ways (Jensvold, 1996). Gender bias within the courtroom, as described by Schafran (1996), can also pose a problem for both clinicians and plaintiffs involved in the legal process.

This chapter has summarized the clinically relevant aspects of the current legal environment. The clinical implications of the legal climate have been described, as well as relevant legal processes, which should be understood by both the victimized person and any treating clinician prior to embarking upon litigation. The clinician's value in helping clients or patients assess the pros and cons of litigation and move smoothly through the litigation process will be discussed in more detail in Chapters 5, 6, and 7. Interpersonal dynamics involved in discriminatory behaviors will be discussed in the next chapter.

CHAPTER 4

The Interpersonal Dynamics of Sexual Harassment and Gender Discrimination

*Sex Discrimination Involving Cultural and Ethnic
    Minority Groups
Secondary Victims of Harassment and Discrimination
Summary*

INTRODUCTION

The psychological consequences of sexual harassment and gender discrimination are the result of a complex series of interactions between the victimized person, the perpetrator(s), the victim's associates and supervisors at work, and the significant people in his or her personal life. If the victimized person is male, gay, or a member of a cultural or ethnic minority, these dynamics may take on special characteristics. This chapter will examine what is known about the nature of these interactions in the context of what is clinically relevant.

Research on specific perpetrator-victim interactions in gender discrimination is relatively new and confined mostly to sexual harassment situations. Many clinicians have, however, identified theoretical links between the dynamics of workplace harassment and discrimination and other forms of abuse against women and girls (Bernstein & Lenhart, 1993; Cleveland & McNamara, 1996; Fitzgerald, 1993; Koss, Goodman, Browne, Fitzgerald, Keita, & Russo, 1996; Schrier, 1996). Childhood sexual abuse, rape, domestic violence, sexual exploitation in professional relationships, and sexual harassment and gender discrimination all reinforce (1) traditional gender role socialization, (2) female subordinate status, (3) sexual objectification and devaluation of women, and (4) social complicity for the exploitation and abuse of women and girls. Bernstein and Lenhart (1993) and Pagelow (1992) have documented the clinical and treatment implications of these similarities. People victimized by these abuses share many common clinical issues, including (1) difficulty in extracting themselves from the abusive situation exacerbated by some form of physical, economic, emotional, or social pressure; (2) difficulty with sociocultural invalidation and nonsupportive bystanders who collude with the abuser; and (3) similarities in psychological sequelae. Specific similarities in resulting psychiatric illness and psychological losses will be described in Chapter 5, which addresses specific psychological consequences.

The dynamic model of domestic violence and battered women is useful in understanding sexual harassment and gender discrimination in terms of (1) the victim-perpetrator characteristics and interactions, and (2) the impact of the external social environment on the interactions. As in domestic violence, there are no solid data to support that sexual harassment and other gender-based discrimination constitute unitary phenomena and fit a specific clinical formulation. Instead, current data suggest the concept of a heterogeneous group of victims and perpetrators affected by a multiplicity of external factors. Like battered women, individuals victimized by sex discrimination vary in terms of (1) their individual histories, (2) their pre-abuse status, (3) the status of their relationship with the perpetrator(s), (4) their status within the work hierarchy or household, (5) the type and severity of the discriminatory treatment they receive, (6) their response to their situation, and (7) the resources and supports available to help them (Cleveland & McNamara, 1996).

Perpetrators similarly cannot be described as unidimensional. Recent research has suggested several potential general typologies applicable to sexual harassment situations. Most significantly, as with battered women, there is no research to support the notion that people victimized by gender discrimination suffer from specific individual psychopathology, which accounts for their adverse experiences in the workplace and academia.

Current research has yielded some relevant data regarding characteristic response patterns in people victimized by sexual harassment, but responses to other forms of gender-based employment or academic discrimination have largely gone unexamined (Cleveland & McNamara, 1996). This is unfortunate because the psychological repercussions of pay and advancement inequities and inadequate or punitive policies regarding maternity leave, child care, elder care, and so on, can be of clinical significance (Lee, 1997, 2002). In addition, various forms of psychological damage can occur in the context of power-based emotional abuse, which remains a prevalent and unaddressed form of gender discrimination. Gender-based emotional abuse can include such behaviors as insults; intimidation; excessive controlling behaviors; repeated unwarranted threats to fire, transfer, or demote; and threats to hit or hurt an employee (Cleveland & McNamara, 1996; Nicarthy, Gottlieb, & Coffman, 1993). Using the domestic violence model as a point of reference, the following sections will summarize what is known about (1) characteristics and response styles of victimized people, (2) perpetrator characteristics and modes of action, and (3) environmental and contextual factors that impact perpetrators' actions and the responses of victimized individuals. Although the existing literature focuses primarily on sexual harassment, applications to other forms of gender discrimination will be discussed. Interactions involving special populations of victimized people, secondary victims, and clinically relevant interactions with significant others in the victimized person's work or academic or personal life will also be explored.

CHARACTERISTICS OF VICTIMIZED PEOPLE

Several authors (Barnett & LaViolette, 1993; Bernstein & Lenhart, 1993; Cleveland & McNamara, 1996) have noted that people who experienced sex discrimination and those victimized by domestic violence are similar. They often share

1. A sense of humiliation and a tendency to conceal the event
2. A sense of betrayal of trust and abuse of power
3. Fears of retaliation and economic hardship if the incident is revealed or reported
4. Physical, economic, or social power differentials between the victimized person and the perpetrator
5. Similar emotional responses and psychiatric sequelae
6. Isolation from support and concealment or minimization of the event by the perpetrator and others in the immediate environment

Young unmarried women are the most likely to be sexually harassed (Fain & Anderson, 1987; Gutek, 1985; U.S. Merits Systems Protection Board, 1981, 1987). There is limited evidence (Gruber & Bjorn, 1986) that women of lower economic status and those occupying low-status or high-visibility positions, or both, are also more vulnerable. This has not been documented to be true of other forms of gender-based discrimination, which can occur at all ages, all socioeconomic levels, and all stages of the career ladder. In fact, it is likely that women are encountering the stiffest forms of gender discrimination at the highest levels and most sought-after positions within their work organizations. Like battered women, those victimized by sex discrimination do not differ from their non-victimized counterparts with regard to previous history of childhood abuse or psychological and personal attributes (Cleveland & McNamara, 1996).

RESPONSE PATTERNS OF VICTIMIZED PEOPLE

The response patterns of people victimized by sexual harassment and of battered women are impacted by similar factors (Cleveland & McNamara, 1996). In my experience, these similarities hold true for people victimized by other forms of gender discrimination as well. They include (1) fear of retaliation or escalation of the situation, (2) fear of not being believed, (3) fear of revenge, (4) fear of economic or other penalties, and (5) hopes for improvement that often surpass what is realistic. Discriminatory or abusive events of a personal or intimate nature raise questions of culpability in the victimized individual. This is heightened by a cultural lack of understanding for why women remain in abusive relationships or work situations that are discriminatory. All of these factors help account for the significant underreporting of these events (Cleveland & McNamara, 1996).

In recent years, empirical research on specific victim responses to sexual harassment have contributed to our clinical understanding. Unfortunately, no similar body of evidence has been accumulated to document responses to other forms of gender discrimination, but much of the sexual harassment data is compatible with case material on other forms of sex discrimination.

In 1997 Knapp, Faley, Ekeberg, and Dubois developed a comprehensive typology of victim responses and described four groups occurring along two intersecting axes. These typologies are based on whether the victimized person focuses her or his efforts on managing internal cognitions and emotions (self-focus) or toward problem solving and altering the external situation (initiator focus). The second axis is defined by whether or not the victimized individual attempts to cope with the situation alone (self response) or via the utilization of another party, such as a superior, a mentor, a physician, a therapist, a spouse, a coworker, a law firm, or an agency (supported response). Gutek and Koss (1996) suggest a similar typology but substitute the terms *indirect* and *direct* for the terms *self-focus* and *initiator focus*, respectively, and *individual involved* versus *other involved* for *self-response* and *supported response*. Figure 4.1 illustrates an integration of these response styles. (See Figure 4.1 at the end of the chapter.)

In reviewing the literature, Gutek and Koss (1996) noted that most employees, including those victimized by harassment, feel that sexual harassment can and should be handled by the individual herself speaking directly with the harasser (self response, initiator focus). This is in direct contrast with multiple and consistent empirical studies that indicate that most victimized people utilize some version of the self response, self-focus style (Bowes-Sperry & Tata, 1999; Gutek & Koss, 1996). Ironically, this style is seldom effective in stopping harassment, which usually persists and even escalates in the absence of a direct response (Dansky & Kilpatrick, 1997; Rabinowitz, 1990). Even so, it is used consistently even for sexual harassment that includes rape. Schneider (1991) found that 81% of the victims raped at work stayed on the job, 67% remained in contact with their rapists, and 21% utilized workplace complaint channels. Of note, 10% of the women in a large study of federal employees chose the drastic step of leaving a job, quitting school, dropping a course, or changing fields to avoid harassment (Loy & Steward, 1984; U.S. Merit Systems Protection Board, 1981). Although this latter step is effective in stopping harassment, it leaves the perpetrator free to target others and leaves the victimized person with additional job and career burdens, including an inability to collect unemployment (Gutek & Koss, 1996). Gruber and Bjorn (1982, 1986) suggest three reasons why the indirect, individual involved responses are popular, despite their ineffectiveness in stopping harassment.

1. They allow the victimized person to manage the situation without disrupting the work or school association or interfering with relationships with mentors, coworkers, and so on.
2. They are perceived by victimized individuals as less risky.
3. Some kinds of harassment are ambiguous and therefore are not likely to induce a direct response.

Individual involved responses focused directly at the initiator are less frequent than individual involved responses focused at the self; however, responses invoking a third party are even less common, perhaps because they require that the victimized person identify the behavior as sexual harassment and make the incident public (Gutek & Koss, 1996). Initiator-focused supported responses are universally the least common response. Formal complaints fall below reporting the incident to a supervisor or asking someone to intervene informally. Studies addressing the use of formal complaint and legal channels usually reveal less than 10% utilization and seldom more than 20%, even for sexual harassment involving rape (Gutek & Koss, 1996). This is ironic because not only are these channels sanctioned by institutions and society, they are considered most effective in stopping harassment. Empirically documented individual reasons for these extremely low utilization rates provide an explanation. They include

1. Failure to recognize the behavior as harassment
2. Lack of knowledge of the avenues for redress
3. Fear of retaliation by the harasser, the supervisor, management, or coworkers
4. Fear of economic or career-development repercussions
5. Shame and humiliation
6. Wishes to protect and not harm the harasser, with whom the victimized person has a relationship
7. Fear that the complaint will not be taken seriously or accomplish anything
8. Fear of negative impact on the family
9. Fears of emotional stress and time connected with reporting
10. Belief that the victimized person should be able to handle the situation herself or himself
11. Hope that the situation will improve
12. Belief that the situation is not serious enough to merit complaint
13. Belief in traditional gender roles
14. Belief that he or she is to blame for the harassment (Bernstein & Lenhart, 1993; Bowes-Sperry & Tata, 1999; Dansky & Kilpatrick, 1997)

Further complicating this situation is the catch-22 scenario described as follows: Direct approaches have been found most effective in stopping harassment. Also, most of the public, most of the victimized individuals, most employers, and the legal system all share the perception that the victimized person should act assertively. The empirical literature, however, does not support this approach as being effective and beneficial for the victimized individuals. In fact, research supports the concerns of many victimized people that reporting has no positive impact on them or worsens the overall situation for them. Dansky and Kilpatrick (1997) present a series of studies documenting that assertive, direct, initiator-focused responses to harassment often result in continued harassment, a high incidence of retaliatory and punitive responses from the harasser and the work environment, and increased psychological and somatic sequelae for the victimized person. Additional research will be necessary to determine whether these more negative outcomes for victimized individuals that have been associated with direct responses are more related to the severity of the events than to the response style, because it has also been proved that victimized people are more likely to respond directly to more severe forms of harassment. A pre-analysis indicated that negative outcomes were present even after the severity of the harassment was statistically controlled, but more definitive research is needed (Dansky & Kilpatrick, 1997).

Other clinical complexities include the fact that sexual harassment and other forms of gender discrimination often occur together, and little is known about how the interaction between the two plays itself out. Existing research has focused on sexual harassment. It seems that the presence of other forms of discrimination would inhibit the victimized person's efficacy in dealing with sexual harassment and vice versa. It also seems likely (1) that the victimized individuals would suffer negative sequelae to either harassment or discrimination, (2) that current research data on sexual harassment could include sequelae related to the presence of other unexamined forms of discrimination, and (3) that other forms of discrimination could enhance the negative effects of sexual harassment. Also, most harassment and discrimination are not one-time events but are rather an experience that unfolds, that waxes and wanes over time. The most effective form of response may vary over time, and a combination of response styles may occur (Fitzgerald, Schullman, et al., 1988). At some times, it may be more important for the victimized individual to manage internal feelings and cognitions and at other times to problem solve or tend to the external situation. Salisbury, Ginorio, Remick, and Stringer (1986) and Gutek and Koss (1996) note that the victimized person's reactions to harassment are progressive, resulting in changes, as well as combinations, in response style. This is an essential concept for psychotherapists and clinicians to grasp. It shifts the focus away from the literature bias that direct assertive responses are somehow more competent and instead provides for an understanding that the victimized person's needs may shift over time, alternating between internal and external issues. This in turn calls for different response styles at different stages of treatment for recovery to be effective (see Chapters 6, 7, and 8). Contextual factors to the work environment may also impact the victimized individual's responses and this will be discussed in the next section of this chapter.

CASE VIGNETTE 4-1

Alternating Internal/External Response Styles

Katerine Santos was a 26-year-old medical student whose senior attending physician, Dr. Ed Payne, had repeatedly pressured her for dates since the onset of her surgery rotation. Katherine's refusals were persistently firm and polite, but the situation escalated when Dr. Payne saw her with her boyfriend at a social event and exploded petulantly, "You think I'm too old for you." After his outburst, he withdrew from the teaching relationship, ignoring Katherine's questions on teaching rounds and in the operating room.

Katherine consulted Dr. Sharon Oaks, a senior resident, who suggested that she switch surgical teams and offered to assist her in the transfer. An appropriate senior faculty member was identified, but when approached, he refused, based on his concern that his colleague Ed might be offended. Katherine then filed a formal sexual harassment complaint with her university. The investigation committee felt they could not substantiate the complaint and therefore took no action. It was also acknowledged privately that Ed was considered a valuable member of the university community. With Sharon's assistance, Joan located three other students who had been harassed by Ed, and together, they filed the complaint that resulted in Ed's removal from the teaching attendings rooster.

ENVIRONMENTAL AND CONTEXTUAL FACTORS AFFECTING THE RESPONSES OF VICTIMIZED PEOPLE

Research addressing the contingent factors influencing people's reactions to being sexually harassed is scarce. Gutek and Koss (1996), in summarizing the existing research, cite several significant studies. Women experiencing the most severe forms of harassment are most likely to respond in direct and assertive ways; the less severely harassed are more likely to respond indirectly, avoiding the harassment, joking about the situation, or minimizing it (Gruber & Bjorn, 1986; Loy & Steward, 1984). Women having higher levels of organizational power, high job skills, high status, or power equal or superior to that of the harasser are also most likely to respond directly and assertively. The converse is also true. There are some data to suggest that women with

few personal resources, low self-esteem, low skills, and a sense of being trapped in the job tend to choose indirect responses (Gutek & Koss,
1996). Women with traditional sex role attitudes were less likely to respond directly to a harasser, as were women who felt they had contributed directly to the harassment situations (Jensen & Gutek, 1982). In
my experience, having a supportive and powerful supervisor or mentor,
visible and credible administrative personnel designated to process complaints, and supportive coworkers, friends or family members positively
impacted a victimized person's decision to report harassment or discrimination. Characteristics of the job that were salient for indirect
responses included (1) a lack of mobility, due to high degree of specialization or the long-term nature of a project; (2) a lack of transfer opportunities; (3) vulnerability to informal blackballing; or (4) loyalty to an
institution, due to a highly valued, high-status, visible position (Gutek
& Koss, 1996). Although these observations are certainly plausible, there
are not yet adequate empirical data to fully understand all of the environmental contingency factors influencing victimized individuals' responses or to understand the interplay between sexual harassment and
other forms of gender discrimination in determining response styles.

PERPETRATOR CHARACTERISTICS

Recent research on the perpetrators of sexual harassment reveals that
like wife batterers, they are a heterogeneous group, with no clearly defined clinical pathology. Instead, individual traits such as heightened
hostility, high levels of anger in conflictual situations, heightened needs
for power and control, and the presence of enabling factors in the environment, which are embedded in the social and cultural environment,
are characteristic for both perpetrators of discrimination and wife
batterers (Cleveland & McNamara, 1997). Bondurant and White (1996)
define and describe an embedded perspective of perpetrator activity for
sexual harassers, emphasizing that an individual's harassing behaviors
are embedded in his relationship with the victimized person, which in
turn is embedded in the policies and practices of the work environment,
which is then embedded in the norms and values of the larger sociocultural environment. Pryor and Whelan (1997) describe situational conditions that are necessary for harassers to act. Some individuals will never
harass, some will harass in the presence of enabling factors that are few
in number, and still others only when the convergence of many enabling

factors is present. Sexual harassment perpetrators are hard to study because many cases go unreported, and, frequently, perpetrators deny any
culpability. Research approaches have included interviews of women
regarding their harassers, asking men about harassing behaviors without labeling them as such, and asking men about their proclivity to sexually harass if they knew they wouldn't get caught (Bondurant & White,
1996). Findings from perpetrator studies have yielded demographic
characteristics, personality traits, and harassing typologies based on
psychological motivation or modes of actions (roles and tactics).

Demographics

Demographically, typical sexual harassers are married coworkers who
are older than those they victimize and of the same racial or ethnic
group, except for African American, Hispanic, and Asian Pacific Is-
lander women, who are usually harassed by men of different ethnic
groups (U.S. Merit Systems Protections Board, 1981). Hostile environment harassers are more common than quid pro quo harassers, sexual
assault perpetrators, or repeated harassers. More serious forms of perpetrator behaviors are committed by supervisors or superiors of the victimized individuals. Also, the more severe the harassment, the more
likely the harasser is to victimize other women as well.

Character Traits

Several scales have been developed, including the Likelihood to Sexually Harass (LSH) and the Modern Sexism Scale, in order to identify
personal characteristics of men with proclivities toward harassment.
These traits include

1. Acceptance of rape myths, such as women's desire and wish to be
   raped
2. Proclivity for sexual violence
3. Belief in antagonistic and adversarial relationships between men and
   women
4. Acceptance of hypermasculine stereotypes
5. Diminished capacity for empathy and ability to appreciate the other
   person's situation
6. Low acceptance of feminist beliefs

7. Tendency to connect sexuality with dominance
8. Desire for status
9. Denial of continuing discrimination and antagonism toward women's demands in the workplace (Pryor, 1987; Swim, Aiken, Hall & Hunter, 1995)

Distinct characteristics for perpetrators of other forms of gender discrimination have not been identified. It is unlikely, given the diversity of these behaviors, that a comparable set of specific trait demographics will emerge. Also, many forms of gender discrimination, such as job segregation and discriminatory institutional policies, do not constitute individual interactions with a specific perpetrator. When individual perpetrators do exist, (1) acceptance of traditional sex role stereotypes, (2) lack of capacity to appreciate another person's situation, and (3) denial of continuing workplace discrimination of women are often characteristic, in my experience. A typology based on the motivation of the perpetrator has been identified for gender-based employment discrimination and will be discussed in the next section.

SEXUAL HARASSMENT AND GENDER DISCRIMINATION TYPOLOGIES

A number of typologies based on the mode of action or motivation for action have been identified for perpetrators of sexual harassment in academic settings and in the workplace. Although they overlap to some degree, they are all useful to clinicians and others interested in understanding the nature of the discriminatory interaction with the victimized person.

Perpetrator Harassment Typologies for Academia

Dziech and Weiner (1984) describe two typologies of academic harassment based on the mode of action. The public harasser is a casual and sociable person who engages in public relationships with students, in which he frequently tells sexual jokes. He is more likely to engage in the less severe forms of sexual harassment. The private harasser appears professional, conservative, and removed in public but, privately, is more likely to engage in more severe forms of quid pro quo sexual harassment and in sexual assault. Within these two typologies, the professor may adopt five different roles to initiate sexual intimacy, as described by Dzeich and Weiner (1984). The counselor-helper takes a flattering personal interest in students but uses the information he gets in the service of initiating unwelcome sexual intimacy. The confidant treats students as equals, provides personal favors, and encourages intimate personal conferences. He shares personal information about himself and either traps his students or leaves them feeling obligated to concede to his wishes. The intellectual seducer first impresses students with his academic prowess and uses academic pretenses to gain personal information about students and their vulnerabilities. The opportunist uses field trips, laboratory work, or meetings in his home as excuses to lower inhibitions, touch students, and pursue further intimacies. The power broker directly utilizes his power over grades, publications, recommendations, and so on, to bargain for sexual favors. Zalk (1990) suggests that the public-private typologies are really extremes along the continuum that in reality may maintain aspects of both. He suggests the following three alternatives.

1. The seducer-demander who actively solicits sexual activity, versus the receptive noninitiator
2. The untouchable who feels superior and entitled to sexual activity with his students, versus the risk taker who knows his behavior is wrong, experiences anxiety in that context, may sadistically abandon a student after sexual encounters
3. The infatuated professor who feels affection and believes he is in love with his student, versus the sexual conqueror who has no personal interest in the student and takes pleasure only in the sexual encounter itself

Zalk (1990) contends that most sexually harassing professors' interactions fall somewhere along the continuum of each of these three axes. Many of these descriptions are similar to the summary provided by me in Bernstein and Lenhart, 1993, regarding the research on sexual exploitation in professional relationships (doctors, dentists, clergymen, lawyers, etc.), and it is likely, but yet to be empirically documented, that these typologies can be found in supervisors and mentors who harass in employment settings. These typologies emphasize problematic behaviors in a superior–subordinate relationship of a fiduciary nature and are not readily applicable to much of the coworker hostile environment harassment that occurs in the workplace.

CASE VIGNETTE 4-2

Seducer-Untouchable-Private Harasser

Janet DiMaggio was a 20-year-old undergraduate student at a highly prestigious university. Her faculty adviser was a 42-year-old professor, Dr. Owen Hall, who offered both expert advice and unique opportunities to co-edit a journal in the highly specialized field she wished to enter after graduation. Owen was highly respected, somewhat aloof, and very impressive in class. Many students coveted Janet's relationship with him. She felt fortunate until Owen began to discuss problems with his marriage during their evening journal editorial meetings. As the year progressed, he began to ask Janet probing questions about her boyfriend and persisted when Janet attempted to redirect the conversation to the editorial work. One evening when they were working alone, Owen approached her from behind, kissed her neck, and rubbed her shoulders. Janet drew away and requested that he stop. Despite her objections, he persisted in this behavior at each of their weekly meetings, saying nothing when Janet pulled away. He continued the work discussions as though nothing had happened. Janet did not wish to endanger this valuable relationship and doubted that anyone would believe this highly regarded professor was capable of such behavior. Feeling immobilized, confused, and distressed, she remained silent for 3 months. She ultimately went to the dean when Owen attempted to fondle her breasts. With the support of the dean, Karen filed a complaint. Owen denied his behaviors, and the formal inquiry was inconclusive. With the dean's assistance, Karen was transferred to another adviser. Karen lost her opportunity to continue as co-editor, as well as her relationship to Owen, who never apologized and treated her coldly whenever they met in class or on campus.

Perpetrator Harassment Typologies Based on the Perspectives of Victimized People

Victimized women reporting on their harassers' behavior emphasize three typologies, based on their perceptions of the motivation of the perpetrator: (1) the male gender role, (2) power, and (3) the psychological characteristics of the harasser. The most common motivation cited was that of power over the victimized individual or of a related fear that the harasser might be losing power at work. Aspects of the male gender role included objectification of women into sexual objects, hostility toward women, and seeing men as the dominant sexual aggressors. Psychological characteristics reported were emotional weakness, insecurity, immaturity, and personal problems. Interestingly, the psychological characteristics were the least likely to be mentioned as a motivation (Crull, 1991).

CASE VIGNETTE 4-3

Male Gender Role/Power/Personality Problems

Sam Watts, a 50-year-old married man with a debilitating chronic illness, was the branch manager of a large and profitable real estate agency whose main offices were located in another state. Because of its isolated location and high productivity, it was seldom visited by senior management, who respected Sam for his yearly high-profit figures. Sam employed 1 male assistant manager and 20 females who served as agents or as office support staff. Sam personally hired each of his employees, usually selecting young attractive women who were undereducated, often in financial distress, and occasionally drug abusers. He told each new employee that he owned this branch office himself and promised them a warm family atmosphere and large financial bonuses on a weekly basis if their work was satisfactory. Initially, he took a personal interest in each employee, praising her work, chatting about her personal life, and immediately offering weekly bonuses. Sam's wife was also employed in the office and sometimes accompanied him to the various workstations, where he would fondle the women employees' breasts, squeeze their buttocks, and call them "his wives." Office parties were often held at Sam's home, and risqué dress, jokes, and illicit drug use were encouraged. Sam had affairs with two of the employees and often engaged in drug use with them. He brought nude photos of these women to work to show other employees. Sam established a policy of allowing the staff to leave early if one of the women would expose her breasts to him. He badgered each new employee to take her turn, stating, "I've seen everyone else's—I need to see yours." If any employee tried to extricate herself, she would be threatened with firing and would receive no bonuses. When an employee appeared to be at the breaking point, Sam would apologize profusely and state that his medical condition and medications affected his judgment. Sam especially seemed to enjoy badgering new employees until they gave in to his demands. Sam sent part of the staff on a pleasure trip at company expense but insisted they wear T-shirts with "Sam's Wives" stamped across the front. Most of the staff members tried to handle the situation by joking, ignoring the behavior, and returning the jokes. Several employees "took him on," determined to be tough enough to take whatever he dished out. Two of the female supervisors confronted Sam and complained to the assistant manager, who said he feared for his job and encouraged them to "wait it out," as Sam was planning to retire. Sam's response was, "If you don't like it, leave. You're easy to replace." A crisis occurred when one of the women became hysterical when Sam exposed himself to her. She left the office, screaming, "I can't take any more of this!" and did not return to work. Feeling guilty about their coworker, several of the women began to document Sam's behavior. They eventually consulted an attorney and filed a lawsuit. Sam was fired but continued to stalk the women at home, insisting that they meet with him and that his affection for them was real.

Perpetrator Harassment Typologies Based on Psychological Function

Pryor and Whelan (1997) suggest four typologies based on the psychological functions that may be served. They suggest that sexual harassment is based on either sexual or hostile intent and that there are two typologies within each of these psychological parameters: sexual exploitation (1) and sexual miscommunication (2) represent sexual intent. Misogyny (3) and homo-anathema (4) represent hostile intent. (1) Sexual exploitation describes situations in which the perpetrator imposes sexual intimacy in the context of a power differential. The power can be (1) organizational (boss–subordinate); (2) status (man's higher status in society); (3) physical (the perpetrator is physically stronger than the victimized individual); or (4) situational (the perpetrator has special information regarding the victimized women that can be used to make her vulnerable). This typology conforms with the previously described professor–student form of exploitation as well as to the traits of merging power and sex and having excessive needs for power, which were included in the Likelihood to Sexually Harass profile.

The second typology is labeled *sexual attraction miscommunication*. In this instance, the perpetrator is interested in establishing a nonexploitative sexual relationship with a woman at work and misperceives her friendliness as sexual interest or is insensitive or unable to interpret her lack of interest. Shotland (1992) has demonstrated how misperceptions of sexual intent can contribute to courtship rape, and *Ellison v. Brady* (1991) demonstrates how this form of harassment can be perceived as threatening by the victimized women. Empirical evidence for this typology is conflictual. Pryer (1994) cites a government study of 2,600 employees, in which three-fourths of the women who reported unwanted sexual attention were not concerned about sexual exploitation but rather were bothered because (1) the behavior was seen as unprofessional, (2) the individual was insensitive to their feelings, or (3) they were not attracted to the individual. Conversely, Frank Saal (1996) described a series of studies that refute the hypothesis that men who misperceive women's friendly behavior as a sign of sexual interest are more likely to endorse and engage in sexual harassment. The sexual miscommunication typology also does not consider Crull's (1991) study of victims who perceive power and the male gender role as the primary motivations of their harassers. It is important for clinicians to recognize that although this is a plausible hypothesis, it is not supported empirically. It also may be used as an excuse to confuse victimized individuals, to discourage them from more assertive responses, or to exonerate perpetrators in court.

The third typology described by Pryor and Whelan, which is based on hostile motivation, is labeled *misogyny*. The perpetrator's intent here is to communicate hostile and degrading attitudes toward women as members of the out-group at work. This tactic may be used as a means of excluding women from the workgroup and impeding their advancement within the work organization. It is common in highly cohesive traditional male workgroups, where women's numbers are small, they are perceived as a growing, threatening minority, or both. It is often combined with nonsexual forms of hostile environment and disparate treatment gender discrimination. Ironically, women with a feminist attitude are less likely to be harassed than are those with careerist attitudes who deny the existence of discrimination (Pryor & Whelan, 1997).

Homo-anathema, the fourth typology, is also based on hostile motivation on the part of the perpetrator, who harasses victims based on the perception that they are homosexual. There is some evidence that men target women they perceive to be gay. There is also evidence of its potential impact on male victims, a special group, which will be discussed in the next section. The following case example illustrates a perpetrator typology based on psychological functioning.

CASE VIGNETTE 4-4

Misogyny

Christine Stamtis was a 30-year-old divorced packer in a small machine parts manufacturing company. She was the only woman working on the machine floor with 35 men but worked in isolation in a small alcove, with little interaction with her coworkers. She ate her lunch with the two female office secretaries and basically kept to herself. She was slightly uncomfortable with the posters and calendars of nude women that hung on company bulletin boards and employee locker doors but basically ignored these aspects of her environment, focusing on the high pay and benefits she received, in comparison to her previous jobs. Because of her high productivity, she was promoted to inspector after 3 years' working with the firm. Her new position involved direct interaction with and supervision of 10 to 15 male employees. Her coworkers immediately responded with hostility, questioning her authority and barraging her with lewd and devaluing comments. "Women aren't worth toilet paper." "Who are you fucking now?" "You're in my way, bitch," and so on. The men told demeaning sexual jokes, speaking loudly and gesturing toward her. Christine constantly found copies of *Hustler* magazine and animal droppings on her desk, which would reappear the day after she discarded them. She complained to her supervisor. His response was that if she wanted the job, she would just have to get used to it. Six months into her new position, she abruptly quit after she opened her locker to find a graphic picture of a woman being raped. It was inscribed, "This is what is going to happen to you." She consulted an attorney and filed a lawsuit. Although she ultimately won a large settlement, she was accused of sexual promiscuousness and lewd behavior during the deposition and the court testimony by a united front of coworkers and managers, who uniformly insisted that she welcomed the behaviors.

Perpetrator Discrimination Typologies for Key Decision Makers

A typology for perpetrators of gender discrimination who hold key decision-making roles within the work organization was developed by labor economist Mary Rowe (1990) and is illustrated in discussions by Bernard (1988) and Rush (1993). Rowe describes the biases against women employees that occur at the level of individual decision makers, which are highly significant because of the power inherent in the decision maker's position in the hierarchy. Although these interactions are not always illegal, they negatively impact morale, self-esteem, job performance, and opportunities for promotion and training. Rowe termed these interactions *micro-inequities* and notes that their impact is cumulative, like drops of water collecting in a bucket. Utilizing the motivation of the perpetrator, Rowe divided micro-inequities into four categories:

1. Unconscious Slights and Invisibility Problems—The perpetrator perceives women's work differently from men's. It may be ignored, devalued, or attributed to a male colleague. The perpetrator leaves women out of both formal and informal work networks. Victimized individuals often do not perceive conscious malice on the part of perpetrators, which creates confusion regarding how to respond.
2. Conscious Slights and Harassment—The perpetrator is overtly hostile toward women, indicating that they are incompetent or inappropriate for their work role, or the perpetrator barrages women with unwanted, devaluing attention based on gender, overscrutinizes their work, or both.
3. Poor Service—The perpetrator does not equitably promote women or provide them with training and educational opportunities. The perpetrator overtly discourages them from opportunities because they are women.
4. Exploitation—The perpetrator pays women less, does not give credit for work done, or places women in positions where they cannot deliver work that would lead to promotion. The perpetrator utilizes women's training and abilities in the intentional services of promoting someone else.

Rowe (1977, 1990) and Lenhart and Evans (1991) have discussed the negative impact of these types of micro-inequities, which include the following factors, summarized by me in Bernstein and Lenhart, 1993, pp. 138–139:

1. The power of negative reinforcement dictates women will perform at the level expected of them and perceive themselves negatively if they receive negative feedback from significant authorities.
2. Micro-inequities make it impossible for capable female employees to perform quality work, overloading them with routine or personal work that stifles creativity and stability.
3. Micro-inequities are irrational, intermittent, and do not occur in the context of merit or striving for excellence. Laboratory studies have shown that such intermittent, unpredictable negative reinforcement creates high levels of anxiety and a sense of helplessness, leading to demoralization.
4. Micro-inequities are difficult to address. If women ignore them, they permit situations to continue that may damage their careers, but if they respond, they may be pegged as overreactive and as troublemakers.
5. Micro-inequities take up time and energy.
6. Micro-inequities exaggerate the polarity between men and women, making it harder for them to work together.
7. Women have few role models to help them deal with methods for redress. Women supervisors often react with a sense of denial, helplessness, or identification with the aggressor.
8. Power politics operate in micro-inequities, in that the perpetrators are often in authority positions and the women are often in subordinate positions.
9. Micro-inequities are especially detrimental if they occur at the vulnerable point when a woman is attempting to consolidate her career and her maternal role at the same time.
10. Many women have been socialized to be sensitive to anger and disapproval directed at them, as well as inhibited in asserting their own anger. This makes the impact of micro-inequities especially significant and difficult to address.
11. Micro-inequities are extremely difficult to stop in skewed groups (groups where women are in a significant minority), due to the intergroup dynamics already described.

Rowe feels that it is more difficult for women to find support in dealing with micro-inequities than it is for White males to find help in dealing with general incivility and work harassment. Continued experience of these destructive situations can lead to unhappy cycles of avoidance behavior, declining self-esteem, withdrawal, resignation, poor work performance, and fantasies of violence. These difficulties are not easily legislated out of existence and are difficult to address within existing complaint channels. The following micro-inequity case examples illustrate the inordinate power of bias at the level of a key decision maker.

CASE VIGNETTE 4-5

Micro-Inequities: Conscious Slights and Poor Service

Mary Kotowski was a 24-year-old third-year medical student who had recently been accepted into a prestigious MD/PhD combined program offered at the Ivy League medical school she was attending. After acceptance to the program, she began meeting with the nine other candidates, of which she was the only female. The group regularly met with Dr. Wall, an internationally renowned researcher, who served as the overall program director. Initially, Dr. Wall was complimentary to Mary, stating his interest in having a female candidate in the program. Mary continued to make good grades and entered the research phase of her program with great enthusiasm. She was assigned to a supervisor she greatly admired and respected and with whom she was quite compatible. All proceeded well until she became pregnant. At this point her program director, Dr. Wall, expressed his strong sentiment that Mary's pregnancy was an unwelcome addition in this highly competitive program and emphasized that his wife had quit her job after their first child was born. He began to express his concerns that Mary would be unable to handle the work involved. Nonetheless, he agreed to her negotiating a 3-month maternity leave, during which she worked intermittently on her research project. Her immediate research supervisor remained enthusiastic about her work. Six months after Mary returned from her maternity leave, Dr. Wall informed her that he was greatly concerned about the quality of her work. Startled, she asked him the basis for his concern, and he was unable to give her a direct answer. She consulted with her research adviser, who was supervising all of her ongoing work. He assured her that her recommendations from him were consistently high. She immediately scheduled a conference between the three of them, during which the program director was jovial and collegial toward both her and her research supervisor. She learned, however, from a friend in the dean's office that the program director continued to voice concern at administrative levels about her viability in the program. She was dismayed when 1 year after her maternity leave, in the midst of a successful ongoing research project, the director informed her that he was recommending her dismissal from the program. He acknowledged that her grades and recommendations had remained high, but he did not feel this was an appropriate slot for her and would not recommend her if she chose to remain in the program. Angry and dismayed, she considered filing a complaint or a lawsuit but was cautioned by her colleagues, her husband, and the dean regarding potential informal retaliation. She ultimately conceded to her program director's wishes, returned to the regular program, completed her medical school education, and graduated with honors, but she developed depression when it came time to apply for specialty training.

CASE VIGNETTE 4-6

Micro-Inequities: Unconscious Slights and Exploitation

Susan Demoli, a 42-year-old mother of three, worked for 10 years as a secretary and receptionist for Dr. James O'Neil, a well-respected family doctor in her community. Despite a low salary, Susan enjoyed the work, found the hours compatible with her family responsibilities, and was able to depend on her husband for the primary family income. In the last 2 years, however, the stress of the job increased, due to the larger volume, complexity of patient billings, and patients' complaints over insurance problems. Susan, as the senior person in the office, had to handle most of these problems and felt proud that James relied on her support. She was distressed at his increased depression, his irritability over the hassles of medicine, and his frequent outbursts at her if the office did not run smoothly. She fluctuated between feeling concerned about him and feeling disappointed by his lack of appreciation for her efforts and empathy for her position. Her situation escalated when, after learning that her husband might be laid off, she approached James for her first salary increase. He was furious and accused her of disloyalty. He then denigrated the quality of her work. She retreated in distress. Susan had no other job experience, and felt conflicted about her loyalty to James and increasingly worried about family finances.

CONTEXTUAL FACTORS AFFECTING PERPETRATORS

As with responses of victimized individuals, perpetrators' behavior is also significantly impacted by environmental factors in the work organization and larger society. Some researchers believe that repeated harassment cannot take place without the presence of facilitating environmental conditions (Pryor & Whelan, 1997). Like perpetrators of domestic violence, sexual harassers usually have some form of power (organizational status, situational, physical) over their victims, who are often isolated. The isolation may be due to the low number of females in the workplace (example: coal miners and surgeons), to the isolating conditions of the job (example: police patrol officer, traveling sales representative), or to the perpetrators' ability to place the victim in an isolated situation (example: secretary or research assistant asked to work late) (Cleveland & McNamara, 1996). The more significant the power differential, the more severe the harassment (Loy & Stewart, 1984). In more serious cases like rape and sexual assault, the sexual harasser, like the batterer, works alone and uses physical force combined with psychological, economical, or political threats to silence the victim; induce fear, shame, and embarrassment; and separate her from validation and support (Bondurant & White, 1996). Organization power differentials are also important to perpetrators of other forms of gender discrimination, as indicated by Rowe's (1977) description of the disproportionate impact of bias toward women at the level of key decision makers. Isolation and low numbers of women in the workplace make it more difficult for the woman to validate her discriminatory experience and seek redress. This type of numerical isolation also leaves a woman vulnerable to gender stereotyping and skewed group dynamics which result in other forms of gender discrimination. (Refer to the discussion in Chapter 2.)

Characteristics of the work or academic environment that increase the likelihood of harassing and discriminatory behavior have also been identified. In an academic setting, Bondurant and White (1996) and Dziech and Weiner (1984) have identified the following factors for sexual harassment:

1. High autonomy and low scrutiny extended to professors, regarding access to students and working conditions
2. The diffusion of authority for faculty members' behavior
3. The absence of guidelines regarding faculty–student relationships
4. In-group loyalties and resistance of peers to report abusive faculty members
5. Low numbers of women faculty members and administrators and associated lack of acceptance of women's concerns
6. Faculty preference for in-depth analysis, rather than action, regarding gender discriminatory issues
7. Lack of a cohesive student voice

The single most important predictor of sexual harassment occurring in graduate training was a department's overall approval of sexual relationships between faculty members and students (Bond, 1991). In nonacademic workplaces the following relevant characteristics, related to management, sex ratios, and organizational factors, have been identified as predictors for sexual harassment:

1. Management encourages or fails to respond to harassment and discrimination.
2. The victimized person is managed by a male boss whose presence, independent of his viewpoint, disinhibits other men from harassing behavior.
3. Ther is a low female-to-male sex ratio in the workplace.
4. There is a low score on equal opportunity ratings within the organization.
5. A woman holds a job that requires her to have frequent contact with men (this applies primarily to blue-collar occupations).
6. A woman holds a job that is considered nontraditional for women.
7. A woman has job that is perceived as difficult to get and high in status.
8. A woman holds a job that is predominantly female and is associated with a woman being perceived as a sex object, such as a secretary and a receptionist.

9. A woman has a job that is low in status.
10. The workplace consists of cohesive male workgroups that perceive women as outsiders (Bondurant & White, 1996; Pryor & Whelan, 1997).

Although identified in association with sexual harassment, many of these factors are applicable to other forms of sex discrimination as well.

Two special factors require particular discussion (1) the unprofessional workplace, and (2) workplaces characterized by cohesive male workgroups that perceive women as outsiders (Bondurant & White, 1996; Pryor & Whelan, 1997). In the unprofessional workplace, the boundaries between work and personal life are blurred. Coworkers may regularly engage in consensual sexual relationships, provocative dress, office flirtations, and sexual jokes. Another version of the unprofessional workplace is less overtly sexualized and is characterized by obscene language, swearing, practical jokes, petty office politics, disrespectful behaviors toward employees and women in particular, and expectations that women will perform non–job related tasks, such as babysitting, making coffee, running errands, shopping, and so on. Gutek (1985) has documented that harassment is likely to increase in both of these types of unprofessional settings. These unprofessional settings have also been associated with higher levels of other forms of discrimination, in accordance with Nieva's (1982) sex role model of discrimination (see Chapter 2).

Social norms condoning and permitting harassment and hostile environment discriminatory action can also occur within cohesive male workgroups that believe that women are outsiders. These attitudes may emanate from an authority figure or from peers within the workgroup. Once a man with proclivities to harass witnesses another man sexually harassing a woman, he is likely to begin harassing women as well (Pryor & Whelan, 1997). This role model effect is persistent in these environments. In a significant minority of cases several men will sexually harass one woman. These are usually coworkers (U.S. Merit Systems Protection Board, 1987). It is possible that harassers operating in this context identify with the group norm and experience less personal responsibility for their behavior. This type of sexual harassment is especially prevalent when a woman is a sole member of a workgroup or she represents a threatening minority in a situation where workers are competing for limited resources (Pryor & Whelan, 1997). This type of situation is often characterized by hostile environment sexual harassment, as well as by other forms of disparate treatment and hostile environment discrimination of a nonsexual nature. These behaviors can serve as a means of driving women from jobs where they were not wanted in the first place (Pryor & Whelan, 1997) and may explain the high turnover rate for women in male-dominated blue-collar jobs (Gutek & Koss, 1996).

Although certain workplace characteristics may facilitate harassment and discrimination, overriding sociocultural norms may impact on any work environment (see Chapter 2). Social scripts that are defined as prescribed ways to behave in certain situations may reinforce workplace behaviors that are discriminating toward women. Traditional and deeply embedded sexual scripts define women as sexual limit setters, subordinates, and nurturers and men as sexual aggressors and superiors who are expected to push the limit. Gutek found evidence of such gender role stereotyping in victim-harasser interactions preceding actual events of sexual harassment. This propensity for gender roles to take precedence over work roles may also explain the phenomena of counter-power sexual harassment, in which women who occupy positions of power in the workplace are still harassed by their subordinates (e.g., female college professors are harassed by male students) (Benson, 1984; Furr, 2002; Gutek & Koss, 1996).

THE POLARIZING DYNAMICS OF SEX DISCRIMINATION

Victimized individuals and those close to them often report on the intense and polarizing impact of sexual harassment and gender discrimination. There is great disparity regarding how people define sexual harassment and gender discrimination and how they react to those who are victimized. These disparate perspectives are accompanied by intense affect. This can be seen as the effect not only of individual and gender differences in perception but also of dynamics of dominant–subordinate interactions. Women are more likely than men to define an event as sexual harassment or gender discrimination and also to perceive the event as threatening, negative, or both, in outcome. Men are more likely to perceive women's friendly behavior as indicative of sexual interest and to see the workplace as an equitable environment. They are joined by a subset of women that focuses primarily on career, minimizes differences in equity in the workplace, and is reluctant to identify with a subordinate group. Miller (1976), Pryor and Whelan (1997), and Wood (1992) have noted that the dominant members of society and work organizations, who are predominantly male, label, organize, and define the social and work realities. They fail to integrate the perceptions and experiences of subordinate groups, rendering them invisible. Dominants also resist and punish those who raise issues. The format of the current complaint system and a litigation process that forces an assignment of blame (who is right and who is wrong), as opposed to mediating a resolution of the situation, further enhances the polarization processes. Victimized individuals may encounter difficulties with validation and support not only within their workplace but also within their personal lives. The embeddedness and unconsciousness of gender-based and dominant–subordinate based differences in perception and the strong association of male with dominant and female with subordinate status make it likely that the intense polarization process surrounding these issues will be long-standing. This impact will be felt by victimized individuals, perpetrators, their superiors, and their coworkers, as well as by significant people in their personal lives. Because of the intensity of this polarization process, significant disruptions in the victimized individuals' work and personal relationships are common in discrimination or harassment situations, especially if the wronged person files a complaint or a lawsuit. Often these disruptions are as traumatic for the victimized person as the discrimination itself was.

Valued mentors and supervisors may be lost if they are the perpetrators of harassment and discrimination or if they fail to support and validate a victimized woman's experience and efforts for redress. Coworkers may ostracize her as a troublemaker or a slut. They may capitalize on any managerial retaliatory actions by taking over her work, her position, or both, if she is demoted. They may side with the perpetrator and the work organization and either retaliate against her directly or fail to validate or support her efforts for redress, even if they have witnessed the events. Coworkers who have been supportive in private may be unwilling to come forward publicly. Others who have suffered discrimination may be too frightened to join in the complaint. The institution may employ the use of "token women" spokespersons who publicly deny discrimination and praise the organization, or it may promote other women to discredit the victimized woman's claims of discrimination. Female mentors may deny the discrimination or become too demoralized to help. Spouses and significant others may identify with the perpetrator or become worried that the woman is having an affair or in some way invited sexual overtures. They may become intrusive into the workplace to protect her or insist upon her taking impulsive legal action. Fathers may overidentify with management and discourage assertive action or overidentify with their daughters and insist that the woman take actions that may not be in their best interest. They may also intrude into their daughters' workplaces to handle the situation themselves. Mothers may feel embarrassed by the public exposure of their daughters in a sexual situation or feel guilty that they did not sufficiently prepare their daughters for the inequities in workplace. Daughters may identify with mothers who are victimized and feel frightened or discouraged. The complexities of the polarization process are unlimited. The mental health implications of this process will be discussed in Chapters 5, 6, and 7. The special polarization dynamics relating to victimized individuals who are gay or members of cultural or ethnic minorities will be discussed in the next section.

CASE VIGNETTE 4-7

Polarizing Dynamics

Arvella Williams was a 35-year-old married mother of two who had worked in a meat-packing plant for 15 years. She was an attractive member of the Black community and attended many church and social affairs. Her first marriage had ended in divorce when she had an extramarital affair in the context of marital strife for which her husband had refused counseling. Her second marriage has remained stable and fulfilling from its onset 8 years ago. Arvella was please with her job, felt appreciated by coworkers, and was proud of the income she could bring to her family. She began experiencing difficulties at work when Dan Horn, a 40-year-old White man, was assigned to her department. Dan approached her persistently for dates, commenting loudly that he'd heard Black women were really "hot."

When Dan's behavior escalated to include after-work harassment, Arvella attempted to file a formal complaint with the union in which both she and Dan were members. Her union steward refused to take the complaint, stating that it was unnecessary, as he would handle the situation personally. A company manager, aware of the situation, reported it to personnel and the company held its own investigation, which resulted in Dan being sanctioned with a suspension. Coworkers, blaming Arvella, ostracized her at work and made hostile comments regarding her disloyalty to a union brother. Union members collected statements documenting her alleged lewd and promiscuous behavior at work. The union succeeded in having Dan's sanctions overturned, and he returned to work.

Dan continued his harassment, and Arvella continued to receive hostile treatment from coworkers. Her tires were slashed in the company parking lot, and her family began receiving anonymous threatening phone calls at night. Her children were frightened and were restricted from playing outside. Her security guard husband vacillated between periods of rage, in which he threatened to shoot Dan; periods when he supported Arvella in her attempts to file a complaint with regional union officials; and periods in which he withdrew from Arvella sexually, raising the issue of the affair in her first marriage and accusing her of cheating on him, too.

When the union officials failed to respond, Arvella filed a lawsuit against the union. Concomitantly, she began to experience depressive and anxiety symptoms and sought counseling from her minister. The minister asked her detailed questions about her sex life and her past marital infidelity and attempted to kiss her during one of their meetings. She promptly terminated the sessions but was fearful of reporting the occurrence to her husband or to members of her church.

Although Arvella subsequently won a large settlement in court, she and her husband separated for a period during the process. She felt forced to seek another job with a reduced salary, she stopped attending church, and she and her children required psychiatric treatment.

SPECIAL VICTIM-PERPETRATOR GROUPS

Sexual harassment and gender discrimination among special populations involves special dynamics, which have been largely unexamined.

This section will review what is known regarding the experiences of victimized individuals who are male, are gay, or represent ethnic or cultural minorities. Secondary victims will also be discussed. The information primarily centers on sexual harassment, as very little empirical work has been done with regard to the broader area of gender-based discrimination.

Same-Sex Harassment and Discrimination of Women

Sexual harassment of women by other women is a relatively uncommon experience. Most survey results parallel those of the U.S. Merit Systems Protection Board, which tracked unwanted sexual experiences among a large number of federal employees in three large-scale studies occurring in 1981, 1987, and 1995. In 1981 only 3% of women victims reported female perpetrators, and by 1995 the numbers decreased to 1% female perpetrators. Special inhibitions in victimized individuals' responses may occur in this unusual type of situation, but empirical data regarding the specifics of the interaction are not yet available. If the victimized woman is heterosexual, she may hesitate to utilize direct methods, such as reporting her harasser if her harasser is a superior or if she is embarrassed or fearful that others may misperceive her as gay. If the victimized woman is gay herself, she may avoid direct complaints because of fear of exposing her sexual orientation in the workplace or encouraging the criticism of her gay community for complaining about one of their own and bringing adverse publicity to the community. Gay women who are already out of the closet are most often tokens within organizations and therefore subject to the discriminatory group dynamics reported in Chapter 2. Their token position within their organization may complicate any complaints they would wish to make. Female mentors and bosses who deny discrimination and identify with dominant norms in the workplace may perpetuate discrimination behaviors via the same mechanisms as their male colleagues. They may also enjoy their token status and wish to eliminate any potential competition from other women (the queen bee syndrome). They may feel embittered by the barriers they encountered and believe their junior colleagues should have to endure the same treatment. All of these behaviors are particularly demoralizing to victimized women.

Same-Sex Harassment and Discrimination of Men

In the same U.S. Merit Systems Protection Boards studies, men victimized by unwanted sexual attention identified male perpetrators in one fourth to one third of the incidences they reported. In a more recent and specific study of male victims by Waldo, Berndahl, and Fitzgerald (1998), there were indications that male-to-male harassment may be more common (approximately 50% of incidences of gender harassment, including unwanted sexual attention). A man who is harassed by a male superior may fear reporting for the same reasons as his female counterpart. A homosexual man victimized by another homosexual man may be inhibited in the same way as his female counterpart. A study by Waldo, Berndahl, and Fitzgerald (1998) demonstrated that a significant proportion of victimized men encounter a different dynamic, which is related less to sexual attention than it is to enforcement of the traditional male stereotype. This results in devaluing or degrading comments that are directed toward men who are perceived as gay or feminine or who are performing traditionally female roles, such as child care. This form of gender discrimination is unique to victimized men and is perceived as more upsetting than is unwanted sexual attention (Waldo, Berndahl, & Fitzgerald, 1998).

Harassment of Men by Women

With the exception of this study by Waldo and associates, most of the research indicates that victimized men are most frequently harassed by women who are coworkers or subordinates. Thus, the women are not in a position to significantly influence the jobs or careers of the men they harass. In addition, in the larger cultural context, male sexual attractiveness and virility are considered enhancing to, rather than detracting from, men's professional competence and status. It is not surprising that in this context, men, in contrast to their female counterparts, often consider sexual harassment flattering, mutual, nonthreatening to their work and career goals, devoid of negative consequences, and therefore not meriting formal complaint or litigation (Gutek, 1985). Nonetheless, they are vulnerable to negative sequelae when their harasser is in a position to damage them at work. There is also some evidence to suggest that as women become more prominent in the workplace, the harassment of men may increase as an expression of abusive power. Kline, in an unpublished study (F. Kline, Kline Associates, Boston, MA, 1993), noted that in one large organization with many female managers and where the CEO condoned discriminatory behavior, the women managers harassed their male subordinates at a significantly higher rate. At this time, however, men are victimized at much lower rates than women are, and their experiences carry fewer of the negative sequelae experienced by women.

Sex Discrimination Involving Cultural and Ethnic Minority Groups

Several issues should be considered in understanding the victim-perpetrator dynamics involving victimized members of racial or cultural minority groups, such as Hispanic, Asian, African American, and Native American individuals. Both the occurrence and the characteristics of these interactions have been widely discussed in the literature but have been grossly understudied. Thus, little can be said with empirical certainty. Many factors have been identified as contributing to the complexity of the discriminatory experiences of women of color by perpetrators who are of the same race or who are Caucasian.

Social stereotypes associated with race may encourage perpetrators to view victims in highly sexualized and nonprofessional ways. Victims may even be perceived as deserving and inviting harassment and discrimination. Examples include the Jezebel and Sapphire stereotypes, which portray African American women as promiscuous, hypersexual, and easily appropriated by white men or as evil, manipulative, amoral, and disloyal. Asian stereotypes of women include features of exotica, passivity, and submission to men. The Latino stereotype of the hot-blooded, passionate woman who submits to a dominant, macho Latin man is also prevalent. Stereotypes of minority women as maids or nannies living in affluent households contribute to their perception as low-skilled workers, who are available for sexual exploitation by their affluent employers and are unsuitable for high-status, highly compensated leadership positions (Adams, 1997).

Other factors strongly associated with racial minority status include low-status and low-pay positions, low social status, cultural and economic marginality, numerical minority, or token status within workgroups. All of these constitute high-risk factors for sexual harassment and discrimination, as well as limited possibilities for redress. They represent the combination of racial and gender discrimination toward women of color (Adams, 1997).

The tradition of sexualizing racial discrimination is characteristic of the African American slave experience, which includes several features (Lerner, 1972):

1. Black women share in all aspects of oppression of Blacks in general.
2. Black women are objects of exploitive sex by White men.
3. The rape of Black women is employed as a weapon of terror directed against the entire Black community.
4. When Black men are prevented through social taboos and violence from defending their own women, the oppression of all Blacks is heightened and institutionalized.
5. When Black men are oppressed economically to an extent that they cannot secure steady employment at decent wages, many Black women are deprived of the support of a male breadwinner and must take on additional economic burdens and psychological burdens (Lerner, 1972, p. 149).

Learner also describes an institutionalized system of racism that includes limited economic opportunities, sexual exploitation, and the devaluing of the relationships between African American men and women. This combination of sex and racial discrimination may be applicable to other racial and ethnic minority groups and can make it difficult for victimized women to determine the difference between sexual harassment and gender discrimination or sexual racism. They may view their experience as racism and thus respond differently than their White counterparts do. Their perception of a lack of protection, a lack of credibility, and a lack of value compared to White women may make it far more likely that they do not report, seek redress, or seek professional help for their problems. The sense that they will not be better treated elsewhere may also prevent them from leaving discriminatory situations. The likelihood of their seeking direct help and redress can also be complicated by religious and cultural values that place high credence on female modesty and virginity and that value domestic roles over work roles. Women coming from cultures such as this may find it difficult to bring attention to their situation and to advocate for better working conditions for themselves. Minority women may also limit the nature of their interpersonal contacts with White men at work, in order to avoid discriminatory behaviors. This may exclude them from career-enhancing relationships. An extreme version of this inhibition is the self-restriction of career patterns. Evans and Herr (1991) present evidence that African American women alter their career patterns in order to escape harassment and discrimination and choose protected fields that serve their communities, such as law, health care, social service, and education. How extensive this self-limiting of career pathways to avoid discrimination is among other minority groups remains to be studied.

If a sexual harassing or discriminatory experience is perpetrated by a member of the same racial or cultural minority as the victimized woman, additional factors may be activated, causing the perpetrator to expect protection and support from his community and the woman to suppress her complaint. If the perpetrator is advancing in the workplace and can be seen as a successful role model, the pressure on the woman to suppress her complaint and not speak out against one of her own race is exacerbated (e.g., *Anita Hill v. Clarence Thomas*). Many minority communities follow the tradition of (1) male leadership, (2) community representation by men, and (3) traditional gender stereotype roles for men. In these circumstances, community advocacy against racism will take priority over advocacy against sexism. Bell (1992) has described an old boys' club within the African American community, which may protect perpetrators for these reasons. Cultural and religious values favoring modesty, virginity, and domestic-centered roles for women may also discourage victimized women from complaining and seeking help.

As previously mentioned, empirical data regarding gender discrimination involving racial minorities are rare. What is known is primarily focused on African Americans and Hispanics and runs contrary to most theoretical hypotheses of higher prevalence and low complaint rates. Barak (1997), in a review of cross-cultural data, did not find significant differences in incidence rates between Caucasian and minority women with regard to sexual harassment. Gruber and Bjorn (1986) and Koss, Gidycz, and Wisniewski (1987) found a larger prevalence of sexual victimization against White women as compared to minority women. Culbertson, Rosenfeld, and Booth-Kewley (1992) found no support for the hypothesis that Black women respond less assertively to complaints than do White women. How much these results are affected by minority individuals' underreporting of sex discrimination, labeling their situations racism rather than sexism, or segregating themselves into low-risk work environments is not known. The scarcity and lack of comprehensiveness of current data do not allow for sweeping conclusions. As the diversification of the workforce intensifies, adequate study and understanding of these interactions will become even more essential.

CASE 4-8

Ethnic Minority Discrimination

Dr. Kathy Johnson was a newly hired assistant professor of endocrinology, with excellent credentials and strong motivation to achieve in academic medicine. As an African American, she had encountered negative stereotypes from colleagues and patients but had always been able to address them in a proactive and constructive manner. Kathy recently received a large federal grant to continue an ongoing project that had already led to several prestigious publications and some national acclaim. In addition, she recently organized a specialty clinic designed to bring substantial revenues to her department. A hospital trustee treated in the clinic praised her clinical style and competence to her department chair. Dr. Joe Brown, a full professor in the department and a prominent researcher, felt that Kathy had great potential and began to mentor her. During lunch in the hospital cafeteria, Joe provided her with helpful tips on obtaining continued grant support, as well as inside information on personalities and departmental practices. He openly complimented her in departmental meetings and encouraged her participation. Susan Raine, another assistant professor in the department for 4 years, was upset that Kathy was receiving opportunities that were not available to her. She began rumors that Kathy was sleeping her way to the top and was receiving extra help because she was an affirmative action hire. Soon, colleagues and support staff memberss were curt and unhelpful. Kathy overheard gossip that she and Joe had begun an affair. Feeling anxious and embarrassed at work, Kathy began isolating herself to avoid contact with others in the department. She recognized that she was becoming less productive and in need of help but felt that talking to Joe or her department head would be too embarrassing.

SECONDARY VICTIMS OF HARASSMENT AND DISCRIMINATION

Secondary victims are those who are not directly involved in an interaction or a discriminatory experience but who witness it at work, usually on a continual basis. Occasionally, these secondary victims file complaints of hostile environment discrimination, and the negative consequences to these individuals can equal or even surpass those affecting the primary victim. The likelihood of this type of victim remaining silent and working in a hostile environment for prolonged length of time is highly likely and places the person at risk for negative psychological consequences, even though he or she was not directly involved in the discriminatory interaction.

SUMMARY

This chapter has described the dynamics of perpetrator-victim interactions, as well as associated interactions in the work and personal environments. The empirical literature has been reviewed with regard to characteristics of perpetrators and victims, as well as environmental factors that exacerbate these interactions. The model of domestic violence has been used as a reference because it also involves a heterogeneous group of victimized individuals, a heterogeneous group of perpetrators, and the high salience of sociocultural and environmental factors in exacerbating the problem. Unique situations involving special populations have also been discussed. The manner in which these interactions impact victimized people and lead to mental health consequences will be discussed in the next chapter.

FIGURE 4.1. Victimized Individuals' Responses to Sexual Harassment

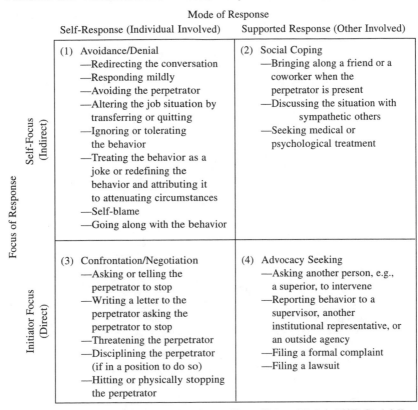

Mode of Response

	Self-Response (Individual Involved)	Supported Response (Other Involved)
Self-Focus (Indirect)	(1) Avoidance/Denial —Redirecting the conversation —Responding mildly —Avoiding the perpetrator —Altering the job situation by transferring or quitting —Ignoring or tolerating the behavior —Treating the behavior as a joke or redefining the behavior and attributing it to attenuating circumstances —Self-blame —Going along with the behavior	(2) Social Coping —Bringing along a friend or a coworker when the perpetrator is present —Discussing the situation with sympathetic others —Seeking medical or psychological treatment
Initiator Focus (Direct)	(3) Confrontation/Negotiation —Asking or telling the perpetrator to stop —Writing a letter to the perpetrator asking the perpetrator to stop —Threatening the perpetrator —Disciplining the perpetrator (if in a position to do so) —Hitting or physically stopping the perpetrator	(4) Advocacy Seeking —Asking another person, e.g., a superior, to intervene —Reporting behavior to a supervisor, another institutional representative, or an outside agency —Filing a formal complaint —Filing a lawsuit

Focus of Response (vertical label spanning the rows)

Adapted from Bowes-Sperry & Tata, 1999, p. 273. *Sources:* Knapp, Ekebert, & Dubois (1997); Gutek & Koss (1996).

CHAPTER 5

Physical and Mental Health Consequences of Sexual Harassment and Gender Discrimination

INTRODUCTION

S exual harassment and other forms of gender discrimination were initially conceptualized as legal problems, essentially as impositions on an individual's civil rights. Academics from the fields of business management and economics then began to address the negative economic and productivity impact of these situations, focusing primarily on sexual harassment. Mental health literature regarding the psychological consequences to victimized individuals is relatively new and has appeared in a fragmented and sporadic fashion. It is also limited almost entirely to sexual harassment. Clinicians have described case histories, symptom profiles, stress factors, and attempts at intervention. Victimized people have reported symptomatology in retrospective surveys. Theoreticians working in the fields of women's development, cognitive functioning, and gender-based traumas, such as rape and childhood sexual abuse, have generated a parallel body of relevant information. The application of their theories to the field of gender discrimination is relatively new, however, and has focused primarily on sexual harassment. Despite significant documentation of the high prevalence of discriminatory events (especially sexual harassment, which has been the basis of most surveys), and despite a growing descriptive literature documenting the negative psychological consequences, few researchers have examined the mental and physical health consequences of gender discrimination. Case Vignette 1-1 (see Chapter 1) illustrates the reluctance of some funding organizations to acknowledge the value of this type of research. Gutek and Koss (1993b), in discussing the scarcity of research on the mental health consequences of sexual harassment, raised the concern that the study of health-related outcomes would limit the definition of sexual harassment to situations in which psychological injury could be proved and thus would limit victimized individuals' capacity to seek legal readdress. In 1993 the Supreme Court ruled in *Harris v. Forklift Systems Inc.* (see Chapter 3) that sexual harassment need not be psychologically damaging to be actionable. Clinicians should be aware that the converse is also true: Harassment and discrimination that do not meet legal criteria can still be psychologically damaging.

Recently, a small number of well-controlled investigations have been conducted and will be summarized in this chapter. Information from my clinical treatment of victimized patients will also be included, to acquaint readers with the broad range of psychological symptomatology and psychiatric diagnoses that can present as a result of discriminatory experiences, and an integrated developmental-trauma model of the impact of gender discrimination will be discussed. Materials will be presented in the following sequence:

1. Review of the existing clinical and research literature on the mental health consequences of harassment and discrimination
2. Presentation of an integrated conceptual model from which the negative psychological sequelae can be viewed

3. Presentations of the reported sequelae of discrimination that create distress for victimized people and require treatment interventions on the part of clinicians

The material in this chapter is intended to acquaint readers with both the wide range and the severity of mental health consequences associated with sexual harassment and gender discrimination and thus provide the background for the treatment interventions described in the three chapters. A word of caution should be noted, however. The empirical study of these mental health consequences is still preliminary, still limited almost entirely to sexual harassment, and still devoid of any hypothesis testing of etiologic models. The solid body of empirical research that should be available for this discussion has yet to be generated.

LITERATURE REVIEW

Numerous theoreticians and clinicians have provided the building blocks toward a model for conceptualizing the mental health consequences of discrimination, and some preliminary models have been introduced. A brief overview of this literature is presented to provide an introductory perspective. Miller (1976) opened the door by describing the psychological impact of women's subordinate role in society and later by elaborating on the importance of maintaining attachments and avoiding conflicts in the context of how women experience anger and power (1983, 1984). Moscarello (1992) discusses these features in relation to gender-based abuse. Gilligan (1982) demonstrated the differences between the moral development of men and that of women, and Riger (1991) applied this concept to problems with sexual harassment complaint procedures, emphasizing how current complaint channels focus on adversarial, right versus wrong outcomes, rather than on outcomes that preserve relationships and allow the victimized person to continue to work in the same setting. Gutek (1985) summarized the ways in which men and women differ in their perceptions of sexual harassment. Carmen, Russo, and Miller (1981) discussed the correlation between a woman's mental health and her subordinate societal role. Bernstein and Lenhart (1993), Hamilton, Alagna, King, and Lloyd (1987), Herman (1993), Koss (1990), Russell (1984), and many others have noted the relationship between harassment and discrimination, rape, battering, sexual exploitation in professional relationships, childhood sexual abuse, and incest. Carmen and Rieker (1989) developed a model for the "victim to patient" process. Multiple authors have applied trauma models to gender-related abuse (Burgess & Holmstrom, 1974; Harvey and Koss, 1987; Herman, 1993; Russell, 1984; Shengold, 1979; Van der Kolk, McFarlane, & Weisaeth, 1996). Raskin and Struening (1976) linked the stress effects of life changes to the subsequent development of illness, and Hamilton, Alagna, King, and Lloyd (1987) applied this concept to this stress impact of sexual harassment.

Numerous clinicians and researchers have contributed to the understanding of the psychological consequences of gender discrimination. Many, however, have focused only on sexual harassment, although much of this literature is applicable to other forms of gender discrimination as well. Charney and Russell (1994) provided a well-referenced psychological overview of sexual harassment. Schrier (1996) compiled a comprehensive summary of the psychiatric aspects of sexual harassment. Dansky and Kilpatrick (1997) and Bowes-Sperry and Tata (1999) summarized the psychological impact of sexual harassment from an etiologic and empirical perspective. Lenhart (1996) provided a summary review of the negative psychological consequences, and Hamilton (1989) and Hamilton, Alagna, King, and Lloyd (1987) focused on emotional and stress-related aspects of sexual harassment from a historical and a treatment perspective. Crull (1981, 1982); Pendergrass, Kimmel, Joesting, Peterson, and Bush (1976), and Salisbury, Ginorio, Remick, and Stringer (1986) discussed consequences in the context of treating victimized patients, emphasizing cultural, racial, and progressive symptom stages, respectively. Esacove (1998) outlined how harassment diminishes the sense of self. Gosselin (1984) described both the psychological and the social implications. Koss (1990) provided a comprehensive literature review documenting the psychological impact of sexual harassment and presented a cognitive etiologic model. Stockdale (1996) summarized processes affecting sexual harassment consequences. Avina and O'Donohue (2002) discussed harassment in relation to the PTSD diagnosis. I presented a preliminary treatment model in Bernstein and Lenhart (1993), adapted later by Shrier and Hamilton (1996). Empirically based investigations and discussions of psychological consequences of sexual harassment have been provided by Fitzgerald (1990, 1993), Fitzgerald and Shullman (1993), Koss (1990), Gutek (1985), Gutek and Koss (1993a, 1993b), Gutek and Morasch (1982), Van Roosmalen and McDaniel (1995), Thacker and Gohman (1996), Schneider, Swan, and Fitzgerald (1997), Richman, Rospenta, Nawyn,

Flaherty, Fenrich, Drum, and Johnson (1999), and the National Women's Study, described by Dansky and Kilpatrick (1997).

CONCEPTUAL MODEL:
A SPECTRUM OF GENDER-BASED ABUSE

Literature on the psychological consequences of sexual harassment and gender discrimination can be best integrated into the existing knowledge base by conceptualizing these experiences as part of an interrelated spectrum of gender-based abuses, including incest, childhood sexual abuse, rape, battering, and sexual exploitation by professionals in the context of fiduciary relationships (e.g., doctors, dentists, clergy, psychologists, therapists, and attorneys). This allows for discussion of parallels and interrelationships in the developmental and dynamic formulations regarding not only the negative psychological outcomes but also the conceptualization of the clinical presentations of symptoms and reactions. All experiences on this abuse spectrum involve harm imposed because of one's gender, occurring in a socioeconomic and cultural climate in which the victimized person often has unequal status and power. Also, they all involve complex interactions between individual, interpersonal, institutional, and societal factors, which greatly influence outcome. Additional significant common themes in these experiences include the following factors:

1. Victimized individuals often depend on their abusers for significant needs, such as mentoring, job security, care and protection, professional services, and so on.
2. The abuse of a power differential and the betrayal of trust have a negative impact on the victimized woman and her sense of self in relation to others.
3. The victimized person perceives the sexual or devaluing content of the experience as humiliating and embarrassing, resulting in a low incidence of disclosure and reporting.
4. Lack of support and collusion with the aggressor or aggressors, the negative organizational climate, or both, by other significant people in the victimized person's life are common and can be as emotionally significant as the original abuse itself.
5. Legal and societal denial or minimization of the significance of the event and the severity of the consequences to the victimized person

leads to options for redress that are limited, ineffective, or unsuited to that individual's needs.

6. External pressure upon the victimized person to internalize blame and accommodate to the abuse results in self-devaluation, self-doubt, a sense of defectiveness, or massive denial.

7. Secondary emotional injuries are commonly produced by legal or reporting processes or by mishandled mental health evaluations and interventions.

8. Retaliation by the aggressor, the organization, or others is likely, especially if the abuse occurs in a setting where the victimized person is in a disempowered position.

9. Similar stress-related psychological and physiological responses occur in people victimized by all forms of abuse.

10. The victimized individual must often maintain an interaction with the perpetrator or the institution for career, economic, or developmental reasons.

11. Current abuse experiences trigger the reactivation of memories, as well as emotional and physiologic sequelae of previous abuse experiences, complicating the response of the victimized person (Lenhart, 1996, pp. 23–24).

The following two case vignettes illustrate how these common themes occurring with people victimized by sex discrimination and other forms of gender-based abuse impact in clinical situations.

CASE VIGNETTE 5-1

Domestic Violence Illustrating Common Abuse Themes

Jean Horowitz was a 38-year-old journalist, a public health advocate, a lecturer, and an author of national prominence who presented for treatment of post-traumatic stress disorder, characterized by nightmares, flashbacks, increased startle response, and feelings of emptiness. She had been married for 10 years to Peter, a prominent attorney. Jean described her marriage as happy during the first 3 years, when they were both actively involved in their careers, and felt that things deteriorated when she expressed her wish for a child. Initially negating her request on the grounds that they were too busy professionally, Peter then became increasingly unpleasant, accusing Jean of a lack of commitment to him. He ultimately stated that she was incompetent and unable to handle motherhood. "You're incapable of caring properly for me. How could you care for a baby?" Always short-tempered, Peter became increasingly devaluing and abusive emotionally. He physically shook Jean when she suggested they obtain marital therapy. Their verbal interactions remained civil when professional commitments kept them apart physically, but quarreling escalated when they were together. Peter accused Jean of being an inadequate wife and threatened to divorce her. One night during an intense argument Peter slapped Jean and pushed her against the wall, shaking his fist at her. Jean was shocked, humiliated, and uncertain as to how to respond. Her mother's glowing praise of Peter's accomplishments and her mother's frequent comments that Jean should deemphasize her work and start a family contributed further to her isolation. Jean considered confiding in a girlfriend, but her social network consisted of other married couples who also were committed to Peter, who always behaved impeccably in public. Jean thought of taking legal action but was ashamed of her situation and fearful of ruining her public reputation. In addition, Peter, as a trust estate attorney, managed all of their assets and was responsible for the bulk of their income. Jean found herself trying to appease her husband, hoping the situation would improve. For 5 years their relationship fluctuated between idyllic getaway vacations and volatile verbal and physical attacks when they were at home. Jean developed headaches, intermittent depression, and an ulcer. When Peter beat her severely during a vacation, she finally consulted a lawyer and filed for divorce. With legal assistance she remained in their house, but Peter canceled credit cards, arranged for utilities to be turned off, transferred assets to his account, and publicly defamed her to friends and professional contacts. Her PTSD symptoms began as she felt increasingly trapped in her home.

CASE VIGNETTE 5-2

Sexual Harassment Illustrating Common Abuse Themes

Sarah Schmidt was a 45-year-old, college-educated, divorced mother of two teenage children, who was delighted to land a well-paying loan officer job at a large branch office of a national bank.

She was the oldest employee working in a division consisting primarily of young attractive women. Frank Kotilla, the division manager, was in his late 50s. Frank and his younger assistant, Tom De Marcus, were the only men. Initially, Sarah found Frank friendly, generous with bonuses, but overly familiar with the staff. Tom appeared low key and tolerant of Frank's frequently demeaning comments. The other women, all in their 20s, appeared unruffled by what soon revealed itself to be a highly sexualized work environment. Frank frequently hugged, kissed, and fondled the young women, calling them his "wives." Sarah learned that one of her coworkers was having a voluntary affair with Frank and that Frank's wife approved of the arrangement. Grateful for the generous weekly pay bonuses that would assist with her children's impending college tuition, Sarah tried to adapt by laughing at the sexual jokes and comments. She rationalized that her young colleagues did not seem unhappy and that her age would protect her from Frank's advances. Her equanimity was badly shaken when 18 months later she discovered a coworker in hysterics in the lady's room. The coworker confided that Frank had attempted to rape her and that she couldn't stand it any longer. Sarah recognized that she had denied many indications of serious behaviors. She felt guilty and anxious and attempted to intervene, by accompanying the young woman whenever Frank was around. Her heightened awareness of the situation and her inability to have a definite impact worried Sarah. Over the next 6 months she developed headaches, sleeplessness, anxiety, and a growing sense of self-disgust for her failure to protect her coworkers, who confided many of Frank's indiscretions to her. She learned that her colleagues were asked to bare their breasts in order to get their weekly bonuses. She and a coworker ultimately chose to approach Tom to report the situation and seek assistance. She was outraged when Tom told her he couldn't risk his job to challenge Frank, who was too well positioned in the central bank hierarchy. Tom urged them to wait it out, stating that Frank was planning to retire. Sarah considered discussing things with her children but was too embarrassed to talk with two teenagers about sexual topics. She also feared they would feel guilty about their college costs. A psychological crisis ensued when Frank escalated his behavior toward her, now directly commenting on her body and joking that he'd be happy to "lay her," even though she was overweight. He joked that she had bccn with him almost 3 years and promised her an anniversary present. One morning when she entered his office to file a report, he grabbed her breast from behind, pulled her against him, and slid his hand down her skirt, penetrating her vagina with his finger. Unable to remain at work, Sarah left immediately, stayed home for 3 days, and presented to her doctor with symptoms of acute post-traumatic stress syndrome.

In addition to this series of common characteristics, gender-related abuses could be conceptualized according to (1) developmental-identity paradigms, and (2) stress-trauma paradigms. Developmental-identity paradigms enhance our understanding of (1) preexisting vulnerabilities to abuse, (2) difficulties with effective coping mechanisms, (3) damage to interpersonal relationships and vocational functioning, and (4) long-term effects involving personal loss and damage to self-esteem and identity. The stress-trauma paradigm also contributes to our understanding of personal losses and identity and self-esteem sequelae. It is uniquely valuable, however, in exploring the physiological and emotional symptom complexes and the psychiatric disorders associated with gender abuse. Although further empirical research is needed to test these conceptual models, they provide an appropriate clinical introduction to the reported mental health consequences of discrimination.

Developmental-Identity Formation Paradigms

Factors related to the differences in female and male identity development play an important role in sexual and gender abuse. They impact on the risk for abuse, personal vulnerabilities complicating abuse, victimized individual's perceptions of the experience, coping styles, and options for resolution. In this section, the factors relating specifically to gender discrimination and harassment will be highlighted. Miller (1976), as well as Carmen, Russo, and Miller (1981), described women's subordinate role in society, with female gender identity developing in an environment that often devalues women and their experiences, especially those experiences outside the home. Women are also defined in terms of male standards and perceptions. This environment imposes compliance with gender roles that are rigidly defined by others. These roles may not correlate with the woman's own self-needs and talents and are often problematic to her in the workplace. These disadvantages are presented as the price for femininity. Women's entrance into higher education and the job force in large numbers is a relatively new phenomenon. They lack a power base and a presence in leadership positions in the workplace and academia, which makes it difficult for them to alter their traditionally imposed roles. In both employment and academic settings, the prevailing structures, leadership types, leadership styles, communication styles, institutional policies and practices, and criteria for advancement are usually based on male standards of fairness and male developmental needs. Women's relational values, their parenting and family responsibilities, and their psychological and moral perspectives have traditionally been excluded. Perceptual biases on the part of key decision makers and leaders, unconscious group dynamics based on low numbers of women, and traditional sex role stereotyping continue to contribute significantly to women's exposure to discriminatory events in the workplace (see Chapter 2).

Miller (1984) and Surrey (1983) defined how women's self-esteem and sense of self develop in the context of their ability to make and maintain relationships. Miller (1976, 1983) discussed the difficulties women have in expressing their anger and in experiencing power and authority, when they perceive it as detrimental to sustaining significant relationships. Early developmental experiences of incest, sexual abuse, rape, and lack of necessary mentoring relationships combine with these normal developmental factors to send many women into the workplace with (1) low self-esteem, (2) self-doubt, (3) excessive reliance on the opinions of others, (4) difficulties with self-assertion and healthy entitlement, (5) empathic concern for others at the expense of their own needs, and (6) blurred sexual boundaries and other traits, which increase their risk for discrimination and harassing behaviors.

Structural and interpersonal aspects of the current work environment may interact negatively with these preexisting factors. Discriminating and harassing experiences present significant challenges to a woman's sense of herself. Her options for resolution of these situations are limited, especially if she is preoccupied with other significant developmental issues such as divorce, pregnancy, parenthood, and career development. The devaluing or aggressive acts that commonly occur in the context of discrimination can disrupt important and valued relationships in the workplace and at home, leaving the relationally oriented woman vulnerable to blaming and devaluing herself or assuming an overly conciliatory and underassertive approach to addressing the situation (see the special section later in this chapter). If the victimized woman feels angry, she may experience it as destructive to her relationships or her femininity. This further damages her sense of herself, especially if she is viewed by others as a "bitch" or a "troublemaker" or is otherwise negatively labeled by coworkers, family, and friends. If she expresses her grievance in the form of a complaint, negative or retaliatory behaviors or both from others are even more likely to occur, and she may lose or destabilize valuable relationships with mentors, coworkers, and work or academic institutions.

Even if a woman is able to maintain a healthy sense of anger, the very acknowledgment of her status as a victim of discrimination can lead to self-stigmatization, isolation, and a sense of being defective or a loser (Koss, 1990). Further damage to her self-identity can occur around attempts at resolution. Complaint channels are often limited in scope and designed for the legal protection of the institution. In addition, current complaint procedures are based on the masculine model of justice, which focuses on objective assessment of guilt and appropriate punishment, rather than upon the female model, which focuses on negotiating for cessation of the behavior and continuation of the work or academic relationship in an improved form. This latter mediation-driven outcome enhances a women's self-esteem but is seldom possible to achieve in the current environment. Even when a woman receives a positive outcome to a formal complaint, she may encounter difficulties, especially if she values her relationship with the perpetrator, the institution, or both. Other problems commonly encountered include collusion of coworkers, lack of family support, and retaliatory behaviors, as previously discussed. The victimized women may emerge from the experience feeling dehumanized and lacking agency (Esacove, 1998).

Self-identity can also be damaged by (1) the destruction of deeply held beliefs and values relating to people, fairness, and work ethics; and (2) the shattering of assumptions and expectations. This can lead to cognitive assimilations of the experience that are either incomplete and therefore destabilizing or negative and therefore destructive. The results of these cognitive problems are more appropriately discussed within the stress-trauma paradigm.

The following case vignette illustrates the clinical value of the developmental-identity paradigm.

CASE VIGNETTE 5-3

Developmental Issues Exacerbate the Impact of Discrimination

Sharon Smith Jones entered treatment for symptoms of anxiety and depression, which began shortly after she accepted a position as a surveyor's assistant in the land acquisitions division of a large coal mining company. The focus of Sharon's presenting concern was her fear that she would be fired from her position and therefore unable to provide college tuition for her two teenage children. She had become depressed in the context of feeling unable to address her concern in an effective manner. Her immediate boss, Joe Moss, had been critical of her since he hired her 3 months previously. He consistently made devaluing comments about women and on several occasions expressed regret at hiring Sharon into the department. Joe remarked that he had wondered about her capabilities from the outset but wanted to give her a chance because he knew she needed the job. In addition to criticizing her work performance, Sharon's boss was critical of her request to leave work on two occasions to assist her daughter in getting to a doctor's appointment. He again focused on his concern that a woman was not appropriate for this particular position. Sharon was also concerned that she was hired at slightly less than full time and thus was ineligible for a benefit package. In addition, her starting salary was approximately $5,000 less than the starting salaries for her two younger male coworkers, who had college degrees equivalent to Sharon's.

In the context of her treatment, it became clear that Sharon's difficulty in finding an effective way to cope with her work situation was related to her own ambivalence about her abilities as a worker and her worth as an individual. In addition, she had never held a salaried position but had been at home full time for the past 12 years. She was therefore unfamiliar with current workplace norms and had no previous experience in negotiating with a boss. Her background and the circumstances in which she entered the workplace were also contributing to her immobilization. Sharon was the younger of two daughters of a prominent chief executive officer of a national corporation. Her mother, a college-educated woman, had remained at home full time in order to support her husband's career. She was constantly available to him and was valued primarily for her skills as a homemaker, an entertainer, a mother, and a social networker. Sharon had followed in her mother's footsteps, excelling in social situations, presiding as prom queen, and viewing her college education primarily as a prerequisite social requirement for finding an eligible mate. While in college, she became engaged to a medical student who was the son of a prominent physician. Like Sharon's father, her fiancé valued her social skills and did not encourage her academic pursuits. She quit college her junior year to marry but ultimately completed her degree by commuting to school at the insistence of her mother, who felt it was important that she have a diploma. Sharon's energies were very soon occupied with raising two young children and remodeling her historic home, which became a showplace for the community's social elite. Although confident of her physical attractiveness and social skills, Sharon always harbored doubts about her intellectual capabilities, especially when she compared herself to her older sister, who was an academic superstar. Sharon valued her role as wife and mother, however, and was content to focus most of her energy on creating a rich home life for her husband and children. She had many friends in the community, and most of her activities outside the home were focused on volunteer organizations related to her husband's hospital. The couple enjoyed an active social life and shared close friendships with several other couples whom they met through her husband's work. Sharon's mother and father were also active in their community and were frequent visitors in Sharon's home.

Sharon was deeply troubled when 15 years into her marriage, her husband began to criticize her for lack of attentiveness to him, stating that he felt she was too wrapped up in her children and her community work. She was devastated when she learned through a friend that her husband was having an affair with a receptionist at the hospital. She confided in her mother, who encouraged her to work harder at the marriage and offered to supply extra cash to relieve the couple of any financial burdens. When Sharon's father died suddenly of a heart attack, her mother became even more insistent that Sharon preserve her marriage, emphasizing how difficult it was for a woman to survive on her own. Despite Sharon's efforts to improve the marriage, her husband requested a divorce in order to marry his new lover. Incapacitated by her wish not to distress her daughters with tales of her husband's infidelity and by her own inability to mobilize her anger at her husband's lack of commitment, Sharon was not able to properly defend herself during the acrimonious divorce proceedings. She left the marriage with scant financial resources and learned afterward that her husband had managed to hide many of his assets. Without her husband, her social standing in the community diminished. She was shocked at the disloyalty of her so-called friends, all of whom secretly empathized with her but publicly supported her husband. Feeling ostracized from her community, she moved to a nearby city. With some financial assistance from her mother, she bought a small house and began to look for a job. She was dismayed by her own lack of confidence, as well as by the lack of opportunities for entry-level positions for a woman in her situation. Her difficulty in obtaining a job frightened her, making it harder to mobilize herself to deal with the difficult circumstances her current employer was imposing on her. With treatment, she was able to objectively assess her own capabilities, free herself from the traditional sex role her parents had prescribed for her, and mobilize her anger at her husband. She returned to court and obtained a better financial settlement that included college tuition for her daughter. She ultimately left her job at the mining company and obtained a position where her skills were valued and where there were opportunities for her advancement.

CASE VIGNETTE 5-4

*Developmental Issues Inhibit Vocational Functioning
and Exacerbate Marital Stress*

Katherine Smith Kelly entered treatment for depression and marital difficulties following the birth of her first child, a daughter who was born with severe developmental disabilities of genetic origin. Katherine's daughter required intensive care, necessitating Katherine's resigning from her position as a computer program developer. Initially, in treatment, Katherine identified the basis of her concern as her daughter's disability and her own sense of defectiveness at having produced a disabled child. She stated that the child's demands had also stressed her marriage, resulting in a decline in sexual activity and constant bickering between her and her husband.

Although she did not mention her job, it became clear in the course of her treatment that a significant component of her depression, as well as of the marital tension, was the result of her lost employment. Katherine stated that her husband had never taken her job seriously and that the family had never needed her income, but she had enjoyed the position tremendously. Unlike her sister Sharon, Katherine had excelled at school and felt awkward in social situations, despite being very attractive. She was frustrated when her father refused to support her request to attend engineering school, despite her excellent grades and College Board scores. Unlike Sharon, Katherine had been closer to her father than to her mother and often accompanied him on business trips as a junior hostess. She enjoyed listening in on the business sessions that were held informally at her father's quarters. Katherine married shortly after her graduation from a regional college-finishing school. Although her husband was the recognized breadwinner, Katherine obtained a low-key position as a computer programmer in a local start-up company. The company's nonhierarchical model allowed for the extension of her activities into a number of interesting areas, and her extraordinary talents were soon utilized and valued by her employer. Outwardly, Katherine maintained the appearance of a traditional wife and mother, the roles prescribed by her family of origin. Inwardly, she was quite conflicted. She managed her conflict by excelling at work and enhancing her skill base under the guise of a low-key position.

Katherine's depression originated when her daughter's condition necessitated her relinquishing this important aspect of herself, which had been deemphasized by both her and her husband. With treatment, she was able to clarify her need to obtain a divorce from a husband for whom she was an unsuitable partner and return to college, supported by high-level child care. Katherine obtained both an MBA and a master's degree in mathematics. She ultimately returned to the workplace, where she met and married a more suitable partner. With her husband's support, she then began her own successful computer company. In the context of her treatment she also became closer to her sister Sharon, as they both discussed the ways in which their "privileged" upbringing, with its ascribed female roles, had negatively impacted upon their adult lives.

Stress and Trauma Paradigms

Similarities in the physiological-physical and in the psychological problems experienced by people victimized by gender discrimination and other forms of gender-based abuse can best be compared in the context of existing stress-trauma models. These models emphasize a complex interplay between individual, interpersonal, societal, and institutional factors, creating an individual psychopathology that is expressed in the context of complicated mind-body interactions. Psychological stress can be defined as a "relationship between the person and the environment that is appraised by the person as being taxing or exceeding his/her resources and endangering his/her well being" (Lazarus & Folkman, 1984, p. 21). Rowe (personal communication, 1994), in applying this concept to gender discrimination, states that the severity of the psychological impact of gender discrimination will depend on the seriousness of the episode as a stressor (stimulus factors), the situational context in which the episode occurs (contextual factors), and the preexisting individual and psychological characteristics of the victimized person (individual factors). (1) Stimulus factors include the objective aspects of the experience, such as frequency, duration, intensity, predictability, and ambiguity. (2) Contextual factors include the organization's tolerance of discrimination, the impotance of the organization to the individuals career or financial stability, the lack of adequate complaint channels, retaliation toward complainants, the power differential between the perpetrator and the victimized person, the perpetrator's ability to directly affect the victimized person's well-being, the quality of the victimized individual's relationship with the perpetrator, and coworker responses. (3) Personal factors include prior exposure to gender-based trauma; high commitment to work for personal or economic reasons; personal resources available; the impact of the experience on deeply held beliefs, values, and sense of self; and the personal losses incurred (Fitzgerald, Swan, and Mugley, 1997; Lenhart, 1996). Sex discrimination usually consists of a cumulative series of escalating and variable experiences involving gender-based devaluations and inequities, sexual behaviors, or any combination of these. The experiences can be the result of a single perpetrator, a group of people, or a faceless combination of institutional policies and communications. In the latter instance, there is usually an individual in immediate authority who is responsible for the cumulative experience of all employees or students within the particular work or academic environment. The accumulation of gender discriminatory experiences often results in a chronic level of stress and affective arousal. This is in contrast to the acute, intense level of arousal that is commonly associated with experiences such as rape, where a single, unexpected attack is accompanied by an immediate fear of death. Intense arousal is also characteristic of (1) sexual harassment involving violent and humiliating sexual assault or the realistic possibility of such assaults); (2) other discriminatory experiences that threaten physical boundaries of legitimate control over the work environment or financial viability; and (3) experiences that reactivate memories and responses to previous sexual trauma (Avina & O'Donohue, 2002). In these situations intense arousal may occur initially, followed by more chronic stress and arousal if the initial victimized person must remain in the discriminatory work or academic environment.

As an individual stressor, Hamilton, Alagna, King, and Lloyd (1987), using Holmes's (1978) Social Adjustment Scale, computed that a life change score of 161 would commonly be associated with sexual harassment experiences, bringing harassment into the range of a mild life crisis associated with adverse health effects in about one third of individuals. More severe harassment has been compared to the stress of a divorce or a major illness. The impact of a harassing experience as a stress factor has been further elaborated by Loy and Steward (1984) and Terpstra and Baker (1987), who provide ratings of

> (1) mild; (2) intermediate; (3) severe stressors correlating numerically to the following experiences: (1) Remarks of a sexual nature, frequent requests for dates, whistles, gestures and staring. (2) Sexual propositions not directly linked to work status and unwanted physical contact of a nonsexual nature. (3) Sexual propositions linked to job or academic enhancement or loss, unwanted physical contact of a sexual nature and sexual assault. (Lenhart, 1996, p. 27)

Similar ratings for other forms of gender discrimination have yet to be elaborated.

A stressful experience is commonly defined as traumatic when the victimized person experiences or witnesses actual or threatened death, serious injury, or threat to the physical integrity of self or others and then responds with intense fear, helplessness, or horror (American Psychiatric Association, 1994). Traumatic experiences are known to result in a variety of serious psychological sequelae and psychiatric illnesses, the most common of which is post-traumatic stress disorder (PTSD). Avina and O'Donohue (2002) summarize empirical studies that indicate that sexual harassment can produce PTSD symptoms in many victimized individuals and that many forms of sexual harassment meet criteria A-1-2 for PTSD by presenting threats to the physical integrity of self and others via threatening financial viability, physical boundaries, and personal control. Stress and trauma can also be conceptualized in terms of abrupt disruptions in significant attachments, followed by characteristic emotional reactions. Sexual harassment and gender discrimination have been associated with multiple acute relational disruptions at home and at work. (See the section on relational disruptions later in this chapter.)

Koss (1990); Taylor (1983); Janoff-Bulman and Frieze (1983); and Dansky and Kilpatrick (1997) elaborate on the cognitive-behavioral aspects of the stress-trauma paradigm of discrimination. They apply classic cognitive models to explain the negative internal psychological sequelae. Shattered values and assumptions regarding (1) the self as worthy and invulnerable to serious harm; (2) others as honest and fair; and (3) the world as just, rational, and predictable cause significant psychological distress. This results in attempts to restore internal equilibrium and control by creating explanations for the events (attributions) that can be ultimately detrimental. For example, a sexually harassed woman may attribute a benign motivation to a harassing coworker or may trivialize the event, in order to safeguard her assumption of personal safety. A woman victimized by gender discrimination may attribute blame to herself for not getting promoted, rather than see her mentor as unfair or experience the work organization as irrational. If these attempts at cognitive coping fail, the victimized person will remain symptomatic, experiencing intrusions of the traumatic event and its associated negative emotions when exposed to any stimuli similar to those present during the event (classical conditioning) and constricting her behaviors to avoid these triggers (instrumental conditioning). Until her core assumptions are altered to accommodate the reality of the event, she will remain symptomatic (Horowitz, 1986). If assimilating the discriminatory event alters the victimized woman's core assumptions in unhealthy ways, such as "all bosses are untrustworthy" or "my personal judgment regarding coworkers is always erroneous," she may remain symptomatic indefinitely. The model of learned helplessness can be used to explain negative altered assumptions arising from uncontrollable situations. If a woman experiencing discrimination cannot remedy her situation, she may develop assumptions that bad outcomes are probable, regardless of effort, and thus acquire an attitude of "learned helplessness."

The conservation of resources model contains elements of the previous models and can be used to explain the occurrence of psychological sequelae when discriminatory events (stressors) lead to a rapid loss of resources that are of the highest value to the victimized individual (Dansky & Kilpatrick, 1997). Hobfoil (1991) suggests five reasons for the rapid loss of resources occurring as a result of a traumatic stressor. (1) It disrupts basic values. (2) It is unexpected. (3) It demands more from victimized people's systems than they are equipped to handle. (4) No previous resources or coping strategies were developed prior to the event. (5) The stressor results in the creation of negative mental images that can be triggered by other cues.

The internal negative cognitive changes described by these various models are not the only problem. Stress-associated declines in work and academic performance can further diminish the internal conceptualization of self-esteem and internal security. Difficulties with cognitive assimilation of the experience and cognitive readjustment contribute to high stress levels that are internally generated and self-escalating. This internal destabilization synergizes negatively with the external economic, vocational, and interpersonal sources of stress created by the discriminating situation. Negative and defensive cognitive attributions and physical symptomatology are the common result.

The negative psychological consequences, reported in association with harassment and discrimination, can be explained in the context of a stress-trauma model, with mild or more transient reactions falling into the spectrum of stress reactions and the more severe and chronic reactions falling into the spectrum of post-traumatic reactions that involve intrusive cognitive flooding, affective numbing, avoidance, and affective hyperarousal. Anxiety disorders, depression, substance-abuse disorders, adjustment disorders, and other diagnostic groups associated with discriminatory behaviors can be conceived as fallout from the initial trauma. Specifically, these associated disorders are related to traumatic losses, traumatic disruptions of attachments, and attempts at self-treating trauma-related affective arousal via alcohol and drugs. The following case vignette illustrates the value of the stress-trauma paradigm.

CASE VIGNETTE 5-5

Trauma-Related Symptoms and Cognitions Complicate a Discriminatory Work Experience

Jennifer Davidson was a 34-year-old corporate attorney who, while in treatment for marital problems, developed dysthymia and post-traumatic stress disorder, characterized by irritability, hyperarousal, sleep disturbance, nightmares, and flashbacks, alternating with social avoidance, lack of connectedness to people, anxiety, depressed mood, and anhedonia. The onset of Jennifer's new symptoms occurred shortly after she had been undercut by two male coworkers who colluded to obtain control of the account of her most lucrative client. They were supported in their takeover by Jennifer's boss, Bob, who had been her most important mentor but recently had expressed concerns that mothers of young children could not "produce" at partner levels.

Prior to the onset of her work-related trauma, Jennifer had entered treatment for mild sexual inhibition, the only flaw in an otherwise happy marriage to her husband, Bob, who was also a successful attorney. In the context of her treatment, Jennifer had provided both a background history and a significant work history. She was the only child of a homemaker mother and a father who operated an independent business. She related her childhood as a happy one, in which she excelled both scholastically and socially. She was close to both parents, whom she felt had contributed greatly to her development. Her mother had emphasized homemaking skills and creativity and had exhibited significant joy in nurturing and empathizing with Jennifer. Her father, who shared his work experiences with his only child, had encouraged her academic excellence. Jennifer stated that her relationship with her parents remained close, although her mother had been ambivalent and somewhat undercutting of her obtaining advanced degrees. She was also ambivalent about Jennifer's success at work, having aspired to work goals of her own, which were not supported by either her father or her husband. Jennifer considered her mother's model crucial in her own view of family life and childrearing. She also stressed the high value she placed on her work role, for which her father had been the model. Although considered highly successful within her firm, Jennifer had experienced some difficulties in combining her family life with her high-powered career. She had managed primarily by overfunctioning. Her high-profile and fast-paced firm did not allow time off for family life, and Jennifer had either worked overtime or had kept her family needs to herself. She had attended her children's school events under the guise of "out-of-the-office meetings." She did not feel able to question the norms of her office; in fact, she felt grateful to be accepted as one of the few women on the partner track. Jennifer found her work exciting and challenging; she accepted as an appropriate reality the notion that she needed to work twice as hard in order to prove herself. She did not question the stress this model placed upon her and her individual needs. She handled her responsibilities as a wife in a similar fashion. She exhibited extreme loyalty to her husband and his needs and expressed extreme gratitude to him for his willingness to assist in household responsibilities. She failed to consider his help as a part of reasonable agreement to which she was entitled. Jennifer also considered her sexual inhibitions to be primarily her problem and failed to notice her husband's contribution. Occasionally, she experienced difficulties around the competitive atmosphere of her office, which often conflicted with her values of empathy and fairness to others.

Jennifer was in the process of exploring these conflicts in relation to her sexual complaint when her PTSD symptoms took center stage. Her symptomatology was complicated by a depression that ensued as a result of her decline in functioning, the direct result of her PTSD. Unaccustomed to not excelling, she was extremely severe and critical of herself and characteristically lacked empathy for her own needs and concerns. Her depression and many of her PTSD symptoms responded to a combination of psychotropic medication and supportive and cognitive behavioral therapies. Ultimately, with the assistance of her therapist, she was able to connect her traumatic symptoms to a childhood attack by a pedophile, who had assaulted both her and her best friend when Jennifer was 8. Jennifer had resisted the pedophile and had spoken to her parents and teachers, who did not appreciate the significance of what she was reporting. Her best friend, who was frightened by the pedophile, did not verify her reports, leaving her to face his retaliatory assaults alone. Her PTSD symptoms subsided with the recovery of this memory and the ancillary use of psychotropic medication. She was able to identify her overfunctioning as the result of her own unconscious and defensive cognitive attributions, in which she blamed herself for not explaining her abuse properly, rather than blaming her family and friends for not understanding and assisting her. She also attributed their lack of response to the notion that she might not be valued or that they thought that she could handle it alone, an underlying component in her lack of empathy for herself as an adult and her willingness to overfunction in a variety of home and work situations. The sexual inhibition that had initially brought her to treatment connected with the childhood fears and the humiliation associated with the sexual assault. Jennifer was able to use these insights to leave her firm, start a small firm of her own, and negotiate a more satisfying sexual and emotional relationship with her husband.

IMMEDIATE AND LONG-TERM CONSEQUENCES OF DISCRIMINATION ON MENTAL HEALTH AND PHYSICAL HEALTH: EMPIRICAL SURVEYS AND CLINICAL REPORTS

Although the literature base on the psychological and physical consequences of gender discrimination is growing, it remains primarily descriptive, citing empirical survey results or case studies, and it focuses primarily on sexual harassment. A broad range of references is available on the health impact of other gender-related abuses from which useful inferences can be made. Treaters must be aware, however, that (1) empirical symptom-specific data, (2) prospective and longitudinal studies, and (3) studies linking the symptomatology associated with sexual harassment and gender discrimination with symptomatology associated with other forms of gender abuse are largely unavailable at this time. This prohibits us from deriving firm conclusions from related literature. Available literature of the health consequences of gender discrimination, combined with my experience, allows sequelae to be divided into the following categories: (1) physical and emotional symptoms, symptom complexes, and psychiatric disorders; (2) problematic coping responses; (3) disruptions in interpersonal relationships and vocational functioning; and (4) psychological reactions related to loss and grief. I first summarized these sequelae in 1996 (Lenhart, 1996, pp. 31–34). Adaptations of this summary, illustrated by case examples, are presented here.

Physical and Emotional Symptoms, Symptom Complexes, and Psychiatric Disorders

A large number of physical symptoms have been reported in relation to discriminatory experiences, including gastrointestinal disorders, jaw tightening, teeth grinding, dizziness, nausea, diarrhea, tics, muscle spasms, fatigue, dyspepsia, neck pain, back pain, pulse changes, headaches, weight loss, weight gain, increased perspiration, cold feet and hands, loss of appetite, binge eating, decreased libido, delayed recovery from illness, sleep disruption, increased respiratory or urinary tract infections, recurrences of chronic illnesses, ulcers, irritable bowel syndrome, migraines, eczema, and urticaria. Often the relationship between these physical symptoms and the discriminatory experience remains unnoted by both the treater and the patient. Psychological reactions that have been reported include persistent sadness, negative outlook, irritability, lability, anergia and hypergia, mood swings, impulsivity, emotional flooding, anxiety, fears of loss of control, excessive guilt and shame, escape fantasies, compulsive thoughts, rage episodes, obsessional fears, crying spells, persistent anger and fear, decreased self-esteem, self-doubt, diminished self-confidence, decreased concentration, anhedonia, and feelings of humiliation, helplessness, vulnerability, and alienation. The psychiatric disorders that have been reported include (1) anxiety disorders, especially generalized anxiety disorder, post-traumatic stress disorder, acute stress disorder, and dissociation disorders; (2) somatization disorders; (3) sleep disorders; (4) sexual dysfunction disorders; (5) psychoactive substance abuse disorders; (6) depressive disorders; (7) adjustment disorders; and (8) *DSM-IV* (American Psychiatric Association, 1994) V code diagnoses associated with marital, occupational, interpersonal, and bereavement issues.

The following case example illustrates how a broad range of physical and emotional symptomatologies can be linked to workplace discrimination.

CASE VIGNETTE 5-6

Physical Symptoms and Psychiatric Disorders Associated with Sexual Harassment

Nicole DiMaggio was a 39-year-old married Italian immigrant mother of three who presented to her family doctor with symptoms of jitteriness, sleeplessness, and diarrhea 6 months after the birth of her third child. Her medical work-up was negative. Her symptoms were treated with low doses of Ativan and attributed to postnatal adjustment problems, despite Nicole's report that she was enjoying her new baby. At the same time, Nicole confessed to her priest that she was having difficulty responding to her husband sexually and was reassured that her difficulties would subside when her baby stopped nursing. Three months later she presented to her physician with a depressed mood, a 10-pound weight loss, decreased libido, crying spells, sleeplessness, anergia, and vague suicidal ideation, which responded only partially to antidepressant treatment. She was referred for further psychiatric evaluation. In the course of her therapy, she revealed that she was working two mornings a week in a local grocery store owned by a distant relative, Angelo, who had hired her as a favor to assist her family economically. Nicole revealed that Angelo's son, Tony, persistently fondled her breasts in the storeroom, and that shame, embarrassment, and loyalty to her relatives had prevented her from speaking up even to her priest. The minimization of the role of paid employment for women within her cultural community had prevented her priest and her physician from identifying the source of her distress.

Maladaptive Coping Responses

The complex nature of discrimination, the limitations in appropriate and timely channels for resolution, the variations in the level of available validation support, and the associated unconscious negative cognitive attributions can result in defensive responses and unproductive coping methods in otherwise psychologically healthy women. These responses can engender further problems. They often result in the victimized woman being discredited or blamed for her experience and isolated from supports. Denial is a common long-standing coping response and leads to the continuance and exacerbation of discrimination. Denial can result in an emotional crisis, in which the accumulated pain or rage related to the discrimination gives rise to emotional flooding and injurious disorganized behavior. This, in turn, diminishes the woman's credibility and inhibits her ability to formulate an effective plan of action.

Coping responses involving impulsive withdrawal from the workplace or academia lead to diminished credibility, economic crisis, career derailment, and exacerbation of family or work conflicts. Many women interpret discriminatory experiences as signals that they do not belong in the workplace and should be at home, caring full time for their families. Coping via internalization of responsibility and blame for discrimination can lead the victimized woman to self-doubt, lowered self-esteem, diminished self-confidence, poor morale, and lowered career aspirations. Chronic ambivalence involving fluctuations between outward anger toward the perpetrator and inward self-doubt can lead to stalemates in both work and academic performance. Displaced anger can result in alienating neutral or supportive figures, such as family members, attorneys, and mentors. Unprocessed surges of anger can lead to injudicious confrontations or impulsive litigations that are not in the woman's best interest. Feelings of guilt or shame may make it difficult for the woman to talk about her experience, leading to isolation, reduced exposure to supports, and limited access to ideas for more productive coping options. Obsessional fears or images or retaliation can paralyze a woman so that she cannot invest in new people or in work that can be more potentially productive.

The following case vignettes illustrate the destructive potential of maladaptive coping mechanisms.

CASE VIGNETTE 5-7

Maladaptive Coping as Illustrated by Impulsive Withdrawal from a Discriminatory Workplace

Dr. Susan Bray was a 26-year-old African-American physician who was recently accepted as a surgical intern in an exclusive and predominantly male residency-training program. Susan was the first in her family to obtain higher education and always felt socially isolated from her academic peers. She had compensated by focusing on her scholastic performance, in which she consistently excelled. This social isolation was compounded by her current situation. She was working in a predominantly male environment, and many of her peers demonstrated marked discomfort in integrating a female coworker. Susan was especially happy and grateful when her chief resident, Dr. Tom Gary, began to take an interest in her professional work. He complimented her on her surgical skills, her commitment to the field, and her capacity to deal with difficult interactional problems with patients. Tom began to mentor Susan by giving her advice on whom she should meet within the hospital, by making her work visible to attending physicians, and by suggesting that she serve on two important hospital committees. Susan received excellent performance evaluations after the completion of her first year. She was devastated to learn, however, that one of the operating room nurses had started a rumor that she was sleeping with Tom. She began noticing that the nurses snickered when she walked by, and she overheard an orderly comment that Black women are good lays. Dr. Connie Brown, the only other female trainee in the program, also began to distance herself from Susan. Her fellow residents began to complain about what they described as favoritism in the on-call schedule. Although Susan was aware that Tom had never displayed anything other than appropriate professional interest in her work, she felt too ashamed to discuss the problem with him and utterly unable to address the innuendoes she was receiving. Her anxiety level rose, and she began having difficulty sleeping. A crisis occurred when she entered the locker room and noted that the word *whore* was scribbled across her locker room door. She abruptly left work, precipitating criticism from Tom. She returned and completed her weekly surgical schedule. Following her on-call night, however, she abruptly left the service and drove to her home 300 miles away. Once at home, she found herself immobilized. She couldn't discuss her situation with her mother, whom she felt would not understand. She felt unable to return to work but was also unable to discuss her situation with Tom and negotiate a leave. On the second day of her absence she agreed to meet with a therapist, with whom she confided her situation. The therapist attempted to intervene on her behalf but was unsuccessful in reaching her department chair. The chair, angered by what he saw as gross negligence and irresponsibility, suspended Susan from the program. Lacking any information, Tom, her primary support, was unable to defend her.

CASE VIGNETTE 5-8

Maladaptive Coping, as Illustrated by Displaced Anger Related to Sexual Harassment

Jane White was a 38-year-old businesswoman who called the employment hotline of her professional association because of difficulties with her attorney, who had filed a sexual harassment complaint against her previous boss at her request. When the volunteer professional counselor manning the hotline returned her call, Jane asked immediately for a referral to an employment attorney, stating that her current attorney was incompetent. The volunteer expressed concern for her situation, as well as concern over her original complaint, which involved a very persistent and severe series of sexually harassing experiences. When the volunteer phoned her the next day with a list of attorneys available in her area, Jane was irritable and critical, stating that the counselor had delayed in returning her call and lacked professionalism in her approach. Jane refused further follow-up from the professional and hung up without thanking her, despite knowledge that she was a volunteer. Jane did, however, contact one of the attorneys on the list that had been furnished to her. The attorney agreed to take her case but found her immediately critical, demanding, and utterly unable to collaborate with him. Consultation with Jane's previous attorney validated the consistency of her hostile reactions. Concerned about her emotional stability, as well as her capacity to cooperate as a client, the attorney suggested to Jane that they employ a psychiatrist as a forensic expert. Jane was insulted and initially refused, stating that such a consultation would diminish her credibility. During her forensic evaluation, Jane was critical of her attorney, as well as of the interviewer. She threatened to terminate the evaluation. The forensic expert recommended referral for psychiatric treatment in the report to Jane's attorney, who agreed to continue working with her only if she went for treatment. Reluctantly, she agreed and ultimately was able to appreciate her displaced anger and become aware of the year she had lost in the litigation process as a result of her inappropriate anger toward those who were trying to help her.

Disruptions in Interpersonal Relationships and Vocational Functioning

Discriminatory experiences are associated with a sense of profound dis-illusionment with previously respected teachers, mentors, supervisors, health professionals, clergy, and other authority figures who either per-petrated the discrimination or harassment or did not support the victim-ized person in appropriate redress. This feeling may be generalized into a lack of trust of or inhibition in dealing with important authority fig-ures in the future, or both. Conversely, many potentially useful male mentors who are sensitized to the current climate of political correct-ness regarding discrimination in the workplace may avoid engaging with promising female students or workers because of anxiety and uncer-tainty regarding acceptable personal and work boundaries. Many also fear that they will be unjustly accused of discrimination. Personal and professional relationships with coworkers are often disrupted, especially if the woman has taken legal action or has filed a formal complaint. Coworkers often fail to validate a woman's experience and to support her in speaking out. They may collude with the harasser and the organi-zation out of fear or in hopes of being rewarded. Often the complainant is ostracized as a troublemaker. Hamilton, Alagna, King, and Lloyd (1987) described the difficult scenario of a harassment complainant whose work was devalued but was subsequently taken over and ex-ploited by other female colleagues, who then received credit for its true value. Relationships are also disrupted with coworkers who confide the truth privately but will not speak out publicly and with female supervi-sors who defend the institution or the harasser and neither validate the woman's experience nor provide her with models for appropriate re-dress. Disappointing reactions from female mentors or coworkers who deny discrimination or are overwhelmed and pessimistic themselves are especially detrimental.

Disruptions in work relationships and diminished trust in work insti-tutions and leaders may directly inhibit work functioning. In addition, anxiety and depressive symptoms may impact work by reducing energy, self-confidence, motivation, and concentration. Missed work time due to sick days for emotional or physical health sequelae further diminishes work capacity. Avoidance reactions and diminished communication with individuals of key importance to work or academic performance are also common. Finally, the work time expended in dealing with the dis-criminatory experience significantly reduces work performance.

Relationships with physicians and other health and mental health professionals may be compromised when these professionals fail to understand the impact of discrimination or imply that the harassment is the victimized person's fault. Clergymen and other professionals who are approached as a means of support also fall into this category.

Relationships with family, friends, and community are complicated in unique ways. Husbands, boyfriends, and male family members may identify with the harasser's or the institution's point of view. They may insist upon the woman filing a complaint or may intrude into her workplace to personally deal with perpetrators. Irritability, depression, sexual dysfunction, or any combination of these on the part of the victimized individual may cause further deterioration in the marital relationship or a relationship with a lover. Daughters may overidentify with their mother's experience and develop negative attitudes toward work, social inhibitions, and problems with self-assertion. Parents of victimized women may feel guilty for not adequately preparing their daughters. Parental overidentification, discomfort, or both, with the sexualized nature of the harassment, the extent of the inequity, and the backlash can cause further discomfort in parent–daughter relationships. For example, a daughter may feel reluctant to tell her parents that she has been accused of being a slut or incompetent in her work. A high-achieving father may take discrimination toward his daughter as a personal insult to his power and integrity and may insist upon intervening for her. In cultural subgroups where traditional sex roles are valued, the victimized woman may be viewed as a dishonor to her family for being the focus of public dispute in a sexual matter. A woman who is ambivalent about combining work and family roles may view discriminatory experiences as proof that her place is in the home or as punishment for neglecting her family. Families who support traditional roles for women may only exacerbate this viewpoint. Family members who support a woman during physical illness may fail to sympathize with the less visible psychological injuries incurred by discrimination. Families unfamiliar with the negative health and psychological consequences may even criticize the woman for neglecting housework or nurturing duties or for being depressed, angry, or spacey at home. Financial crisis precipitated by loss of job, diminished income, or high litigation costs may cause family strain. The extra time that must be devoted to litigation or complaint procedures can be equivalent to another part-time job and can disrupt time with the family. The following cases exemplify the seriousness of these issues.

CASE VIGNETTE 5-9

Significant Family and Work Relationships Disrupted by Gender Discrimination

Dr. Rachel Teem was an associate professor of pathology in a large urban medical school. She is the mother of two grown children and the wife of a department chair. She has worked successfully in her department for over 20 years and was a pioneer woman doctor both in her departmental position and in her area of expertise. She took pride in her ability to combine work and family and in the cordial, respectful relationships she enjoyed with colleagues. She often commented on how smoothly her career had gone, how well she had been treated, and how little discrimination she had encountered. She was shocked one day when she discovered accidentally from a secretary that she was being paid $12,000 less than a junior male colleague. She confronted her department head, Dr. John Howe, who cited her lesser number of publications, a statement that she accepted. Three months later, she discovered in the library that her publications actually exceeded her colleague's. Her department head chuckled at her confrontation, stating, "Come on, Dr. Teem, don't rock the boat. You don't need the money and, besides, we know your family has always come first." Rachel was speechless and noticed with embarrassment and surprise her own feelings of anxiety. When she discussed the encounter with her husband, he identified with John, sympathizing with a department chair's need to save money and minimizing the inequity to Rachel. He emphasized what great opportunities the department had given her, warning her strongly against litigation or making a stink. He noted the embarrassment it would cause him in his position and the danger of informal blackballing to her. He suggested that she handle it with gracious good humor and let it drop, if necessary, in order to preserve her position. She agreed that it was solid advice but found herself feeling increasingly anxious over the next several weeks, reacting strongly to a group of students who complained about sexism in their lectures. She began to worry that she had dismissed similar student complaints in the past. Two months passed and she was still unable to address the issue with John or to make peace with her salary inequity. She thought of the issue constantly, yet was unable to resolve it. Her marital relationship deteriorated, and she began to avoid her boss, quarrel with her husband, and withdraw from her female students.

CASE VIGNETTE 5-10

Significant Work and Family Relationships Disrupted by Sexual Harassment

Gwen Aimes was a 34-year-old divorced and then remarried African American woman who worked for a courier service as a delivery truck driver. Approximately 2 years after accepting her position, she filed a sexual harassment suit with her union representative, citing a hostile work environment. Gwen reported that her coworkers made lewd remarks and gestures when she walked by them, told sexual jokes using her name as the protagonist, drew lewd sexual pictures on her delivery receipts, and encouraged Sam, one of her coworkers, to persist in making sexual overtures to her while on the job. Gwen's husband, Fred, supported her in filing the suit. As he read the details of her descriptions, he became suspicious of her fidelity toward him and embarrassed that he was being made a fool of within their small African American community. Fred's suspiciousness and negative reaction impacted upon the couple's sex life, which up until this point had been quite satisfactory. In addition, Fred began to accuse Gwen of being promiscuous, citing a confession she had made to him that she had had an affair during the time that she was married to her first husband because the marriage was so unsatisfactory. Despite Gwen's distress at his accusations and her insistence on her marital satisfaction with him, Fred continued to withdraw in the relationship. Gwen found his reaction especially upsetting given the retaliation she was receiving from her coworkers for having filed the sexual harassment suit. Gwen's mother was also embarrassed that her daughter was becoming the center of community discussion and chided her gently about causing too much trouble. Feeling anxious and very unsupported, Gwen consulted her minister, because the family's cultural background did not support mental health counseling. Gwen confided her marital difficulties, as well as her humiliation at the sexual experiences she was confronting at work to her clergyman. He initially provided comforting advice and reassurance but under the pretense of offering a "supportive hug" he attempted to kiss her and fondle her breasts. Gwen was shocked and felt betrayed. She worried that neither her mother nor her husband would believe her if she reported this incident. She became depressed, isolated, and even more reluctant to seek treatment. Her husband interpreted her withdrawal as further proof that she was being unfaithful. The couple was in the process of filing for divorce when Gwen sought treatment for severe depression.

Psychological Reactions Related to Loss and Grief

Even if a harassment experience is ultimately resolved in a positive manner, the victimized person is highly likely to suffer both internal and external losses. Internal losses may include the loss of a sense of self as a competent and relational person; loss of faith in people, institutions, and standards of fairness and equity; and loss of a sense of enjoyment and commitment to work. External losses may include loss of a job, loss of income, loss of economic security, loss of important opportunities for career development, loss of important mentoring relationships, deterioration in interpersonal relationships, loss of opportunities for specialized training and education, and loss of seniority or expected promotions. Women grieve and mourn when they become fully aware of the impact of these losses. Seldom is their grief acknowledged and supported by others, and often it is denied by the women themselves. This is especially true if they have received a positive outcome to formal complaints or litigation. Such denial can lead to unresolved mourning, severely complicating their adjustment. The following case example illustrates these issues.

CASE VIGNETTE 5-11

Unresolved Grief Related to Discrimination

Sandra Jones and five of her work colleagues had been involved in a 6-year litigation battle with a pharmaceutical company. Sandra and her close colleagues, all midlevel executives, had filed charges for both sexual harassment and gender discrimination. Although the litigation was prolonged, the women had remained in close contact during the process and were supported by their husbands and families. Sandra obtained work as a manager in another pharmaceutical company after filing her suit and remained steadily and happily employed throughout the litigation. At several points in the legal process, she had developed symptoms of anxiety and depression, usually related to difficult deposition and trial experiences. She had received appropriate treatment and had terminated satisfactorily with her psychiatrist. Ultimately, the group succeeded in winning its litigation, obtaining one of the highest reported punitive awards for damages and making the national news. The win was followed by a round of celebratory parties, and Sandra was interviewed by several reporters and cited in a number of business journals for having made a significant contribution to the cessation of gender-related employment discrimination. Sandra's husband was especially happy to have their family life return to normal and scheduled a week's vacation in Hawaii with Sandra. During the vacation, Sandra became depressed in a way that both puzzled and frustrated her husband. Upon return from her vacation, the family resumed a "normal routine," but Sandra's spirits did not improve. Six months after winning the lawsuit, Sandra was hospitalized for depression. Unbeknownst to her family, friends, and previous therapist, she had become preoccupied with the loss of her co-litigant colleagues, whom she now no longer saw on a regular basis and who had been both valued work colleagues and a primary source of support during the litigation. She also had been preoccupied with the amount of time and energy and the 6 years of her life that had been lost in the process, something that she had not considered when she was mobilizing herself for the trial. Her family and friends focused on the positive outcome of the trial and never spoke with her about the downside, leaving her feeling isolated with her sense of loss.

CONSEQUENCES RELATED TO SPECIAL POPULATIONS

If the victimized individual and the perpetrator are members of the same ethnic or religious minority or are both gay, their social community may criticize them for filing a formal complaint and exposing their community to public scrutiny and adverse publicity, rather than settling the matter confidentially within the community. For example, Anita Hill was criticized for reporting Clarence Thomas and thus diminishing the chances for an African American to sit on the Supreme Court. The victimized person's legitimate complaints may even be viewed by the community as racial or ethnic slurs. Victimized individuals who are members of the same ethnic or racial minority group as the perpetrator may be personally reluctant to expose their perpetrator to redress in the legal system. Problems with internalizing negative self-concepts after discrimination are also compounded by previously existing internalized negative racial stereotypes. Often, minority women are unsure whether to label their experience sex discrimination or racial discrimination. Racial and ethnic stereotypes characterizing women of certain groups as promiscuous or highly libidinous may target these women for increased sexual harassment or may result in their being blamed for any harassment that occurs. Finally, in cases of employment discrimination based on racial and ethnic factors, it is even more likely that a person from such a subgroup who is being harassed will be at the very bottom of the work power hierarchy and thus perceived as less valuable to the organization than the harasser is.

Among Hispanics and other cultures that accept traditional, rigidly polarized sex roles, victimized women may be viewed as dishonored, no longer pure, an embarrassment to their family, or all of these. Illegal aliens may fear endangering their immigration status by filing complaints.

Homosexual men and women victimized by same-sex harassers may fear that a complaint will expose their sexual orientation or will result in adverse criticism from the gay community for complaining about one of their own or bringing adverse publicity to the community.

Heterosexual men vary in their vulnerability to harassment sequelae. They are harassed much less frequently than are women. Their harassers are much less likely to be in a superior position or to be able to impact their work status, and men often perceive the harassment as flattering and mutual, rather than humiliating and devaluing. Nonetheless, they are vulnerable to negative sequelae when their harasser is in a position to damage them at work or when the event is humiliating and devaluing (see Chapter 5). There is also some evidence to suggest that as women become more prominent in the workplace, the harassment of men may increase as an expression of abuse of power. Klein, in an unpublished study (F. Klein, Klein Associates, Boston, MA, 1993), noted that in one organization characterized by a high number of female managers and a male CEO who condoned discriminatory attitudes, the women managers harassed their male subordinates at a significantly higher rate than usual.

CONCLUSION

The high prevalence of discriminatory experiences has been documented since the 1970s, and a descriptive literature has emerged regarding the physical and mental health consequences of these experiences. Conceptual models drawn from other forms of gender-based abuse and expressed in terms of developmental-identity paradigms and stress-trauma paradigms can be utilized to understand and predict psychological sequelae and design treatment interventions. Further work is crucially needed with regard to (1) longitudinal and prospective studies, (2) studies linking gender discrimination with other forms of gender abuses, and (3) studies linking gender discrimination with specific psychiatric disorders. A specific model for treatment intervention based on the conceptual models and targeting the common groups of sequelae discussed in this chapter will be presented in Chapter 7.

CHAPTER 6

Conceptualizing Treatment of Sexual Harassment and Gender Discrimination

The Initial Stages of Alliance Building and Crisis Intervention

INTRODUCTION

The treatment of sexual harassment and other forms of gender discrimination is a complex and challenging clinical task about which relatively little has been written. Victimized individuals enter treatment (1) at different stages of the discriminatory experience, requiring different intervention styles and focuses; (2) with differing levels of insight and motivation, requiring a variety of alliance-building techniques; and (3) with diverse and variable symptom complexes of different degrees of severity, requiring a broad range of treatment modalities. In general, the degree of psychological distress and psychiatric illness in the patient or client will depend upon (1) the nature of the experience, (2) the context in which it occurs, and (3) the preexisting condition of the victimized person with regard to both external and internal resources and vulnerabilities (Mary Rowe, Personal Communication, 1994). For example, a severe response would be anticipated if a socially isolated, financially strapped woman with a past history of sexual abuse was exposed to prolonged discrimination involving both sexual assaults and severe work inequities from a respected mentor, in the context of a highly specialized, nontransferable career track, in which the woman was highly invested both financially and emotionally. In contrast, a mild response would be anticipated if a psychologically healthy, economically stable woman with a supportive family and coworkers was exposed to critical gender-focused remarks and negative differential treatment during quarterly public meetings with an off-site manager who had little impact on her job evaluations and with whom all contact would cease in 3 months, when she is being promoted to a new work station. The literature addressing the negative consequences of sexual harassment and gender discrimination has evolved from early accounts that focused primarily on economic and productivity losses, to more recent accounts that address medical and psychological consequences from multiple perspectives (Avina & O'Donohue, 2002; Bernstein & Lenhart, 1993; Charney & Russell, 1994; Clark & Lewis, 1977; Esacove, 1998; Fitzgerald, 1993; Gutek, 1985; Gutek & Koss, 1993a; Hamilton, 1989; Hamilton & Jensvold, 1992; Hughes & Sandler, 1986; Klein, 1988, 1989; Koss et al., 1994; Lenhart & Evans, 1991; Powell, 1999a, 1999b; Richman, Rospenda et al., 1999; Roy, 1974; Russell, 1984; Sandroff, 1988; Sanford, 1981; Schneider, Swan, &

Fitzgerald, 1997; Shrier, 1996; Stockdale, 1996; Thacker & Gohmann, 1996; U.S. Merit Systems Protection Board, 1987, 1995; Van Roosmalen & McDaniel, 1998).

Despite the encouraging proliferation of the literature, there is still a limited amount devoted to treatment of victimized people (Bernstein & Lenhart, 1993; Charney & Russell, 1994; Crull, 1982; Koss, 1990; Paludi, 1990; Pendergrass et al., 1976; Quina & Carlson, 1989; Rabinowitz, 1990; Shrier, 1992, 1996; Salisbury et al., 1986). Related literature on the treatment of psychological trauma and other forms of sexual abuse, such as incest, rape, sexual exploitation, and battering, can also be valuable in conceptualizing treatment approaches (Bernstein & Lenhart, 1993; Burgess & Holmstrom, 1974; Carmen & Rieker, 1989; Courtois, 1988; Figley, 1985, 1986; Foreman, 1980; Gabbard, 1989; Herman, 1981, 1993; Herman & Schatzow, 1993; Horowitz, 1986; Kilpatrick, Veronen, & Resnick, 1981; Kluft, 1989; Krystal, 1988; Marmar, Foy, Kagan, & Pynoos, 1991, 1993; McFarlane, 1994; Notman & Nadelson, 1980; Powell, 1999a, 1999b; Renshaw, 1989; Rose, 1986; Schwartz & Prout, 1991; Silverman & Apfel, 1983; Stockdale, 1996; Sutherland & Davidson, 1989; Taylor, 1983; Tomb, 1994; Van der Kolk, 1987; Van der Kolk et al., 1996; Wilson & Raphael, 1993; Yalom, 1975).

This chapter will provide a multidimensional approach to treatment that integrates (1) the existing literature on the treatment of sexual harassment and discrimination; (2) relevant preexisting literature on psychopharmacology, psychodynamic therapy, cognitive behavioral therapy, group therapy, and trauma and grief therapies; and (3) my clinical experience. The model is a revision of an approach to sexual harassment that I initially developed and presented in Bernstein and Lenhart (1993). This version incorporates new data and experiences appropriate to both sexual harassment and other forms of gender discrimination. It provides illustrative and related information necessary for proper case management, such as (1) available resources, (2) modes of resolution, (3) relevant legal issues, (4) types and styles of presenting symptomatology, (5) appropriate therapeutic stance for treaters, and (6) formats for initial evaluations. It can be utilized by a single treating clinician or a collaboration of treating clinicians such as an individual therapist, a medication doctor, a group therapist, an EAP counselor, and so on, who handle various stages of treatment according to their areas of expertise. The model can be outlined in nine steps or stages, as follows:

*Multidimensional Treatment Model for Sexual Harassment
and Gender Discrimination*

1. Establishment of the appropriate therapeutic alliance and clarification of the clinician's role.
2. Assessment of the severity of the immediate crisis and appropriate validation and support regarding the challenges presented.
3. Evaluation and treatment of immediate physical and psychological symptoms presented and establishment of therapeutic contract for periodic monitoring of symptoms throughout treatment.
4. Ventilation of feelings and exploration of self-cognitions and goals.
5. Reestablishment of a sense of control via the development of effective coping strategies and formulation and enactment of a realistic plan of action.
6. Assessment of potential personal losses and retaliatory behaviors from others and institution of proactive protective measures.
7. Identification of and appropriate mourning of inevitable losses.
8. Reestablishment of investment in preexisting or newly formulated goals and activities.
9. Attention to long-term and other significant therapy and treatment issues.

This model is presented in sequential steps but is intended to be flexible and adaptable to the wide variation of patients, problems, points of entry into treatment, and constant changes in status with which clinicians must deal. This chapter will focus on issues related to the initiation of effective treatment: Steps 1–3. Chapter 7 will discuss approaches to helping the patient deal with both the internal psychological and the external situational challenges, Steps 4–6. Chapter 8 will explore issues related to aftermath, recovery, and reinvestment, Steps 7–9. It will also present issues related to specific populations.

STEP 1: ESTABLISHMENT OF THE THERAPEUTIC
ALLIANCE AND CLARIFICATION OF THE CLINICIAN'S ROLE

Managing the Initial Referral

Patients and clients enter treatment related to discriminatory experiences with differing levels of motivation and insight and from a variety of referral sources. Some may be unaware that their physical and emotional symptoms are related to a discriminatory experience, or they uncover the experience in the context of ongoing treatment that is focused on other issues. Others may be focused on issues of sexual harassment and unaware that other forms of discrimination or other psychological issues are a primary or a contributory cause of their distress. Some may already be involved in the litigation or complaint process, which often exacerbates symptomatology and blurs treatment goals. They may seek consultation for forensic or treatment objectives, or both, or be unclear regarding the distinction. A small group may enter treatment for unrelated problems or for problems such as marital discord and unresolved grief, which are the aftermaths of discriminatory and harassing events.

Referrals may also arise from a variety of outside sources. Physicians such as internists, primary care doctors, and obstetricians or gynecologists may refer patients for symptom management. Because many physicians still do not take work histories from woman, they may be unaware of the work or academic trauma that has transpired. Conversely, they may be the first professional in whom the woman confides. Employee Assistance Program (EAP) professionals may refer clients or patients when their symptomatology is severe, cannot be resolved within the time-limited period in which they are authorized to treat, or both. Mental health clinicians who are unfamiliar with this area of treatment or who are anxious about involvement with potential legal aspects of a case may seek consultation or referral. Attorneys may legitimately refer clients for a variety of issues: (1) treatment of psychiatric symptoms related to discrimination, (2) management of the stress involved in litigation, and (3) forensic assessment and expert testimony. Occasionally, attorneys unduly pressure the clinician to act as both therapist and expert witness, to maximize psychological injuries, or both. Employment and human resource personnel may make empathic and appropriate treatment referrals but may also attempt to intrude upon the treatment with institutional goals, such as discouraging litigation. In instances where the clinician is an employee of the work or academic institution where the incident occurred or when the evaluation or treatment is mandated or financed, or both, by that institution, the potential for a conflict of interest and the misuse of the clinician's role is further heightened unless the boundaries of confidentiality and disclosure are established at the outset with both the patient and the institution. Employee Assistance Program clinicians are often the first to evaluate a sexual harassment or discrimination client. They can play an invaluable role in addressing initial symptomatology, understanding the institution's complaint procedures, and making appropriate referrals for longer-term treatment when necessary.

Clarifying the Clinician's Role and the Boundaries of Treatment

Clarification of the clinician's role and disclosure of and discussion of any potential conflicts of interest or limits to confidentiality are essential first steps in treatment. This promotes the therapeutic alliance and affords the patient or client the opportunity to truly give informed consent for the treatment. If the patient or client is engaged in or would consider legal remedies for her situation, she should be informed of the possibility that her clinician, her treatment records, or both may be subpoenaed. If she realizes only later, in the context of treatment, that discrimination has occurred, these issues should be addressed at that time. (See Chapter 3 for complete details.) Potential strategies for protecting confidentiality should be discussed and mutually agreed upon. Any preset limits to confidentiality, such as employment reports, conferences, and so on, should be disclosed. The treatment record should be kept in a concise medical and legal mode, free of speculation and other material that could be misused: (1) diagnosis and symptoms targeted for treatment, (2) rationale and type of treatment methods employed, and (3) treatment outcomes and changes in the patient's clinical status.

If the patient or client is already involved in litigation, the clinician should emphasize the critical need for the patient's attorney to retain a separate forensic evaluation by another professional to (1) document relevant historical information, (2) correlate discriminatory events with symptoms, (3) discuss the patient's symptoms relative to her pre-event character, (4) evaluate allowable issues related to credibility, (5) review the existing medical and psychiatric records, and (6) determine emotional damages and treatment needs (see Chapter 3). This provides the best, but not an absolute, safeguard that the clinician's views or the treatment record will not be unduly publicized or utilized in court in a manner that would compromise or destroy the therapeutic alliance. The vast differences and conflicts of interest between the role of the forensic expert and the treating clinician should be clarified with the referring attorney and the patient, along with an explanation as to why the treating clinician cannot accept both roles (see Chapter 3).

If the treatment is being financed or mandated by the involved work or academic institution, the following issues should be discussed with the patient: (1) the stated purpose of the institutional referral, (2) the type of reporting contract the clinician is expected to have with the institution, (3) the purpose of any mandated reports or discussions, and (4) the clinician's relationship and obligation to the institution. The patient and the clinician can agree to mutually discuss the contents of any verbal or written reports, records, or other communications with the institution prior to their disclosure and afterward. If the patient is initially too distressed to fully appreciate these issues, they should be reviewed again when she has stabilized. The clinician should seek consultation and, if necessary, refer the patient to another treater when conflicts of interest are interfering with proper treatment.

Assuming an Appropriate Therapeutic Stance

The most appropriate therapeutic stance for beginning treatment is that of empathic validation. It is important for the treater to take an actively supportive and educative position during the initial sessions. The patient will respond well if the clinician initially communicates a willingness to believe the following: (1) that her perspective has validity; (2) that she deserves help; (3) that she is not "crazy," and that any initial symptoms and impairment are more likely the result of her real experience than caused by any premorbid pathology; and (4) that she has suffered retaliation in some form if she has filed a complaint or taken legal action (Hamilton & Shrier, 1996; Pendergass et al., 1976). Conversely, the patient or client may suffer secondary traumatization, with an exacerbation in symptomatology, if the clinician initially takes any of the following stances: (1) disbelief, vigorous questioning, or both of her report and credibility; (2) preoccupation with whether the experience meets legal criteria for discrimination, rather than focusing on the patient's distress level; (3) undue focus on sexual harassment and failure to elucidate other forms of discrimination; (4) a rigid analytic stance that fails to acknowledge the significance of real external events, that overemphasizes the contribution of internal psychological issues, and that implies the patient is to blame for her distress; or (5) minimization of the discriminatory event and attempts to identify other issues as the focus for treatment (Hamilton et al., 1987; Shrier & Hamilton, 1996).

The clinician can better assess if the patient is distorting the events or exhibiting inappropriate or self-destructive behaviors and motives that are contributing to her suffering after an alliance has been formed, some stabilization has occurred, and more complete information is available. Documentation of false claims is rare, in comparison to underreporting of legitimate claims. It is true that some women distort, exaggerate, or engage in provocative or other destructive workplace behaviors (1) as a frequent result of earlier sexual traumas; (2) as a result of other characterological or affective pathology, and, occasionally, (3) as part of a psychotic delusion. Although it is important for the clinician to identify and treat these problems, it is essential that these issues are addressed in a supportive and timely manner. Early in treatment, they should be presented as a means of enhancing the woman's effectiveness in coping with her situation and preventing her from taking inappropriate steps toward resolution. Later in treatment, after her current situation has been resolved, they can also be presented as a preventative measure to help her avoid future distress and vulnerability. The patient or client can and should be asked if she feels that other psychological or external factors are contributing to her distress, but this should be done in a manner that communicates a wish to target all sources of stress, as opposed to questioning the validity of her perceptions.

Common countertransference reactions may also influence the formation of therapeutic alliance. Overidentification with the perpetrator's or the institution's viewpoint or lack of awareness of the prevalence of discriminatory events can lead to some common therapy errors: (1) denial/disbelief regarding the abuse of power and/or irrational stereotyping inherent in these situations, or both; (2) overemphasis of the patient's pathology; (3) focusing undue concern on the legal definition of discrimination or the harasser's or institution's reputation, while denying or minimizing the patient's injuries; and (4) failure to identify, and to address the detrimental effects of lack of support from friends, coworkers, family, and the work/academic institution. Overidentification with the victimized person can result in (1) failure to address the patient's contributing behaviors, ineffective coping strategies or any underlying pathology; or (2) failure to assist in avoiding premature or suboptimal forms of action, based upon incomplete processing of anger and other affects. Therapists should also be aware of any personal gender stereotypes and conflicts of interest that they are bringing to the treatment (Simon, 1996).

Providing the patient with a cognitive framework for treatment is helpful in forming an alliance for patients and clients who are in acute distress or confused. Marmar (1991) and Marmar et al. (1993) present an overview of the therapist's role, based upon the trauma model, in which the therapist (1) assists in altering negative cognitive attributions, (2) assists with the modulation and the processing of affect, (3) assists the patient in identifying the unconscious meaning of the trauma, and (4) assists the patient in developing strategies to contain the trauma without resorting to maladaptive or avoidance behaviors. The clinician should describe these functions in lay terms at the onset of treatment. An example of what that information might be is as follows:

> Experiences like the one you have just described to me are often harmful to people's mental health, their views of themselves, their relationships, and their work functioning. I can help you assess if you are being affected negatively in any way. If so, we can work together to reverse these changes. I can also help you to assess the possible ways in which you could deal with your situation so that you can choose the approach that best suits your needs. I can support you in enacting your plan and in dealing with any stress associated with your taking action. We can then review the outcome and deal with anything that is preventing you from reinvesting in your life and work. Your treatment will involve our reviewing your current situation, obtaining background history, and assessing how you are coping as you work on resolving your situation. If at any time you develop symptoms such as depression or anxiety, we can utilize medication or cognitive and behavioral techniques to help you so that you can feel your best and function at your best at all times. We can work on this at your own pace and continue to meet until the situation is fully resolved and your life and work have returned to "normal."

The following case example illustrates issues involved in clarifying the clinician's role and establishing a therapeutic alliance.

CASE VIGNETTE 6-1

Problems Related to Clarification of Clinician's Role

Janet Jones was a 26-year-old graduate student who entered treatment for symptoms of anxiety and depression after filing a formal, institutional sexual harassment complaint against her mentor-professor, an illustrious, internationally known scientist.

In the context of investigating her complaint, Janet had received excellent advice from the dean of the graduate school, who ultimately recommended treatment. The dean negotiated on behalf of Janet for the school to pay for the costs of her treatment. Janet's therapist legitimately discussed the nature of the treatment contract with the institution at the onset of therapy and received verification from both Janet and the dean that the treatment would be entirely confidential and that the only statements required from the therapist would be to certify that continued treatment was indicated and to submit bills. This agreement was satisfactory to the therapist, Janet, and the dean, who was authorized to represent the school. Treatment focused initially on containment of the anxiety and the depressive symptomatology by a combination of psychotropic medication and psychotherapy. The therapist focused on assisting Janet in assessing and implementing a transfer of her graduate work to another mentor, a move that was well supported by her dean. As both she and her therapist began to explore some residual depressive symptomatology, Janet became more resistant to the treatment, especially when they mutually identified conflicts with her father as the source of her residual symptoms.

Janet's father, himself a noted professor, had been killed unexpectantly in an auto accident 5 years earlier, leaving many unresolved issues between him and his daughter. Janet's father had always adopted a punitive, rigid, and devaluing stance toward his daughter, a position that was passively supported by Janet's mother. Although Janet had begun to address these issues with her father, his untimely death had abruptly terminated her attempts and enhanced problems related to the idealization of him by both her mother and herself.

Janet's therapist clarified that these were longer-term therapy issues but important ones in terms of her potential vulnerability to relationships with male authorities. Janet was asked if she wished to embark upon this segment of treatment or to conclude the therapy now that her presenting symptoms were greatly relieved and her immediate situation had been rectified. Janet informed her therapist that she wished to continue the treatment but after six sessions informed her therapist that an excellent opportunity to study abroad for 8 weeks had presented itself. She expressed the wish to temporarily discontinue her treatment and resume after her study abroad. She and her therapist agreed to a termination at that point, and the treatment was concluded after two additional sessions, to the satisfaction of both the therapist and Janet, who expressed great appreciation for the help she had received.

The therapist heard no further from Janet until 6 months later, when she received a call from an attorney representing Janet in a lawsuit against her institution. The attorney requested the therapist to testify on Janet's behalf. The therapist explained that she could not serve as an expert witness, given that she had already had a treatment relationship with Janet and her understanding was that treatment, though temporarily on hold, was still ongoing. She recommended that a forensic evaluation be performed by another clinician. The therapist also explained to the attorney that the initial treatment contract with Janet had included an understanding that she would never serve as an expert witness. The attorney remarked that Janet was well aware of the agreement but felt that her therapist was in the best position to help her, and she did not have money to support a forensic expert. The therapist suggested a joint conference between Janet, the attorney, and herself, but Janet refused the conference, again for monetary reasons.

Despite the therapist warning the attorney that she might have information regarding Janet that might prove detrimental, the attorney named the therapist as a factual witness, and she was subpoenaed for deposition. During the deposition, the defense attorney questioned the therapist regarding the reasons for Janet's termination of treatment, and the therapist responded by explaining the educational opportunity that had presented itself to study abroad. The defense attorney informed the therapist that Janet had not traveled abroad and asked how she, the therapist, could explain this. The therapist was circumspect but shocked. The case went to trial, and the therapist unwittingly became the defense's primary witness. The explanation Janet gave her therapist for discontinuing treatment was utilized in the service of diminishing her credibility with regard to her sexual harassment complaint. Janet was crushed and developed a depression, in which she expressed a deep sense of betrayal by her therapist, whom she idealized. She had great difficulties (1) in appreciating her unrealistic expectations that her therapist would rescue her, (2) in engaging with a new therapist, and (3) in properly placing her experience into perspective and completing her treatment regarding issues with her father.

CASE VIGNETTE 6-2

Nontherapeutic Stance by Clinician

Katherine Glid was a 32-year-old attorney who sought treatment for depression, which arose in the context of being involuntarily transferred, along with four other female colleagues, to what was derisively labeled "the dead end division" of her law firm. Katherine had entered the large urban firm with high hopes and excellent academic credentials. She had spent 7 years working intensively to develop a career in her chosen subspecialty. The lateral transfer would make it impossible for her to reap the benefits of her past work and pursue this specialty.

The problem had first surfaced during Katherine's maternity leave, which had occurred 2 years previously. Following her pregnancy, 3 months' maternity leave, and return to work, she had been treated as though she had no strong commitment to work and as though her potential was limited. This change of attitude greatly distressed her. She was assigned to less important cases and not put forward as a candidate for teaming with some of the firm's more illustrious partners.

As Katherine described these themes in her therapy, her therapist began to focus not on the disparate treatment in the external situation but rather on Katherine's denial of the problem as a major issue in her current situation. This stance caused Katherine to blame herself and become even more critical in her expectations of herself than she had been prior to her treatment. Without soliciting Katherine's ideas and wishes or reviewing possible options, her therapist focused on the unlikelihood of winning a lawsuit. The therapist considered this stance supportive, in the sense that it would save Katherine undo distress. Also intending to be helpful, the therapist suggested that this might provide an unexpected opportunity for her to get better acquainted with her new baby and to take advantage of her husband's sympathetic stance and ability to support the family financially without Katherine's income. By pursuing this theme, the therapist failed to identify that the primary cause of Katherine's distress was the loss of a potential career track with which she was highly identified and which she had worked hard to obtain. He also inadvertently heightened her conflicts regarding the demands of her work and family life. In addition, he took a rigid stance with regard to treatment hours, insisting on regular treatment hours with no changes. This situation created stress for Katherine, whose work often required that she travel out of state. The therapist further exacerbated the situation by frequently traveling himself to lecture at various locations throughout the country, without acknowledging the disruption this created for his patient or the contradiction in his messages.

When Katherine's symptoms failed to respond to treatment and her depression became more prolonged, the therapist became irritated and began to more directly blame Katherine for her situation. By mutual consent, a consultation was obtained. The consultant recommended terminating the treatment and switching therapists. The therapist initially agreed to the consultation but later attempted to undercut the transfer, further exacerbating Katherine's distress. Treatment with her next therapist progressed painfully. Much time and energy needed to be devoted to the misconceptions and internalized blame created by the first therapy, allowing little opportunity or energy in the therapy, to be devoted to Katherine's external situation. This caused her further frustration and self-blame, because her initial motivation for treatment was to obtain support in coping with and mastering the work situation.

STEP 2: ASSESSMENT OF THE SEVERITY OF THE IMMEDIATE CRISIS AND APPROPRIATE VALIDATION AND SUPPORT REGARDING THE CHALLENGES PRESENTED

After the establishment of a therapeutic alliance, there needs to be an assessment of the nature of the immediate crisis in terms of (1) safety, (2) threats to employment or academic status, (3) severity of presenting somatic and emotional symptoms, (4) disruptions in important relationships, and (5) threats to financial viability. This assessment, combined with validation of the serious reality of the patient's or client's situation, is a good way to begin treatment. Starting in this context helps the clinician to ascertain areas of stress and begin to structure an appropriate course of treatment. This also encourages the patient to realistically assess, rather than deny the reality of, her external situation and to mobilize coping responses and problem-solving strategies, rather than regress to a depressed, helpless, and devalued state. Usually, some aspects of the patient's or client's story have already been reviewed, but it is important at this time to explain that some detailed information will need to be collected in order to plan treatment. This includes (1) a detailed account of the events; (2) a developmental family, marital, sexual, and work history; (3) a past medical and psychiatric history; and (4) a mental status exam. The evaluation should be conducted with emphasis placed on assessing the severity of the immediate crisis so that appropriate preventative interventions can be made regarding extenuating external circumstances, debilitating symptomatology, or both. It is important that the clinician not assume that the patient's current emotional state is the cause of her discrimination or harassing experience (Hollander, Sherer, Newman, et al., 1993). Following is a suggested interview format that integrates earlier materials developed by Hollander, Sherer, Newman, et al. (1993) with my materials.

Sample Evaluation Format

Chief Complaint and History of Present Illness

1. Tell me your story regarding what has happened.
   A. Incidents of discrimination?
   B. When did they occur?
   C. Where did they occur?
   D. Who was present?
   E. Who has been informed?
   F. Has a complaint been filed or any other action taken?
   G. Have you kept a record of your experience?
2. What has brought you to the point of coming to see me?
3. How is this experience affecting you?
   A. Symptoms: emotional and physical
   B. Relationships: at work and in your personal life
   C. Work functioning: motivation, attendance, performance
   D. Economic situation
4. Do you have sick or personal time accrued?
5. Do you consider yourself to be in a crisis situation? If so, regarding what issues?
   A. Your safety
   B. Your family's safety

    C. Your job and career

    D. Your finances

    E. The status of your relationship with your spouse or other significant person

    F. Thoughts of hurting self or others

    G. Other

6. Do you consider yourself to be at risk in any way?
7. Who are the people whom you can count on for support?

    A. At home

    B. At work

8. Have you told any of these people about your situation? If so, what was their reaction? If not, why?
9. Have you told anyone else? What has been that person's response?
10. How long have you been in this situation?
11. Have you experienced any other instances of harassment or discrimination at this job?
12. Did you take any action?
13. Describe the action.
14. Have you consulted an attorney? Have you filed a lawsuit?
15. Do you know of anyone in your current work setting who is having similar experiences?
16. What actions has this person taken and what has been the result?
17. In the past, were you having any troubles at work unrelated to this situation?
18. In the context of this situation, have you been given an increased workload, been ostracized, skipped over for promotion, received a detrimental assignment or transfer, or in any other way suffered retaliation?
19. What evaluations or other evidence of your work performance is available prior to these events?
20. Have you been documenting your work performance since the events?
21. Are there any immediate changes you could make in your work or academics to alleviate the situation without cost to you?

    A. Transfer job, stop seeing this client, customer, or colleague

    B. Transfer reporting responsibilities

    C. Transfer location

    D. Drop courses

    E. Other

Concomitant Stresses

1. Are there any other situations causing stress in your life at this time?
   A. Marital
   B. Parenting/family
   C. Health (physical and mental)
   D. Finances
   E. Legal
   F. Other

Relevant Past History

1. What other jobs have you held?
2. Have you experienced harassment and discrimination in any of these positions? If so, describe.
   A. How did you respond?
   B. What was the outcome?
3. What has been your previous work performance? Documentation?
4. Have you ever filed for Workmen's Compensation, filed a lawsuit or been sued?
5. Does this experience remind you of any other relationship in your life?
6. Does this harassment or discrimination experience remind you of any other experiences in your life?
7. Have you ever had any of the following experiences? (time, age, duration)
   A. Physical abuse (by a spouse or partner, date, parent, or family member, etc.)
   B. Emotional abuse
   C. Verbal abuse
   D. Childhood incest or molestation
   E. Rape or coercive sex, date rape
   F. Sexual exploitation by a professional such as a physician, a lawyer, clergy, and so on
   G. How did you cope with this situation?

(A standard developmental and family history review should also be performed with the patient at this point.)

Medical and Psychiatric History

1. Have you ever experienced your current symptoms in the past? If so, when?
2. Past psychiatric treatment: when, what, outcome?
3. Current medical treatment and medications
4. Are your currently using alcohol or drugs? Has this increased in your current situation?
5. Have you used alcohol or drugs in the past?
6. What is your current medical symptomatology and what is its chronological relation to you work situation?
7. How do you feel about what has been happening to you?
8. Why do you think this is happening?
9. Do you think you have contributed to your situation? If so, how? What would you do differently?
10. Is anyone trying to make you feel guilty?
11. What would you consider to be the ideal outcome in this situation?
12. Do you think it will be possible to achieve this?
13. What do you hope to get from treatment?

Relevant Cultural and Economic Factors to Consider

The therapist must be familiar with relevant cultural and economic issues in order to collaborate properly with the patient or client in this preliminary assessment of her circumstances. The following factors are important to consider at this stage of the treatment.

1. Most women work out of economic necessity.
2. Most women are in junior or lower-status jobs, and their perpetrators are likely to have some authority or status advantage over them in the work hierarchy if a confrontation occurs. If a woman holds a higher-status position, she is likely to be outnumbered by male peers who might identify with the perpetrator or minimize the significance of her experience.
3. Cultural norms place women in a no-win situation. If a woman rejects a harasser's advances, she is challenging his masculinity. If she tactfully ignores him, she may be misinterpreted as being coy,

and he may increase his attentions. Similarly, if she challenges discriminatory behaviors, she may be labeled a troublemaker and be blackballed. If she is silent, she may lose any opportunity for promotion, salary equity, expert mentoring, and so on.

4. Culturally, women may still hold responsibility for controlling men's sexual behavior and are encouraged to internalize blame for any sexual misconduct. Similarly, they are socialized to accept nurturing subordinate roles and to internalize responsibility for maintaining relationships, even when those roles and relationships may be discriminatory toward them.

5. Women are expected to put families before jobs and may interpret sexual harassment and other forms of gender discrimination as a reminder that they should be at home with their families, even if they are working out of economic necessity.

6. Gender discrimination and sexual harassment reinforce the low self-confidence and difficulty in judging one's own abilities that most women bring to the workplace as a result of negative stereotypes they are taught at an early age.

7. Students and professional women may depend on the perpetrator of the discriminatory behavior for valuable education and training experiences, verbal or written evaluations and references, and opportunities for career advancement. Informal blackballing instigated by the perpetrator or another representative of the institution can be extremely difficult to combat effectually in this instance. Blue-collar and public service women breaking into traditional male occupations depend on their coworkers for safety, job training, support, and advancement, and they face similar difficulties.

8. Victimized people in highly specialized positions or with special training or women with significant financial needs and minimal work or educational backgrounds cannot easily transfer, change jobs, or find alternative tutors or mentors. In these circumstances the victimized individual may be forced to deal with the stress of continued interaction with the perpetrator or suffer severe educational, economic, job, and career-development losses.

9. Victimized people from ethnic or racial minority groups may be subjected to withdrawal of support, community sanctions, or both, because of cultural mandates (1) not to speak publicly about sexuality; (2) to settle these issues privately within the community, rather than speak out publicly against one of her own (e.g., Anita Hill and Clarence Thomas); (3) to value domestic roles over work roles;

and (4) to give advocacy against racism priority over advocacy against sexism (see Chapter 4).

10. Homosexuals and bisexuals may be vulnerable to the same community inhibitions as other minority groups and, in addition, may fear unwanted invasions of their privacy, negative reactions toward them, or both, due to exposure of their sexual preference (see Chapter 4).

11. Family and marital problems, losses, and other life stresses may complicate the patient's or client's work or academic situation.

12. Support systems vary with regard to family, coworkers, superiors, and friends. Problems with supports may contribute both to psychological symptoms and to difficulties with resolution of discriminatory events.

13. A significant number of victimized individuals will have histories of previous sexual traumas, increasing their vulnerability to severe symptomatology, flooding of repressed memories, or both. (See the special section on the treatment of pretraumatized individuals in Chapter 8.)

14. Although sexual harassment has received the most public attention, other forms of gender discrimination are even more common and may accompany and complicate the resolution of harassment or may be the sole or main cause of the patient's distress.

15. Studies indicate that if a patient is complaining of harassment and discrimination, it is likely to have occurred because most workers are reluctant to complain. Although her institution may currently be alleging incompetence in the victimized woman's work and academic performance, it is likely to have been adequate or superior prior to the event. The longer her problem has persisted, the more likely her performance has deteriorated.

16. Disruption and conflict in significant relationships with spouse, family, friends, coworkers, mentors, and others are common, highly significant sequelae of harassment and discrimination situations (Bernstein & Lenhart, 1993, pp. 319–320; Crull, 1982, p. 542; Hollander, Scherer, et al., 1993).

Review of the complicated personal, economic, employment, and cultural circumstances helps both patient and clinician develop respect for the severity of the challenge. They can identify special areas of stress that are immediate and need to be targeted or are anticipated and may require attention in the future. This also helps them to avoid the following countertransference errors common at this stage of treatment: (1)

devaluing a patient or client for an initial inability to take action, or (2) erroneously supporting the patient or client in taking immediate or impulsive action that may be ineffective or not in her best interest. It is also possible at this point for the clinician to identify victimized individuals who have minimal symptomatology, healthy coping skills, and good supports, who may require little or no treatment. They may be referred to self-help and education resources or seen supportively on an intermittent or an as-needed basis, to assist them in formulating or enacting a plan of action and dealing with any symptoms that arise. Informal grassroots support groups, as well as formal structured support groups, can be especially helpful in this respect. Additional resources are available from national organizations and agencies, some of which are listed as follows:

1. The Institute for Research on Women's Health, Suite 109, Washington, DC 20009-2530, (202) 483-8643
2. The National Council for Research on Women (NCRW), 530 Broadway, 10th Floor, New York, NY 10012-3920, (212) 274-0730
3. The Women's Legal Defense Fund, 1875 Connecticut Ave. NW, Washington, DC 20009-5728, (202) 986-2600
4. Legal Resource Kit: Employment Sexual Harassment can br ordered from NOW/LDEF, 99 Hudson St., New York, NY 10013-2815, (212) 925-6635.

In an earlier book (Bernstein & Lenhart, 1993) I presented supportive and educational guidelines to assist individuals with minimal symptoms. They included the following steps.

Guidelines for Effective Individual Responses to Sexual Harassment and Gender Discrimination

1. Define the problem as clearly as you can and document the situation.
   A. Is the problem disparate treatment, disparate impact, or a hostile environment? Is it sexual harassment, another form of gender discrimination, or both?
   B. Could it be conceptualized as sexism, skewed group behavior, or micro-inequity?

    C. Is it sexual harassment or another form of illegal gender discrimination, or is the behavior destructive but not illegal?

    D. How severe is the impact on you?

    E. Is the impact temporary or long term?

    F. Is the behavior directed toward others, as well as you?

    G. Have others witnessed the behavior?

    H. Document all incidences in writing as completely and objectively as possible, including dates and any attempts you have made to remedy your situation.

2. Assess your emotional status.

    A. Have you developed depression, psychosomatic complaints, anxiety, panic, rage reactions, or post-traumatic reactions? If so, get professional help.

    B. Have you developed some problematic defensive reactions, for example, displaced anger, withdrawal, self-blame, isolation, chronic ambivalence, lowered goals? If so, try to contain these and work on a more effective response.

3. Get help and support. Don't isolate yourself. Discuss your situation with a trusted friend, a colleague, a peer, the AMWA hotline, a mentor, and so on. Be sure to check whether an institutional official must file a compulsory report or a complaint before you discuss the situation. You want to maintain control.

4. Maintain a high level of job or school performance and document this.

5. Clarify your goals in working out a solution.

    A. Do you want the behavior to stop?

    B. Do you want not to work with this person?

    C. Do you want a grade or an evaluation to be changed?

    D. Do you want financial reimbursement for losses?

    E. Do you want institutional sanctions against the individual?

    F. What were your original career, work, and personal goals and how can they best be served? (Revenge is not a productive goal and usually means your anger is not yet in perspective.)

6. What are your responsibilities, given your role within your institution? Do these conflict with your personal goals for resolution? If so, how could this conflict be resolved?

7. List all possible strategies for dealing with your situationn and list the potential risks and benefits of each strategy. Get input from others you trust.

8. Which strategy best fits your overall personal goals, without substantial risk to you?
9. What back-up strategy could you use if your first strategy fails?
10. What steps could you take to minimize the potential risks of your first-line strategy?
11. Proceed with your best strategy at your own pace, in a manner that protects you from further losses.
12. Be prepared for a mourning period. Some loss is experienced with discrimination, no matter how well the situation is handled. Share your sadness and get support from others.

The following case example illustrates the importance of properly addressing the immediate crisis.

CASE VIGNETTE 6-3

Assessment of the Immediate Crisis and Special Cultural Challenges

Tamar Gregorian was a 25-year-old married woman referred by her family doctor for acute symptoms of agoraphobia and depression. Mr. Alexander Gregorian reported that his wife had abruptly refused to return to work, had sequestered herself in the bedroom, was eating and drinking very little, and would not speak to him about whatever was going on. The situation was exacerbated by the fact that the couple was greatly isolated and in a stressful situation.

Both Tamar and Alexander had recently come to the United States as immigrants from the Middle East. Their departure from their native country had been chaotic and traumatic, the result of major political and religious differences with their families of origin. Although both Tamar and Alexander had been schooled in the United States, their initial plan was to return to their homeland and to build a life there. This unexpected fracture from their family of origin had been greatly distressing to both of them and had precipitated a flight, which had not allowed them time to properly plan an appropriate move to the United States. Fortunately, Alexander, a scientist, had obtained a position in a computer start-up company with the help of a colleague from school. Tamar had also been helped by this friend, who assisted her in obtaining a position in the supply division of the company.

The couple's economic situation was near crisis. Although both had obtained jobs with benefits, the cost of moving and the lack of possessions, combined with the lower-status jobs that they were able to obtain, had left the couple in need of both salaries, a factor that greatly concerned Tamar's husband.

The partners were also stressed over their abrupt and disruptive disconnection from their families of origin. Tamar, in particular, had many conflicts regarding the change in her role—specifically, the fact that neither she nor her husband were practicing the Moslem dress code and that she had broken strict family traditions in entering the workplace. Alexander was agitated by his wife's condition but freely acknowledged that the stress of the new move, the newness of the country, and his own economic worries were exacerbating his response to his wife's illness.

On initial evaluation, Tamar was quite constricted in affect and very reluctant to speak to her therapist. She did agree to antianxiety and antidepressant medication but was very reluctant to meet with the therapist. She did, however, at the insistence of her husband, acquiesce and arranged to be on sick leave for 1 week. The leave was accomplished with the assistance of the couple's friend. Alexander was especially anxious about the outcome, fearful that his wife would lose her job and that the relationship with their friend would be strained by this additional request for special treatment. Tamar agreed to several therapy meetings during the week of her leave. In the context of the frequent meetings she was able to give a more complete history, initially focusing on (1) the difficulties of the adjustment to the United States, (2) her sadness and anxiety with regard to her fractured relationships with her family, and (3) concerns for the couple's economic viability. She was initially unable to ascertain the reason for her agoraphobic stance.

In the context of discussing how the move had impacted on the marital, emotional, and sexual relationship, Tamar became agitated and ultimately revealed that a courier delivering laboratory supplies to the corporation had approached her sexually. Without her permission, he had fondled her breasts. This precipitated her abrupt departure from the workplace, as well as an intense sense of shame and guilt. She stated that in her country, such an act would bring dishonor upon the entire family and that she had been disobeying Moslem Law by not covering her body properly and by entering the workplace. Although she saw her husband as supportive and was consciously aware of his breach with the family religion, she nonetheless imagined that he would have a punitive reaction to her situation, as she was certain her father would have.

With her therapist, she identified the immediate goal of not losing her job or her relationship with her husband, who was her only source of support, both emotionally and economically. With her therapist's assistance, she was able to explain the situation to her husband in a joint conference and to name it as sexual harassment. Neither Tamar nor Alexander wished to jeopardize their positions within their new company by filing any type of complaint. With the assistance of their American friend, Tamar was able to transfer from the warehouse to the telecommunications section of the supply division and effectively remove herself from contact with the courier. After dealing effectively with the initial crises and challenges, she was able to continue her therapy at a less frequent pace and to address longer-term issues related to her family of origin and her immigration status.

STEP 3: EVALUATION AND TREATMENT OF IMMEDIATE SYMPTOMATOLOGY AND NEGOTIATION OF A THERAPEUTIC CONTRACT FOR ONGOING COLLABORATIVE MONITORING OF SYMPTOMS

Physical and psychological symptoms of varying severity are common in people victimized by sexual harassment and other forms of gender discrimination and may vary or exacerbate at different stages of treatment, as the patient deals with prolonged litigation, traumatic confrontations, significant losses, withdrawal of support, and other commonly associated stresses. If the patient is in crisis at the time of the initial evaluation or has endured a prolonged experience, it is likely she will have some configuration of debilitating symptoms, requiring immediate attention. A small minority of patients may have or may acquire suicidal or homicidal symptoms.

Eliciting the patient's primary complaints and reviewing the most common symptomatology allow the therapist to identify the immediate problems that require treatment. It is also important at this time to educate the patient as to the need for continual monitoring of the common symptoms, given the likelihood that symptoms may change or exacerbate as the woman experiences stress and change over the course of treatment. Common symptoms to review include: distractibility, psychomotor agitation or retardation, appetite change, insomnia, hyperinsomnia, decreased libido, hypersexuality, impaired functioning (social or occupational), disorientation, memory loss, phobias, obsessions, compulsions, ruminations, hallucinations, delusions, racing thoughts, dysphoria, apprehensive expectations, anxiety, dyspnea, palpitations, chest pain, choking sensations, vertigo, feelings of unreality, paresthesias, sweats, fainting, trembling, suicidal or homicidal ideation, reexperiencing traumatic events (flashbacks), constricted affect, difficulty concentrating, hypervigilance, avoidance, psychophysiologic symptoms, exaggerated startle response, irritability, detachment, pessimism, social withdrawal, crying, depression, logorrhea, indecisiveness, guilt, feelings of worthlessness and inadequacy, loss of interest or ability to enjoy life, loss of energy, crying spells, drug and alcohol abuse, headaches, diarrhea, muscle spasm, nausea, panic attacks, headaches, diarrhea, or dyspepsia.

Some of the most common psychological problems requiring treatment include (1) anxiety or post-traumatic stress, along with depressive and substance abuse disorders; and (2) psychosomatic symptoms and complaints. (Chapter 5 contains a complete discussion of the negative psychological sequelae and should be reviewed at this time.)

Problematic anxiety and depressive and post-traumatic symptoms can be treated effectively with adjunctive psychotropic medications selected on the basis of the most disruptive target symptoms. Although controlled studies are limited to general traumatic and depressive experiences, rather than harassment or discrimination, they provide some guidelines regarding choice of medication. Hamilton and Shrier (1996, pp. 109–110) recommend several approaches: (1) low-dose antianxiety medications can be helpful for daytime anxiety, panic, and agitation, provided they do not trigger dissociative states; (2) SSRIs (selective serotonin reuptake inhibitors) preferentially, but also tricyclic and MAO antidepressants, can reduce depression, mixtures of depression and anxiety, and obsessive ruminations; (3) mood stabilizers alone or in combination with antidepressants can be effective in patients complaining of hostility, irritability, and hyperactivity; (4) sleep medications are helpful for transient uncomplicated insomnia; and (5) meditation or a variety of behavioral relaxation techniques may also prove valuable.

Occasionally, patients or clients may present for treatment with these complaints but do not connect them with workplace or academic situations. In this case, it is important for the clinician to elicit further history, as the individual may be denying or minimizing her situation or may simply be unaware of the connection between her physical symptoms and her experience at work or school. Victimized individuals should be asked specifically about suicidal ideation and destructive feelings toward themselves, especially if they are depressed. Homicidal ideation should also be elicited. These behaviors are rare but have occurred in this context, especially in clients or patients with previous sexual traumas (see Chapter 8). Interventions for symptom relief should be placed in the context of enabling the client or patient to function optimally so that she can maintain credibility at work and devise the best strategy for resolution. The following case example demonstrates the importance of proper diagnosis and treatment of initial symptomatology and ongoing collaboration of monitoring of symptoms.

CASE VIGNETTE 6-4

Treatment of Initial and Ongoing Symptomatology
That Is Key to Resolving Sexual Harassment

Cynthia Jones was a 35-year-old corporate executive who was referred for therapy by her attorney, for symptoms of anxiety and agitation that had exacerbated in the context of litigation proceedings involving her former company, against which she had filed a sexual harassment lawsuit. Cynthia had been recruited to the area to join a small start-up firm specializing in her area of technical expertise. Tom, one of the senior executives of the corporation, was especially helpful to her in negotiating her position and in assisting her move to a new city. Six months after Cynthia began work, Tom began to pressure her for dates. He became irritated when she persistently and firmly declined. He ceased asking and withdrew from contact with her. Worried about losing his valued patronship, Cynthia volunteered for extra work, agreed to overtime hours, and strove to become conciliatory. Despite her efforts, Tom criticized her work in public business meetings and pressured her immediate boss for a reevaluation of her performance. Tom's criticisms were reflected in her new evaluation, which occurred 4 months prior to the regular period. She also did not receive assignments to the types of work that had been promised her at her hiring.

Shortly thereafter, another senior executive approached Cynthia to report vague complaints from secretaries and various business clients regarding her attitude and deportment. She was told that she did not fit in with the company culture, and it was suggested that she seek another position. When she challenged this position, she was told that she left them no other choice than to document her significant deficits, which might jeopardize her in finding a new position.

Three months later she was fired and was read a list of short-comings, most of which she felt were inaccurate. She was asked to remove her belongings from the premises and to vacate immediately. Stunned, she began to pack but was interrupted by Tom, who entered her office and smugly told her of his satisfaction in ruining her career. He then began to further devalue her work. Enraged, she attempted to pass by him and out the door. He pushed her back, stating that he was not finished with her and that she had a lot more coming to her. She retains no memory of the remainder of the conversation. Once at her apartment, Cynthia was obsessed with the memory of Tom's hands on her and was too furious and anxious to sleep. She invited a friend to stay with her, who also recommended that she consult an attorney specializing in discrimination. The following morning she visited the attorney and immediately filed suit. Although active and focused in her sessions with her attorney, Cynthia began experiencing panic attacks, explosive episodes, and sleep disturbance at home. She became so anxious when her attorney was preparing to file suit that he referred her for therapy.

On initial evaluation, Cynthia reported that she was extremely anxious at bedtime and often unable to fall asleep. During the day, she experienced panic attacks, combined with explosive outbursts of anger directed toward friends and occasionally toward her attorney. Initially, she was phobic regarding medication but was ultimately able to control her panic symptoms by using antianxiety medications and behavioral relaxation techniques. At the suggestion of her therapist, she instructed her attorney to postpone legal proceedings until she stabilized. Therapy initially focused on controlling her symptomatology, stabilizing her in a new job she had been offered, and creating a supportive network of friends in her new city. Her symptoms diminished, and she saw her therapist less frequently for medication monitoring and support at work.

Three months later, Cynthia became symptomatic again when her attorney reactivated her case. Although she permitted him to file the complaint, her fears escalated when she considered the necessity of giving a deposition. In the context of exploring these fears, she began having nightmares that she ultimately associated with being raped by a date at age 15, an experience she had tried not to think of. Over a 4-month period, she was able to explore the current harassment experience in the context of her parents' reaction when she told them about her date rape. Her mother had been ashamed and encouraged her to minimize the experience, and her father had accused her of being deliberately seductive and had instituted a punitive curfew. Integration of this material enabled Cynthia to give a deposition against her corporation and ultimately to receive a settlement.

This chapter has presented a conceptual model for the treatment of people victimized by sexual harassment and gender discrimination. The initial stages of treatment have been reviewed in detail: (1) establishment of a therapeutic alliance and clarification of the clinician's role, (2) assessment of the severity of the immediate crisis, and (3) evaluation and treatment of immediate symptoms and establishment of therapeutic contact for periodic monitoring of symptoms throughout treatment. These steps are necessary before the patient can effectively formulate an effective plan of action. Even if the patient has already taken action prior to entering treatment, these initial steps should still be reviewed. If she is symptomatic or in crisis, the action she has taken is not likely to be well thought out or effective or she may be in crisis related to retaliatory actions taken against her. If so, she will need to rethink her action plan when she has been stabilized. Chapter 7 will review the therapeutic process involved in helping a patient to formulate and enact an effective plan of action and to protect herself against retaliatory behaviors.

CHAPTER 7

Conceptualizing Treatment of Sexual Harassment and Gender Discrimination

The Intermediate Stages of Processing Affects and Cognitions and Formulating an Effective Plan of Action

INTRODUCTION

When a treatment alliance has been formed and any initial debilitating symptoms or external crises have been stabilized, it is appropriate for the clinician to assist the patient or client in formulating her plan for dealing with the discriminatory experience. This is crucial for reestablishing her sense of autonomy and internal control. Given the complexities of the issues involved, there is no perfect plan for any particular situation. The goal is, therefore, to assist the patient or client in identifying a plan that best suits *her* needs, goals, and style and best protects her against retaliatory actions and significant losses. The emphasis on *her* is crucial. To be restorative to the patient's sense of control, autonomy, and integrity, the plan must be *hers,* not the therapist's. The role of the clinician at this stage of treatment is to provide a safe, stabilizing environment for the patient or client (1) to thoughtfully review the pros and cons of possible actions in terms of her needs and goals, and (2) to proactively anticipate and plan protective measures against any possible losses or retaliatory behaviors that may result from her actions. This process usually involves three steps, which will be discussed in this chapter: (1) ventilation of feelings, processing of negative self-perceptions and attributions, and clarification of outcome goals; (2) a review of the pros and cons of possible responses to the discrimination, as well as the formulation and enactment of a realistic plan of action; and (3) an assessment of potential losses and retaliatory behaviors and the institution of protective measures.

STEP 4: VENTILATION OF FEELINGS, EXPLORATION OF NEGATIVE PERCEPTIONS, AND FORMULATION OF REALISTIC OUTCOME GOALS

Intense feelings and related cognitions, such as anxiety, fear, confusion, disbelief, guilt, shame, anger, sadness and disillusionment, self-blame, self-devaluation, and so on, are common in victimized individuals (Bernstein & Lenhart, 1993). A wide spectrum of emotional responses is common and usually unfolds in progressive stages, which will be discussed further on (Bernstein & Lenhart, 1993; Gutek & Koss, 1996; Shrier & Hamilton, 1996). Treatment should provide a safe place for full exploration and ventilation of these feelings, not only to relieve the client's distress, but also to prevent the following common adverse outcomes: (1) impulsive actions that are not in the client's best interest and do not lead to effective resolution; (2) emotional displays in the workplace, which can lead to decreased credibility, termination of employment, or exposure of the client's vulnerabilities to unsupportive people; and (3) displacement of negative affect onto potentially supportive individuals, such as spouses, mentors, treating clinicians, and attorneys.

Stages of Reactions

Feelings of confusion and disbelief are common early on and are often related to a wish to believe that the behaviors will stop or that they are not detrimental. A review of the factual realities of her situation, as well as the provision of educational information regarding the nature and the frequency of gender discrimination and power inequities at work, will support the victimized individual in facing her problem. This will also help to "normalize" the experience and prevent the development of a sense of isolation or narcissistic injury, which can be problematic later.

The ventilation of feelings of fear, anxiety, and occasionally paranoia will help to clarify and process threats of physical injury, job loss, economic ruin; derailment from crucial career and educational pathways, loss of key relationships and supports, and retaliatory actions. This stabilizes the client or patient and prevents impulsive withdrawal from the workplace or abrupt changes in career. It also prepares her for developing a plan of action that will minimize and protect her from future trauma. It is important to appreciate that paranoia is not an uncommon response to discriminatory events. It is also important at this stage not to assume that paranoia is indicative of more severe pathology. Antianxiety medication and behavior relaxation techniques can be useful to contain severe anxiety reactions.

The unobstructed ventilation of feelings of shame, guilt, and self-blame serves several important functions. It allows for a realistic discussion and an adaptive resolution of any preexisting concerns regarding intrinsic work or academic ability triggered by the experience. Culturally induced shame regarding women's roles, sexual orientation, or the public discussion of sexual issues can be alleviated prior to the disclosure or complaint proceedings. Realistic or unrealistic concerns regarding the client's or patient's contributions to her situation can be addressed and appropriate action taken to rectify any inappropriate or contradictory behavior on her part, for example, previously colluding with or encouraging the behavior. Victimized women, as well as the public in general, often view gender discrimination as something the individual can and should be able to handle directly and assertively, despite empirical evidence to the contrary (see Chapter 4). This perception often exacerbates guilt in the victimized individual and exposes her to direct and subtle blame from others. If indeed the woman has lied, distorted, or fabricated the events, she can be discouraged from further action, and the motivations for her behavior can be explored in the privacy and safety of her therapy. Work, family, and other women's role conflicts aggravated by the situation can be put into proper perspective, decreasing the chance of an impulsive and detrimental flight from the workplace based on guilt.

Direct expression of anger at the perpetrator or the institution is often impossible or detrimental. Impulsive expressions of anger through litigation, verbal confrontations, and obsessional thoughts of revenge are destructive. It is wise to give the patient or client ample opportunity to express her grievances in detail, explore her anger, and bring it into perspective before she takes any action. Some victimized individuals fear legitimate anger in themselves, which inhibits their ability to be properly assertive and take appropriate action. If, on the other hand, the woman's anger is due to a distortion of the event or a displacement from other issues, it cannot be effectively resolved via workplace complaints, which might correctly be identified as frivolous and therefore ultimately detrimental to her credibility and well-being. In this instance, detrimental action can be avoided and significant issues properly identified and addressed in the safety and privacy of therapy.

Sadness, depression, and disillusionment resulting from (1) shattered beliefs; (2) immediate or potential losses; and (3) the experience of being discredited, unsupported, and devalued by powerful individuals should be resolved within the therapy so that these do not interfere with the client's or patient's energy and ability to assert herself on her own behalf. Appropriate grieving can be facilitated, and medication can be used to target depressive symptoms that are interfering with the victimized individual's ability to cope.

Processing of Negative Perceptions

Negative changes in the internal perception of self, others, and the world may accompany the patient's strong feelings in accordance with the progressive emotional stages just described or independently. In addition, negative internal cognitions regarding the discrimination may trigger negative cognitions from the patient's past experiences, further intensifying the impact (see Chapter 5). Common negative self-concepts and central beliefs resulting from harassment and discrimination include

1. Personal sense of helplessness and incompetence
2. Lowered self-esteem
3. Generalized self-doubt
4. Devalued sense of skills and talents
5. Belief that she has chosen the wrong job, profession, or academic focus
6. Loss of faith in people
7. Disillusionment with mentors, superiors, institutions
8. Exacerbation of inner conflicts regarding home and work balance, accompanied by a belief that harassment and discrimination are punishment for neglecting her family or proof that she belongs at home, rather than in the workplace
9. Belief that she caused the harassment and discrimination
10. Belief that taking action on her own behalf would be unfair or harmful to the perpetrator
11. Destruction of a sense of justice
12. Belief that hard work, ability, or loyalty will never be rewarded

Clinicians who are aware of the high potential for these maladaptive changes in internal perceptions can address them directly as they appear, with or without their affective components. Clinicians can also proactively educate and caution their patients regarding the frequency of these reactions and the need to self-monitor and openly discuss any such changes with their therapist. Unfortunately, these perceptions are often reinforced by the subtle and overt blame the victimized person is likely to encounter in her work and her social communications. If the clinician overlooks this important aspect of treatment, permanent and maladaptive changes in internal perceptions can result, accompanied by serious long-term consequences for the client or patient (see Chapter 5).

In addition to negative perceptual changes, intense affect can also result in maladaptive coping responses. The presence of these nonproductive behaviors can be an indication of the intensity of underlying affect that needs to be explored. The most common of these behaviors include

1. Impulsive confrontation and litigation
2. Impulsive withdrawal involving job, career, or academic changes
3. Displacement of legitimate anger onto supportive or neutral people
4. Internalization of blame, with self-punitive behaviors or persistent nonproductive attempts to make the situation better
5. Isolation and secrecy regarding the events
6. Chronic ambivalence, fluctuating between anger toward the perpetrator and self-doubts regarding her work capability and career choices
7. Denial of the seriousness of the situation and failure to act

Obviously, intense feelings, negative cognitions, and maladaptive coping responses may arise and recede at various points in the treatment process. They require continued monitoring by the patient and the therapist. Providing ongoing opportunities for the patient to explore and ventilate prepares her for developing a realistic and effective plan of action, free of emotional distortion. This process also educates her regarding common emotional reactions that may hinder her and allies her with her therapist in identifying and monitoring her affect as treatment progresses. (1) If a patient's emotional responses are extreme or prolonged; (2) if they do not respond to supportive approaches; or (3) if the patient cannot move on to develop a plan of action, underlying issues related to self-esteem, self-assertion, or entitlement may need to be uncovered and addressed without implication or blame. Treatment should be presented in terms of helping her face her current situation from a position of strength and removing undue distress that could interfere with her coping adequately.

Patients with previous abuse experiences, such as rape, physical abuse, emotional abuse, sexual abuse, or sexual exploration within a professional relationship, may also demonstrate intense emotional responses. They represent special cases, which will be discussed later in this chapter. The following case exemplifies the importance of allowing for sufficient ventilation of feeling within the therapy.

CASE VIGNETTE 7-1

Inadequate Ventilation of Affect Inhibits Resolution
of Sexual Harassment or Assault

Sandra Stewart was a 25-year-old single secretary for a midsized shipping company. She entered treatment immediately following her departure from that job, complaining of symptoms of anxiety, depression, and an inability to resolve her ambivalence about filing a lawsuit against her former boss, who had raped her on the job. Although she was distressed and considered the incident significant, she repeatedly reiterated to her therapist that he was such a nice guy and that she was ultimately to blame. Sandra reported that she had been working for the firm approximately 3 months when her boss approached her for a date, in what she felt was an appropriate and friendly fashion. Finding him attractive, she accepted, and they began a mutually gratifying social and sexual relationship, which lasted approximately 6 months. Sandra broke off the relationship when she learned her boss had not yet finalized his divorce from his wife. She stated that her departure from the relationship had hurt him deeply and that she had great regrets regarding her actions. He had initially pleaded with her to continue the relationship and then had withdrawn and avoided contact with her. Their relationship had ultimately become so strained that she requested a new assignment. He had reluctantly agreed, and Sandra was ultimately positioned on a different floor. She saw little of him but heard through her social network that he was suffering greatly in the context of the acrimonious divorce proceedings, which were now upon him. Still feeling attached, Sandra was tempted to comfort him, but she was fearful that this would reactivate her own feelings of attachment, as well as his.

One month later she was working late in the office, and her old boss approached her in a friendly fashion. They chatted casually, but the conversation escalated, and, according to Sandra, he "poured his heart out" and begged her to continue the relationship, inviting her to spend the night with him in his apartment. Sandra attempted to interrupt the conversation and join a friend who was leaving the office, but her old boss intervened, pleading with her to remain. When her friend left the building, he asked her if she would make love to him. When she refused, he pushed her onto the desk and forced her to have intercourse with him. During the assault, he blamed her for toying with him and taking advantage of his vulnerability. He then abruptly left the office. Sandra was greatly shaken by the experience and found herself uncomfortable returning to work. Not wishing to cause additional trouble for her ex-lover, she ultimately left the position and obtained a job in a similar firm with very little difficulty. A friend with whom she had recently confided the situation was appalled that she had taken no action. In this context she began to consider the possibility of a sexual harassment suit but felt unable either to proceed or to lay the matter to rest.

Sandra's therapist focused on her internalization of blame for the incident, encouraging her to move forward with her lawsuit and obtain adequate restitution for her assault. Any doubts on Sandra's part were interpreted as further indication that she was assuming undue responsibility for her ex-lover's behavior. Her therapist repeatedly clarified the distinction between having an affair, ending it, and then being raped. Sandra filed a lawsuit, felt somewhat better, and left treatment, with the understanding that she could return if she developed symptoms or concerns in the context of any upcoming legal proceedings. Both she and her therapist agreed this might be a stressful time for her. Her therapist was not surprised when she returned 6 months later in the context of the discovery period of her lawsuit. She had become symptomatic again after giving her deposition. Again, Sandra focused on her sense of guilt and responsibility. Again, her therapist reiterated the importance of not internalizing blame for the situation. Sandra proceeded with her lawsuit, won, received a sizable settlement, but remained depressed, a fact that puzzled the therapist.

Following the conclusion of the suit, Sandra still did not recover but instead became more critical and self-punitive. She engaged in a number of self-defeating behaviors, including dating a man who did not treat her well. She failed to use any of her settlement money to assist her in moving to a better apartment, despite having multiple difficulties with heat and rodents. Having treated Sandra for approximately 1 year with very little success, the therapist arranged for a consultation, which Sandra interpreted as additional evidence of her failure.

In the context of her consultation, she revealed that despite her sophisticated veneer, she came from a conservative religious background and considered her sexual activity with her boss as adulterous. Her negative self-concept was exacerbated by her family's persistence in urging her to return to her town of origin, as opposed to pursuing a career in the city, and her mother's constant complaint that Sandra had abandoned them. Instead of allowing Sandra to ventilate her feelings of guilt regarding her boss, her therapist had prematurely attempted to bring them to closure. The therapist inadvertently exacerbated the situation rather than assisting Sandra in identifying and resolving the underlying conflicts regarding her abandoning her religion and her family. This preexisting negative perception had made coping with her sexual harassment-assault situation difficult and impossible to resolve.

STEP 5: REESTABLISHMENT OF A SENSE OF AUTONOMY AND CONTROL VIA THE DEVELOPMENT OF EFFECTIVE COPING STRATEGIES AND THE FORMULATION OF AN EFFECTIVE PLAN OF ACTION

Once the client's feelings have been explored and processed, she is positioned to develop a plan for action. The clinician's role at this point in the treatment is to refrain from recommending a specific course and instead to assist the client in developing her own plan, based on her individual needs and goals. The client's sense of control can be reestablished by encouraging her (1) to review her coping mechanisms and address any inappropriate responses in light of what she has learned about her feelings and perceptions; (2) to review all possible options for resolution of the situation, along with the pros and cons of each; (3) to choose the option that best suits her own needs and goals, provided they are realistic; (4) to proceed with her plan at her own pace; (5) to develop protective measures against further discrimination or retaliation; and (6) to proceed in a manner that will minimize further losses.

Although no therapist can hope to be familiar with the multitude of state and federal laws and the wide variety of institutional and corporate formal complaint procedures, it is important to have a general knowledge of the types of options and grievance formats so that the clinician can provide a cognitive framework from which the patient can construct her personal plan. In general, there are five approaches to the resolution of discrimination experiences: (1) direct, (2) indirect, (3) formal complaint, (4) litigation, and (5) special. The first four of the approaches are routinely recommended in the literature and by organizational consultants. These approaches correspond to the (1) confrontation-negotiating, and (2) advocacy-seeking categories of victim responses, discussed in Chapter 4. Because these externally directed, assertive response styles have been documented as effective in stopping discriminatory behaviors, it has sometimes been assumed that they are also the healthiest responses from a psychological standpoint. There is evidence, however, that these responses can result in negative outcomes for the victimized person (see Chapter 4). From a clinical standpoint, the description of a healthy, assertive response needs to be broadened to include a response in which the client thoughtfully, and without denial or avoidance, acts assertively to protect her own best interests (her internal psychological health and her external goals and needs). This calls for a fifth category of approach, which will be considered "special responses," to encompass situations in which it may not be in the client's self-interest to utilize the standard methods of action for resolving her difficulties. She may also initially utilize a special form of response to stabilize herself and then move on to utilize a more traditional plan of action.

Each of the five approaches has pros and cons, which should be carefully considered. Back-up approaches should also be planned, in case the initial strategy fails. No clinician should offer legal advice and should refer the patient to an attorney to assess the possibilities for litigation or to discuss the legal aspects of any plan of action. Many attorneys are skilled not only in employment law and litigation strategies but also in being supportive to victimized individuals' treatment and sensitive to their emotional distress. Following is a summary of the literature on responses to discrimination, which can be useful to clinicians in discussing options with patients.

Possible Methods of Action

Direct Method of Response

(Adapted from Hughes & Sandler, 1986, pp. 4–5)
(Written for sexual harassment but applicable to other forms of gender discrimination)

Direct approaches involve direct action by the victimized person toward the problematic individual. Direct action via the most appropriate institutional representative can be utilized if the discrimination is complicated and arises from many sources. Direct approaches work well if the victimized individual assesses that the discrimination is not conscious and that the perpetrator or the most appropriate institutional representative is reasonable and has been respectful and supportive to her in the past.

Mary Rowe, a labor economist, has outlined the following potential advantages of a direct approach to sexual harassment. She offers the following list of reasons for considering a direct approach:

1. To give the offended and the offender a chance, usually for the first time, to see things the same way. Because neither person may have any understanding of how the other sees the problem, discussion may help. Entry of a third party at this stage usually further polarizes the views of the opposing persons.
2. To give those who are wrongly accused the chance to defend themselves.
3. To give those who are correctly, or to some extent correctly, accused the chance to make amends. (This may not be possible in serious cases.)
4. To provide some evidence of the offense, because usually there is no substantive evidence at all. This step is vital if higher management or the courts must later take action.
5. To give sexual harassers who do not understand what they were doing a fair warning, if this is appropriate.
6. To provide the offended employee with a chance to get the harassment stopped without provoking public counterattack, experiencing public embarrassment, harming third parties, damaging the company's reputation, or causing the offender to lose face. In my experience, the aggrieved person almost always considers these points important.
7. To provide offended persons with a way to demonstrate that they tried all reasonable means to get the offender to stop. This step may be convincing later to supervisors, spouses, and others who become involved.
8. To encourage ambivalent complainants, as well as those who have inadvertently given misunderstood signals, to present a consistent and clear message.

9. To encourage those who exaggerate to be more responsible (Mary
   Rowe, 1981, p. 43).

Direct approaches to other forms of gender discrimination, such as
salary and promotional inequities, can be helpful for similar reasons.

1. They provide victimized individuals with an opportunity to present
   both their qualifications and the inequities to a potentially supportive supervisor, who may not be conscious of the problem. The supervisor may be willing to negotiate a solution if the situation is
   presented clearly in a firm, respectful, and professional manner.
2. They allow the discriminatory situation to be resolved privately, without embarrassment or damage to the reputation of the victimized
   person, the supervisors, or the organization.
3. They provide a way for the victimized woman to document that she
   has tried a reasonable approach to a remedy.
4. They provide a way for a group of aggrieved people to negotiate for
   a policy or a behavioral change in an organization.

Rowe also suggests a written approach to sexual harassment, in
which the victimized person writes a concise, polite, and low-key letter
to the perpetrator, using the format described as follows:

> Writing a letter: One method that works quite consistently, even
> when many verbal requests have failed, is for the offended person
> to write a letter to the accused. I usually recommend a polite, low-
> key letter (which may necessitate many drafts).
>
> The letter I recommend has three parts. The first part should be
> a detailed statement of facts as the writer sees them: "This is what I
> think happened. . . ." I encourage a precise rendition of all facts
> and dates relevant to the alleged harassment. This section is some-
> times very long.
>
> In the second part of the letter, writers should describe their
> feelings and what damage they think has been done. This is where
> opinions belong. "Your action made me feel terrible"; "I am deeply
> embarrassed and worried that my parents will hear about this"; "You
> have caused me to ask for a transfer (change my career objective,
> drop out of the training course, take excessive time off, or what-
> ever)." The writer should mention any perceived or actual costs and

damages, along with feelings of dismay, distrust, revulsion, misery, and so on.

Finally, I recommend a short statement of what the accuser would like to have happen next. Since most persons only want the harassment to end, the letter might finish by saying so: "I ask that our relationship from now on be on a purely professional basis." Someone who knows that he or she contributed to the problem does well to say so: "Although we once were happy dating, it is important to me that we now reestablish a formal and professional relationship, and I ask you to do so."

If the letter writer believes some remedy or recompense is in order, this is the place to say so: "Please withdraw my last evaluation until we can work out a fair one"; "I will need a written answer as to the reference you will provide from now on"; and statements of that type. (Mary Rowe, 1981, p. 43)

The use of letters of a different format may be helpful in addressing other forms of gender discrimination. A letter can be prepared directly and politely, stating the individual's wish to be considered for a raise, a promotion, a job or education opportunity, and so on, and stating her qualifications and justification for the request, as well as any supportive institutional policies. The letter can be used as a prelude or a follow-up to a face-to-face meeting. It is an effective way to document the individual's serious intent to protect against any future denial by the organization that a request was made and justifications provided.

Writing an appropriate letter, even if the patient or client decides not to send it, can be a valuable exercise to review in treatment because it helps her organize her thinking, express her feelings in a responsible manner, and focus on realistic goals for resolution.

It cannot be emphasized enough that direct approaches, both verbal and written, should be expressed thoughtfully, politely, calmly, firmly, explicitly, and appropriately. Otherwise, the victimized individual is likely to be ineffective and also vulnerable, in some cases, to libel charges. The main disadvantage to the direct approach is that it may anger, rather than sensitize, the perpetrator or the organizational representative. It may also escalate the discriminatory behavior. It may expose the woman's vulnerability in an unsupportive setting, thus traumatizing her further. The offended party should be prepared to terminate the interaction quickly if it backfires, document the negative interaction, and move immediately to a backup plan.

Indirect Method of Response

(Adapted from Hughes & Sandler, 1986, p. 5)

Indirect approaches require the victimized person (1) to identify a supportive third party or parties with formal authority or informal influence within the work or academic environment; and (2) to request that the identified party or parties intervene in her behalf, either directly with the perpetrator or, in cases of other forms of discrimination, via the appropriate institutional representative. She may attempt to maintain control over the process by requesting the third party to intervene in a specific or limited way. She may request that the third party communicate specifically with the perpetrator, or that a responsible authority in the work hierarchy address the issue. One way is to send out a general communication, such as a memo, reiterating departmental policies and giving the offending experience as an example of a violation without naming the parties. The victimized woman may also distance herself and leave the third party to exercise his or her own discretion regarding intervention approaches. Informal channels can also be utilized to ascertain (1) if others in the workplace have complained or experienced similar problems; (2) to ascertain the offender's status or vulnerability within the organization; and (3) to determine the organization's official stance and past history of dealing with discrimination. Indirect approaches have several advantages: (1) They eliminate the risks of individual confrontation. (2) Confidentiality and privacy can often be maintained. (3) The victimized person can effect resolution with minimal time and effort. (4) The effort is focused on reconciliation, rather than on sanctions. This latter point is significant for both individuals and institutions. Victimized people are often more interested in resolving the problem than in ascribing blame and punishing individuals or institutions. In a significant number of cases, they only want the discriminatory activities to stop without disrupting their work or academic activities and disrupting their work relationships.

Disadvantages to the indirect approach include (1) the inability to maintain control of the process, (2) the risk that the third party will be unsympathetic, and (3) the possibility that institutional policies may mandate that the third party institute formal complaint procedures, despite the victimized individual's wishes. Anyone considering this approach should be counseled to explore in advance the institution's policies regarding issues of guaranteed confidentiality. She should be prepared to approach another potential advocate if her first choice proves unhelpful. If a person agrees to help the victimized woman, she should negotiate how and when the third party will intervene, when they both can meet to discuss the outcome, and what other approaches the third party would recommend.

Formal Complaints

(Adapted from Hughes & Sandler, 1986, pp. 5–6)
Formal complaint procedures have deadlines for filing and involve prescribed steps for the complainant and the institution. The victimized individual files a complaint, which is usually written. The institution then conducts a formal investigation that commits to protecting the rights of any individuals accused, as well as those of the complainant (this includes protection against retaliation). A hearing is held to discuss the results of the investigation and to determine what sanctions will be applied if the accused individual or individuals are found responsible. Either side may institute an appeals process if it finds the outcome unacceptable. Because law mandates policies regarding discrimination, almost all institutions have sexual harassment and discrimination policies. Some have separate policies for sexual harassment versus other forms of gender discrimination; some combine the two; and, occasionally, an institution will have no policy because it falls outside the legal mandates or because it is negligent.

Formal complaint channels are often preferred in more serious incidents of discrimination, when multiple victims are involved, or when both of these occur. They may empower the complainant by providing her with a means of taking definitive action, in which the nature of the process can be known in advance. The patient or client should be counseled to stay in control of the procedure as much as possible. She should ask prior to filing a complaint whether she is allowed to file and then opt for another approach later in the process. She should also ask what the time frame will be; who will conduct the investigation and under what circumstances; whether an attorney and a cross-examination will be involved, and whether she will be informed of the results; and what, in general, have been the outcomes and durations of other similar grievance proceedings.

Disadvantages to consider are (1) The procedure is public and exposes the complainant to informal ostracization and negative labeling such as "trouble maker," "whistle blower," "seductress," or "mental case"; (2) The complainant must compile substantial evidence, which is difficult if records and documentation have not been kept; (3) The process can be time-consuming, intimidating, exhausting, and traumatic; (4) Institutions can stall the procedure informally, if they do not wish to act; (5) Coworkers' and superiors' support can be minimal and their negative reactions intense and prolonged; and (6) Sanctions may be minimal, especially if the accused is valuable to the institution or if the top leadership is not committed to the policy.

Legal Action

(Adapted from Hughes & Sandler, 1986, pp. 7–8)
Harassment and discriminatory behavior may violate federal or state civil rights laws, or both, as well as criminal or civil laws, such as assault, intentional infliction of emotional distress, interference with a contract, defamation, breech of contract, negligent intent, and so on (see Chapter 2). Suits may be filed against an individual, an institution, or both. Legal action can be effective as a means of empowerment or in obtaining monetary restitution. If the victimized person is no longer affiliated with the institution or has suffered serious economic or other losses that cannot be resolved by other means, litigation may be the best option. Some attorneys will work on a contingency basis, if the client is financially strapped. Legal proceedings allow women to expose and directly face the perpetrator or institution in a setting outside the institution, a setting where case law sets precedents and treatment can be more objective. This can be psychologically healing for those victimized individuals with unshakable determination to do everything possible to seek vindication for themselves and to improve the workplace for others.

Legal action also has many disadvantages. Suits can be extremely costly, time-consuming, and highly adversarial. Some last 6 to 8 years and expose the plaintiff to severe financial or emotional stress, with no guarantee of outcome. Civil suits are vulnerable to countersuits. Lengthy legal proceedings can significantly delay or inhibit a woman's resolution process and her return to a normal life. Negative outcomes may result in sense of profound loss and complicated mourning reactions. If the goals of litigation are unrealistic, even a positive outcome can be disappointing. Legal proceedings, especially involving professional women, can result in permanent blackballing within their fields via informal networks. It is next to impossible to continue to work effectively within the institution being sued, so that retaining one's position is not often viable. Clients or patients should be advised against unrealistic/ impulsive litigation and attorneys who place litigating and winning a settlement above the client's best interests. Therapists should not offer legal advice but can help by referring patients to an appropriate attorney. The decision to litigate should be an informed choice that goes well beyond whether the attorney believes that a client has a good case, to include a careful assessment of the economic, emotional, interpersonal, and career costs of litigation (Lenhart & Schrier, 1996).

Special Approach Methods

Therapists should encourage patients or clients to generate options outside the standard procedures, in order to maximize the chance of a positive resolution based on realistic goals, available resources, and overall best interests (internal psychological health and external goals and needs). Women who are in transient work or school situations may find it best to do nothing or to delay addressing the situation until their training or work rotation is over. This resolution can also be appropriate if the woman faces too many additional life stresses or if the perpetrator or discriminatory policy has minimal impact on her long-term work or school goals. Some women choose to become active on an organizational or educational basis, joining women's groups and organizing workshops and work-gender issues committees within their institution rather than focusing on their specific case. These activities are inappropriate if they lead to an avoidance or displacement regarding the individual's situation. Conversely, they are empowering if a woman feels that her organizational role mandates a broader response. A woman can also efficiently resolve a situation by minimizing contact with the problematic person, initiating a transfer within the institution, changing her reporting status, transferring an offending client's account, or making a thoughtfully planned departure to a more gender-friendly environment. Some women create their own environment by starting their own businesses or professional practices or by partnering with other like-minded individuals. None of these maneuvers are an avoidance if (1) they are well thought out and either represent a realistic assessment of the unlikelihood of a positive result to a more direct approach, or (2) meet the woman's overall needs and goals, with the least expenditure of psychological energy. Mediation is an underutilized but growing form of action that is appealing to many women because it focuses on resolution of the issues, rather than on adversarial positions. It can be requested and is even mandated by some organizations. Others have effected or enhanced their resolution process via the utilization of art forms such as dance, music, sculpture, art, writing, and poetry. One woman who was unable to extricate herself from a discriminatory setting was able to take action after creating an abstract quilt symbolizing her experience. The quilt now hangs in the lobby of her institution's human resource department. Often, a special approach developed by a patient or client in a safe therapy environment will prove to be a better plan of action than the traditional approaches previously described. Sometimes a special approach is needed first to allow the victimized individual time to stabilize emotionally, gather her resources, and review her options, in order to move on to a more direct response aimed at the specific discriminatory behavior. The following case vignette illustrates how therapy can provide a safe structure for review of the various options that have been discussed and the development of an effective and appropriate plan for action.

CASE VIGNETTE 7-2

Effective Use of Special Approaches in Discrimination

Susan Smith, a master's degree chemist, had held a midlevel executive position in the marketing division of a chemical company for 6 years. During her tenure, she experienced the following events, which she considered discriminatory: (1) Four of her male coworkers were promoted above her. (2) Two of her most successful projects were handed over to male coworkers, who took credit for her work. (3) She twice received significantly lower salary increases than her two current male coworkers, who each had 3 years' less seniority. Armed with her consistently high performance reviews, Susan approached her boss, requesting his support in applying for a specific promotional opportunity. He initially agreed to put her name forward, but she later learned that he had recommended a junior male colleague. In response to her inquiry regarding this issue, he stated that he did not believe a woman could establish the proper credibility in this male-dominated field.

Angry and frustrated, Susan consulted an attorney but then became fearful that she would jeopardize her job. Stalemated between anxiety and depression, she consulted a therapist, who encouraged her to halt the legal process until she stabilized. Susan was treated with antianxiety and antidepressant medication. She underwent weekly therapy sessions over the next month, during which she stabilized her symptomatology and fully ventilated her anger regarding the perceived discrimination. She also clarified her goal to remain an employee of her current company, which was paying for courses toward her PhD degree and providing excellent health benefits that were unavailable at her husband's company. With her therapist, she was able to identify how her anger toward her boss had blinded her to other sources of support and opportunity within the company.

She halted her lawsuit and instead aimed her goals at making a lateral move to a division that would provide better opportunities. With her therapist, she identified several potential supporters with whom to speak. She chose to focus on career goals, rather than on dissatisfaction with her current boss; to present herself in a positive position; and to maintain corporate relationships. Her good work had been visible to others, and she was able to negotiate a transfer within 4 months. Her new boss agreed to regular performance reviews and access to promotional opportunities as a stipulation of her new position. By presenting her transfer as a career opportunity, she was able to maintain an amicable relationship with her old boss, who ultimately became more supportive.

STEP 6: ASSESSMENT OF POTENTIAL PERSONAL LOSSES AND RETALIATORY BEHAVIORS AND INSTITUTION OF PROTECTIVE MEASURES

Once a patient or client has developed an action strategy, it is important to collaborate with her in anticipating potential losses and retaliatory behaviors. This will allow her to prepare and institute protective strategies as she begins to act upon her overall plan. Examples of important protective actions include (1) identifying and neutralizing potential opponents; (2) documenting work quality; (3) maintaining an impeccable attendance record; (4) meeting deadlines; (5) identifying and utilizing supportive people and advocates within the workplace; (6) locating witnesses; (7) collaborating with other victimized people, when appropriate; and (8) identifying possibilities for work or school transfers or for changing supervisors or mentors. The patient or client should also try to identify who will be most supportive among her family and friends and engage them in helping her. Identifying unsupportive family and friends in advance is also important, so that they can be neutralized as much as possible. Professional and women's organizations can be useful sources of support and information at this point.

A therapist can provide additional help at this stage by assisting the woman in setting goals that are realistic to achieve and by guiding her in processing underlying feelings that are likely to result in further disappointments or losses. For example, revenge as a major goal is unlikely to bring satisfaction and is often the result of unresolved anger. The therapist can also educate the patient regarding the common reactions of institutions, families, friends, and workers, thus enhancing her ability to anticipate and cope with their problematic responses (see Chapter 4 for common responses). Often these disruptions in significant relationships are as emotionally damaging as the discriminatory experience was. The real possibility of individual and institutional retaliatory responses to complaints should be carefully reviewed. Similarly, the therapist can review other potential risks of the patient's action plan, providing advanced preparation for avoiding or coping with potential difficulties. Treaters can also provide information regarding the litigation and complaint processes and potential forms of stress or refer the woman to her attorney or union or EEOC representative for additional information.

By utilizing the theoretical material in Chapter 2 to help the patient objectively assess the external conditions of work or school environments that increase the risk of harassment or gender discrimination, the therapist can assist her in protecting herself within her own environment or selecting the best environment for herself if she is considering either transferring locations within her work or school institution or leaving it for a new work or school environment.

Special Proactive Measures during Litigation

The potential for loss, retraumatization, and retaliatory behaviors during the litigation process is especially high. Special assistance is needed in preparing protective measures. It is important for the therapist to implement the following steps:

1. Reviewing the potential impact of litigation on the therapy, and collaboratively forming a plan to protect the confidentiality of the

therapy and the therapeutic alliance to the degree possible.

2. Reviewing the need for the patient's attorney to retain a forensic expert, separate from the therapist, to testify regarding clinical issues (see the discussion of Step 1 in Chapter 6).

3. Providing assistance in assessing the emotional, interpersonal, and economic costs of litigation and in formulating realistic goals for the outcome.

4. Giving support in managing exacerbations in symptomatology and in handling stressful experiences, such as depositions and courtroom testimony. Behavioral visualization exercises can be helpful at this stage.

5. Assisting the patient in maintaining control over the litigation process.

6. Encouraging the patient to seek support from significant others.

7. Assisting the patient in focusing her energy on restoring her life, independent of the litigation process (Lenhart & Schrier, 1996).

Therapists can play an important role by asking patients to clarify what they would like to accomplish via litigation and then directly discussing those goals that are unlikely to be accomplished. (1) Unfocused anger, (2) wishes for revenge, (3) displacement of other abusive experiences into the case, (4) idealistic wishes for the resolution of truth and justice and denial of the adversarial nature of litigation, and (5) a desire to gain financial security via an unrealistically high settlement are common problems (Lenhart & Schrier, 1996).

The emotional costs versus the benefits in litigation can be summarized as follows. Potential costs include (1) disruption of ongoing psychotherapy, (2) exacerbation of somatic and psychosomatic symptoms, (3) psychological retraumatization, and (4) obsessive focusing of time and energy on the legal process and the outcome, at the expense of maintaining a healthy life balance. Potential benefits include (1) obtaining just compensation and emotional validation regarding the discriminatory event; (2) gaining a large settlement, having a productive impact on the institution's policies and procedures for dealing with victimized people, or both; (3) obtaining a sense of mutual support and validation by joining colleagues in a collective lawsuit; (4) obtaining clear closure on the event through a positive outcome to litigation or, alternatively, through a sense that one has done everything possible if the outcome is negative; and (5) obtaining a sense that the lawsuit will benefit one's daughters or other women (Lenhart & Scheier, 1996).

Gaining support or losing support in key relationships can account for the difference between a lawsuit that benefits the psychological well-being of the patient and one that is traumatic. Polarization of opinion and retaliation by coworkers and supervisors or mentors, combined with an organized institutionalized stance against complainants, often result in feelings of ostracization and invalidation. Coworkers who previously shared similar concerns or experiences may refuse to come forward to support the victimized individuals. Understandable fear of retaliation may account for their refusals. The victimized person nonetheless may feel personally betrayed, especially if it was coworkers' encouragement that led her to proceed with her complaint. Other coworkers may not hesitate to benefit from the victimized woman's dilemma, assuming her work assignments and activities. The leadership may specifically pressure and reward other female employees to replace the plaintiff or to speak out in support of the institution. Poor performance evaluations, demotions, withdrawal of mentor support, adverse job transfers, dismissals, verbal threats, and persona non grata status are common retaliations against plaintiffs. These behaviors can lead the victimized individual to self-doubt, diminished self-confidence, ambivalence regarding her career or job, disillusionment with the institution and the leadership, a reduced ability to trust, and impulsive withdrawal. Conversely, if the victimized individual is able to garner support from coworkers or key authorities, the experience can be empowering, even when the verdict is unfavorable.

Personal relationships can also be disrupted or strengthened by a lawsuit. Spouses or lovers may identify with the harasser or the discriminatory stance or may experience rage, guilt, and shame that they were unable to protect the woman. They may resent the disruption in family life, finances, or sexual relations that can accompany prolonged litigation. They may be harassed within the same company for "allowing" their partner to file a complaint. Children may be frightened by threats, disrupted by moves related to job changes, and distressed by the increased stress levels within the family. Mothers and other female relatives can experience the woman's complaint as embarrassing or entitled and indicative that she should have remained a homemaker. They may experience guilt and a sense of responsibility for not properly warning and protecting her. Daughters may identify with mothers' shame or become pessimistic about the workplace. If the plaintiff is a member of a cultural minority, she may be perceived as bringing shame to her community or as attacking one of her own. Conversely, if a plaintiff receives constant support from significant people in her personal life, she can feel enhanced and oblivious to the stress of the lawsuit (Lenhart & Schrier, 1996).

The emotional impact of possible job loss, career derailment, and financial stress should also be discussed with potential litigants. A woman may win in court but lose the larger battle, due to formal and informal blackballing, which can extend well beyond her immediate work institution. Prolonged litigation can disrupt work functioning and can also prove emotionally distressing and demoralizing, leaving plaintiffs doubtful of their competence and original career goals. They may become totally disillusioned with their institutions, their mentors, and the leaders of the organization or the professional fields who either perpetrate or collude with the discrimination and the retaliation. The final settlement may not outweigh the expenses. Shouldering the cost of litigation, combined with loss of income due to retaliatory dismissal, can lead to adverse credit ratings, bankruptcy, and intense family stress. Conversely, a large settlement can ultimately lift financial burdens, finance job retraining or relocation, force institutions to constructively change their policies, and provide internal validation for the victimized person. If support has been successfully solicited from credible individuals and leaders in the field of expertise, blackballing can be neutralized. Plaintiffs may emerge with financial security, expanded career networks, and a sense of empowerment and self-confidence that can lead to further workplace success.

This section has reviewed the importance of considering potential retaliatory reactions and self-protective measurements in advance of taking action. Special protective considerations regarding legal action have also been discussed. The following case vignette exemplifies many of these issues.

CASE VIGNETTE 7-3

Combined Formal Complaint and Special Approaches to Sexual Harassment

Katherine Good, a 32-year-old OR nurse, entered treatment for severe depression that occurred in the context of her filing a formal complaint of sexual harassment against Dr. Ken Wood, a staff surgeon. Shortly after Katherine arrived as a new employee, Ken began rubbing her breasts and buttocks in the operating room and called her his favorite Barbie Toy. One evening at work he pressed her against the wall of the scrub room and fondled her breasts and genitals beneath her scrub gown. No one witnessed the latter event, but multiple coworkers expressed disgust at Ken's OR antics and encouraged Katherine to file a complaint. Katherine was then shocked when no one would agree to come forward with corroborating information on her behalf. Ken had flatly denied fondling Katherine and accused her of being jealous of his girlfriend. He also warned Katherine's coworkers not to cause him trouble. He explained that he had the full support of the surgery chief, a statement that appeared valid when the chief publicly complimented Ken for his contributions to the department at an all-staff meeting. Frightened, Katherine spoke to an HR representative regarding withdrawing her complaint but was told that her accusation was serious enough to necessitate a full investigation for the protection of the hospital. Tension in the OR increased, and Katherine was devastated when a coworker accused her of being a troublemaking newcomer who was wrecking the environment and putting everyone's job at risk. Katherine consulted with the coworker who had recommended that she file the complaint. Her friend stated that she had no idea of the trouble that would arise. She apologized for recommending the plan and for lacking the courage to risk her job to support Katherine. She then avoided Katherine at work, leaving her even more isolated.

At her therapist's recommendation, Katherine consulted an attorney regarding her legal rights to be protected from retaliation. Her therapist also provided educational material regarding the commonness of retaliatory measures. This reassured Katherine, and she was able to engage in a discussion regarding a new plan of action based on her current situation. She considered the pros and cons of staying in her department or requesting a transfer. Armed with information from her attorney and documentation of the retaliatory backlash, she requested a transfer to another department. Now removed from the tension of the immediate situation, she was able to thoughtfully assess the tenuousness of her situation, given the lack of support. With her therapist she began to plan a strategy for locating a new job, utilizing contacts from her nursing school. In a thoughtful fashion, she determined which of her contacts would be safe to confide the entirety of her situation and which would need to be approached from a purely professional career prospective. Her therapist prepared her in advance for the possibility that some of her contacts would not be supportive. Energized by her capacity to act, she was undeterred by some minor setbacks in her job-seeking strategy and was ultimately able to locate an appropriate position via a nursing school classmate. Katherine was offered the job after a series of interviews but needed to wait 3 months until it became available. Again with her therapist's support, she was able to minimize her investment in her current job and in the ongoing complaint process and focus her energy on supportive relationships with her fiancé and girlfriends. Utilizing all of her accumulated time off to take a lengthy vacation also helped her to maintain her equilibrium until the transfer could take place.

When the findings of the complaint were inconclusive, based on a lack of evidence, Katherine did not suffer an emotional setback but instead focused on planning for her new job. Two weeks later she was able to tender her resignation and move into her new position. She agreed in retrospect that she had not considered the pros and cons of filing the complaint at the outset but was appreciative of her therapist's assistance in helping her process the aftermath and formulate a new plan in a thoughtful fashion.

SUMMARY

This chapter has reviewed the treatment steps that are useful in helping patients formulate and enact an effective plan of action, as well as the importance of adequately ventilating feelings, processing negative perceptions, and arriving at realistic outcome goals as a prerequisite for developing an action plan. The pros and cons of five potential action plans have been reviewed, with emphasis placed on determining which plan best addresses the victimized individual's internal well-being and external needs and goals. Strategies have been presented for proactively evaluating and protecting against potential retaliatory behaviors and other losses associated with taking action. Special emphasis has been placed on identifying protective measures before taking legal action. The next chapter will deal with the final stages of the treatment process.

CHAPTER 8

Conceptualizing Treatment of Sexual Harassment and Gender Discrimination

The Final Stages of Mourning, Recovery, and Reinvestment

Step 7: Identification and Appropriate Mourning of Inevitable Losses
Step 8: Reestablishment of Investment in Preexisting or Newly Formulated Goals and Activities
Step 9: Attention to Long-Term and Other Significant Therapy Issues
Specialized Techniques for Pretraumatized Patients
Summary

Recovery from a discriminatory experience is a complicated process that is often overlooked by both clinicians and patients. Therapeutic work does not end with the identification and implementation of an effective plan of action, yet this is often the point at which treatment is terminated by mutual consent. Full recovery involves more than just attending to the work or academic crisis that prompted the patient to seek help. Three final steps are needed to complete the process:

1. Identification and appropriate mourning of inevitable loss
2. Reestablishment of and investment in prior or newly formulated life goals and activities
3. Attention to other significant therapy and treatment issues

This chapter will address these essential but often-neglected aspects of treatment, including the special challenges presented by clients with prior histories of sexual trauma.

STEP 7: IDENTIFICATION AND APPROPRIATE MOURNING OF INEVITABLE LOSSES

A final piece of therapeutic work for victimized individuals involves coming to terms with what they have lost. Most women suffer significant losses in the course of dealing with their discriminatory experiences, even if they have handled their situations well, and their plans of action have had a positive outcome. These losses must be properly identified and grieved before a woman can reinvest energy in her life and move forward. Often, family members and even mental health professionals are unaware of the prevalence and significance of these inevitable losses. This can leave the woman alone to mourn her losses or to deny them. Clinicians can intervene effectively at this point by asking the client to talk about what has changed for her as a result of the harassment and discrimination. This allows the client to safely approach the process of grief and mourning. Common work-related losses are loss of job; loss of income; loss of significant work or academic relationships, such as mentors, teachers, coworkers, and superiors; career and job derailments; loss of time from personal and career development; loss of opportunities for specialized training; loss of motivation, self-confidence, and enthusiasm for job or school activities; and loss of confidence in career or job choice.

Common personal losses are marital stress, sexual dysfunction, divorce, withdrawal of family or community support, social ostracism, parenting conflicts, financial stress, and disruption of friendships and family relationships. Economic losses, due to loss of job, demotions, absenteeism, treatment, legal costs, relocations, and career changes, can be significant. Financial crises may necessitate significant lifestyle changes and further losses.

Internal losses in the form of shattered beliefs in self, in others, in work institutions, and in value systems related to fairness and equality are also common. Defensive or self-destructive attributions, such as (1) self-blame (internal attribution); (2) viewing the experience as due to factors that are impossible to change, such as character and bad luck, rather than as transient or addressable (stable vs. unstable attributions); and (3) expecting that the current experience will be repeated in any work or academic setting (global vs. specific attributions) are other internal changes that are crucial to address in treatment (Janoff-Bulman & Frieze, 1983). Schrier and Hamilton (1996) and Taylor (1983) suggest specific cognitive-behavioral approaches to these issues, involving (1) a search for the meaning of the experience; (2) attempts to regain mastery and control and prevent reoccurrence; (3) efforts to promote self-enhancement and greater confidence, mature perspective, sensitivity, self-control, and so on.

In general, the therapist's role at this point is crucial in helping the patient to acknowledge significant losses and to share them with her therapist and other supportive and important people. Supporting the patient clinically through the grief process, including (1) management of depression and other symptoms, (2) properly utilizing complementary self-help or focused supportive therapy, and (3) applying cognitive interventions appropriately will ultimately prepare her to reinvest in new life and work situations. Supportive group therapy may also be helpful at this stage, especially if the group has a workplace focus. Traditional grief and mourning groups often fail to identify and empathize properly with work-related losses. The following case examples illustrate the potential destructiveness of an unresolved mourning process and the complexity of losses, which may need to be resolved.

CASE VIGNETTE 8-1

Unresolved Grief Prevents Resolution of Discrimination

Dr. Karen Horn was a 42-year-old married tenured professor of environmental biology at a large urban university. Her career was proceeding smoothly. Her well-funded research was highly regarded and her goal of ultimately being appointed departmental chair appeared viable, especially because her current chair, Dr. Greg Wood, confided to her that he planned to retire in 5 years. Dr. Horn had a strong commitment to her current institution and had been encouraged by the chairs of several related departments to aim for the goal of becoming the first woman department head. Karen had encountered some discrimination early in her career. Several of her male competitors had remarked that her family obligations rendered her less capable as a principal investigator, and she had often been excluded from informal departmental communications. She believed, however, that she was beyond these experiences, especially given the joint work project she had developed with Greg over the last 5 years. The project, in her opinion, had cemented their relationship and her credibility as his protégé and a contender for the chair position upon his retirement.

Karen was disappointed when a change in schedule prevented her from presenting her portion of the project at a major conference but was reassured when Greg told her he would present the research on her behalf. She was distressed to learn from a colleague that Greg presented her data as his. When she spoke with him regarding this, he denied it. He also mentioned casually that he wished to consolidate their data and had instructed his research assistant to transfer her data to his computer. Furious, Karen consulted a colleague, who sympathized with her chair, stating, "After all, he initiated the project. It's his, not yours. He's been good to you. Most women never make full professor. Start something else." Karen began to work on a different project but found that she was unable to remain silent when her chair published an article based on her data, without discussing it with her or citing her as a coauthor. With the support of a women's scientific organization, she filed a lawsuit to gain control of her intellectual work. In the 4 years of litigation that ensued, Karen exhausted her personal resources on legal funds and was marginalized in her department by most of her colleagues, who clearly sided with their chair. The few colleagues who supported her in private strongly advised her to transfer institutions and launch a new research initiative. Her husband urged her to follow their advice, but Karen was unable to let go of the 5 years of work she had invested in the project with Greg. She eventually won her case; however, the award did not cover her full legal fees and did not restore her credibility in her department. When Greg retired, he recommended a male colleague junior to Karen as his replacement. The department complied with his wishes. The new chair was openly hostile to Karen. Unable to grieve her loss and start fresh, she began a series of out-of-town lectures for a scientific organization and spent another 4 years maintaining her faculty appointment. She also began giving talks on gender discrimination for women's organizations, telling her story repeatedly with unrelenting intensity. Her inability to disengage and grieve the loss of her research project and the department chair position resulted in her spending 8 years of her life in an unproductive struggle. Her husband, initially supportive of her "courage," became critical of her efforts and disillusioned with their marriage. Karen ultimately entered treatment for depression, the result of her unresolved grief.

CASE VIGNETTE 8-2

Severe Losses Complicate the Resolution of Discrimination

Susan Ward was a 40-year-old marketing executive for an elite sporting equipment company. Susan joined the company 12 years ago, after returning from the competition circuit as a professional skier. Although lacking a college degree, Susan had risen rapidly to a lucrative position in the company because her professional career as an athlete made her a knowledgeable and credible addition to the marketing and sales division. As the only female executive in the relatively small company, she had also been successful in developing and marketing a line of equipment especially designed for female athletes. She was rewarded for her advancement with a significant salary increase and an opportunity to transfer to an elite ski community, where she could "mingle" with the clients and manage the company's first female sports equipment boutique. Unmarried and accustomed to an active and exotic international social life among an elite group of athletes and clients, Susan was thrilled with her new assignment. Her new salary permitted her to purchase an expensive condominium, and the company provided her with a car and a generous expense account to permit her to socialize with clients. Within a year the boutique was a huge success, and Susan received a generous bonus. Given her high productivity with the company, Susan was not especially worried when she learned that the company had been sold and would now be run as a division of a much larger corporation. She was further reassured when the president of her company praised her work and stated that he had made her value clear to the new management.

Things continued unchanged during the 6-month transition period, except that Susan was no longer included in the top-level management meetings. When Bill Green, her new boss, a retired

Olympian, flew out to meet her, Susan was disappointed when he insisted that she show him "a good time on the town" and asked very little about her work. The visit was cordial, however, and her boss promised to review her marketing strategy for the upcoming year on his next visit, remarking that she had done incredibly well for a woman in sports. Bill returned in 1 month accompanied by Jim Wayne, a junior executive whom Susan was to "fully brief" on her operations. Bill criticized her marketing strategy, stating that it was not compatible with the company's overall plan. He asked her directly if she felt that a woman could manage the less client-centered, hard-ball bottom line strategy, emphasizing that this was the "philosophy in play." Susan assured him she could but had some misgivings when she learned that "deal making" with major outlets would take precedence over demonstrating the superiority of the product. Susan's productivity remained high, but she was concerned when she was not informed about an opportunity to apply for a newly created management position for which she had appropriate experience. In response to a polite request to be considered, she was given a cursory interview but was not surprised when Jim received the position, making him her official boss.

Shortly thereafter, Jim informed her that Bill was unhappy with her productivity and disappointed that she had appeared unprofessional and only interested in having a good time at their first meeting. She defended herself tactfully and appropriately but began to fear for her job. Susan consulted an attorney, who agreed that the sexist remarks and lack of information regarding the promotional opportunity were discriminatory but that a successful lawsuit was unlikely. Within 2 weeks, Susan received a letter from Bill informing her of their wish to terminate her contract at the end of the year. Susan's attempts to negotiate a suitable severance package failed, and she received a final offer via mail, along with notification that she would be terminated at the end of the month. With the assistance of her attorney, she negotiated a larger severance package but was still unable to afford the home she had bought. Given the specialization of her market and her lack of a college degree, she was unable to find a comparable position, despite her marketing experience. She entered treatment severely depressed at the loss of her career, her social network, and her home.

CASE VIGNETTE 8-3

Unrealistic Goals Exacerbate the Loss Associated with Sexual Harassment

Joan Warren was a 24-year-old graduate student whose thesis adviser, Dr. Sam Poll, had repeatedly pressured her for dates since the onset of their relationship. Her refusals were persistently firm and polite, but the situation escalated when her adviser saw her with her boyfriend at a social event and exploded petulantly, "Now I see why you have no time for me." After his outburst, he withdrew from the mentoring relationship, canceling meetings and failing to provide feedback regarding Joan's thesis.

Joan consulted Dr. Kimberly Olds, a trusted female professor, who suggested that she switch thesis advisers and offered to assist her in the transfer. An appropriate senior faculty member was identified, but when approached, he refused, based on his concern that his colleague Kevin might be offended. Joan then filed a formal sexual harassment complaint with her university. The investigation committee, in reviewing the complaint, found that harassment had occurred but did not feel it could intervene. It was also acknowledged that Kevin was considered a valuable member of the university community. With Kimberly's assistance, Joan obtained a research position in another department. She located three other students who had been harassed by Kevin, and together, they filed a lawsuit with the full support of their families and friends. After a prolonged suit, the women won a large settlement that resulted in a major revision of the university's sexual harassment policy.

Initially, Joan was thrilled with her achievement. Now financially comfortable, she left her teaching position and took a 1-month tour of Europe. She returned home to a new condo and a series of celebratory gatherings, hosted by family and friends who were sincerely pleased by her "success." In this context, Joan then developed a deep depression, which puzzled her and her many supporters. After several months of therapy, she was able to express her sadness at never achieving her PhD and her sense that in the 5-year interim, her field had changed dramatically, making it unlikely that she could return to her graduate work, a goal she had secretly maintained but never realistically assessed in the context of her plans for litigation.

STEP 8: REESTABLISHMENT OF INVESTMENT IN PREEXISTING OR NEWLY FORMULATED GOALS AND ACTIVITIES

If treatment has proceeded effectively, the client will develop a sense of stability and will spontaneously exhibit energy and motivation in her personal life and in her new work or school situation. She will reinvest herself in working to achieve old goals and commit herself to new goals she may have formulated.

If a client is unable to reinvest, this should be actively addressed as a problem and the unresolved issues identified. These issues might be residual depression, unresolved losses, negative cognitive attributions, the reactivation of old losses, and early issues around self-esteem, assertion, and entitlement. Previous sexual abuse or trauma might be revealed at this time and may be appropriately addressed in longer-term treatment. If there is no additional work to be done and the client is asymptomatic and actively engaged in her life, the treatment can be terminated at this point, with the understanding that treatment can be resumed if issues arise in the future.

CASE VIGNETTE 8-4

Unresolved Childhood Issues Complicate Recovery from Sexual Harassment

Kate Shaw was a 38-year-old attorney on track for a partnership in a large urban law firm. She was happily married to a successful businessman and only marginally distressed when Jim Oreolano, a fellow attorney, began making casual but unwanted comments regarding her personal appearance and attractiveness. Kate consistently ignored the comments and finally redirected the conversation back to work-related topics. Her colleague nonetheless persisted in his compliments. His behavior escalated and he began to frequent her office, rubbing her shoulders or brushing her cheek with his hand whenever he approached her. Annoyed, but determined to remain professional, Kate firmly requested that he stop, explaining clearly that she found his behavior offensive. When he continued to persist, she threatened to file a formal complaint. Jim made no comment but left her office and did not return for several days. Relieved, Kate shared her experience with her husband, who felt she had handled the situation well but encouraged her to proceed with a complaint if Jim resumed his harassment. All went well for several weeks. Kate was working late in her office one evening, when Jim appeared, smiled at her, and exposed himself, then left the office. The next morning Kate filed a formal complaint. The senior partners and, in particular, her mentor were supportive, and Jim was asked to leave the firm. Kate avoided him during his final month and toasted his departure at a special dinner with her husband.

Perceiving all to be well, Kate proceeded with her life. Over the next 6 months she lost two cases in a row, prompting her mentor to tease her that she had "lost her touch." Her work performance continued to decline, along with her enthusiasm for a political campaign she had been actively supporting in collaboration with her mentor. Concerned, he offered to meet with her to help her get back on track. Kate declined and instead began to distance herself from him. Six months later she was informed that her partnership status was on hold. Depressed, she entered treatment feeling pessimistic and disturbed. With the assistance of her therapist, she identified the source of he difficulties. Shortly after Jim's departure, she learned via office gossip that her mentor had assisted Jim in obtaining a position with another law firm. Wishing to avoid any unpleasantness with a man she respected who had been helpful to her, Kate had minimized the significance of the information. In her therapy she was able to clarify her angry feelings toward her mentor and his resemblance to her father, who had indulged her brother's bad behavior while maintaining strict standards for her. With the help of her therapist, she was able to assert herself and to discuss these issues appropriately with both her father and her mentor. She then was able to resume her previous high level of work performance with enthusiasm.

CASE VIGNETTE 8-5

*Unresolved Negative Cognitions Interfere with Recovery
from Sexual Harassment*

John Guy was a 23-year-old college graduate who had worked 1 year as a sales representative for the regional branch of a national mobile phone company. His immediate supervisor, Kathy Jones, age 30, had consistently teased him about his great body, often joking in front of coworkers that she would like to have "a piece of him." John also overheard Kathy gossiping with some of the female employees about what a "great lay" he would be. Soon, whenever he entered the home office, the female employees would giggle and snicker. Embarrassed and utterly uncertain about what to do, John consulted with Larry Reed, the regional manager, who laughed and told him to "enjoy himself." Kathy's harassment escalated when she patted John on the behind and commented, "Nice buns" in front of the office staff. John asked Larry if he could arrange a transfer. Larry promised John that he would be moved within 2 months. When the transfer did not materialize, John again complained to Larry in the presence of Frank Lipinsky, another sales rep. Larry again assured him of a transfer. When this finally occurred, John found himself working under Sally Jones, Kathy's sister, who told him she'd heard all about him and began a similar harassment pattern. After attending a compelling sexual harassment education program sponsored by the national office, John filed a formal sexual harassment complaint with Larry. Frank was present as a witness. John soon found his work being criticized by both Sally and Larry. When his contract was terminated 2 months later, John found a new job and filed a lawsuit. While in the discovery phase of his lawsuit, he entered treatment for symptoms of anxiety, depression, and sexual inhibition. He had given up his apartment, had moved back in with his parents, and was avoiding his friends and constricting his social life. With therapy and medication, he gradually reversed this negative trend and managed a highly stressful series of depositions with aplomb. After reaching a satisfactory pretrial settlement to his lawsuit, he abruptly left treatment. During the next year, he was laid off from his new job, successfully obtained another position but stayed at home and remained socially inactive, avoiding appropriate and sincere overtures from several attractive women.

John returned to treatment in an attempt to understand why he was unable to resume his previously active and satisfactory dating and sexual relationships with women. It was only at this point that he was able to remember the details of Larry's response to his filing a formal sexual harassment complaint. Larry actively discouraged him from going forward and alluded to Frank that John must be gay because he didn't "enjoy" Kathy's attention.

Frank and the other men at the office began to avoid John, a situation he found to be humiliating and painful. He was too embarrassed to discuss the situation with anyone, including his female attorney and his female therapist. The ability to restructure his perception of this event as a reflection of Larry's manipulative and unethical behavior, rather than as some unidentified "wimpiness" in him, allowed John to successfully pursue a satisfactory sexual relationship with a new girlfriend.

STEP 9: ATTENTION TO LONG-TERM AND OTHER SIGNIFICANT THERAPY ISSUES

Treatment for sex discrimination may intersect with other treatment issues in several ways: (1) The patient may enter treatment for sex discrimination and in the context of that focus uncover significant long-term issues that need to be addressed when the immediate work or academic situation has been resolved; (2) The patient may encounter discrimination in the context of ongoing therapy focused on other issues; (3) Several crises may be occurring at once. In any case, it is unlikely that the patient will be able to focus on other issues while she is trying to cope with the crisis of her immediate work or academic situation and protect herself from retaliation. This should be acknowledged and validated directly by the clinician. The clinician can also reassure the patient that other significant treatment issues can receive attention after the immediate discriminatory situation has been resolved. In the event that several crises are occurring at once—for example, physical harassment in the marriage and sexual abuse at work—the situations need to be addressed in the order of priority, based on the woman's safety and overall well-being. Mobilizing the psychological energy to file a complaint of sexual harassment may be impossible if the patient is in an abusive marriage, has a critically ill child, and so on. In this case, helping the patient minimize the stress of the work situation by avoiding the harasser, temporarily tolerating or minimizing the situation, may be necessary for her to focus her energy on the more serious crisis. Conversely, treatment initially focused on dealing with the stress of caring for an aging relative or a boyfriend's difficulty with intimacy may need to be postponed in order to allow the patient to focus on her more immediate discriminatory situation. If the woman has a preexisting history of another type of gender-related abuse or psychological trauma, her work or academic situation may precipitate a psychological crisis and might require a specialized approach. This will be true for a significant number of victimized individuals.

Specialized Techniques for Pretraumatized Patients

If the patient was previously victimized by rape, incest, childhood sexual abuse, sexual exploitation, or another trauma, she may have difficulty coping with even the mildest forms of sexual harassment and gender discrimination. Significant symptomatology is common in these instances, especially anxiety, depression, substance abuse, and traumatic reactions. Difficulties with self-esteem, self-assertion, self-confidence, and confusion regarding the boundaries of power, authority, and sexuality may also be present and will severely inhibit her capacity to resolve her current situation. She may have a prior history of difficulties with work or personal boundaries, including repeated injudicious workplace affairs. Previous problems with self-esteem, self-assertion, and healthy entitlement may have already led to her placement in a low-level work position. All of these qualities may predispose her to being targeted for sexual harassment, gender discrimination, or both. They will also inhibit her capacity to cope and reduce her credibility, placing her at risk for being blamed for any situations that occur. Often, the discriminating experience, especially if sexual in nature, will act as a precipitate for the depression caused by previously forgotten traumatic experiences. In this instance she may develop a diagnosable post-traumatic stress disorder with nightmares, flashbacks, panic, anxiety and depression, dissociative episodes, affective numbing, and strong urges to flee or withdraw. In addition to being compromised in coping with her current situation, she must also deal with a new disorder, which is often misunderstood and may lead to her being labeled hysterical, crazy, or oversensitive. In these instances, an immediate intervention is needed, and the treatment plan should be reformulated to focus on the following.

Short-Term Stabilization

Short-term stabilization of symptomatology. This can be accomplished with psychotropic medication, relaxation techniques, and cognitive education aimed at helping the patient appreciate what is happening to her. Meditation and behavioral techniques can be utilized to help the patient control the flooding of memories. She may be unable to deal with her current situation until she has stabilized and may require either time off from work or special assignments involving minimal contact with the discriminatory situation, perpetrator, or both.

Coping with the Current Sexual Harassment or Discriminatory Situation

When the patient has stabilized, she may be assisted in dealing with her current situation by the therapist's utilizing the format previously described. Helping her to pace her plan of action so that she does not become overwhelmed and assisting her to adequately protect herself from retaliation are crucial. Transferring or otherwise removing herself from the presence of the perpetrator may be advisable.

Exploration of Her Previous Trauma History and Its Impact on Her Current Life

Longer-term treatment, including elucidation of past memories of abuse and of its insidious effects, should only be undertaken when the immediate situation has been resolved, when the patient has established a solid relationship with her therapist, and when she has both the time and its resources to complete treatment.

CASE VIGNETTE 8-6

Prior Traumatic Loss Complicates Recovery from Discrimination

Janet Ell was a 36-year-old sales representative who had worked with great satisfaction and intensity for 10 years for a large pharmaceutical firm. Her career had been a series of successes until a promotion placed her under the management of a new regional vice president. Jim Been, her new boss, was having an affair with his secretary and openly stated that he liked "real women who didn't try to be men." Although he was initially cordial to Janet, he avoided individual conferences with her. He provided her with little information about her new sales territory and made no effort to discuss strategies and goals with her, he overscrutinized her work, and he micromanaged her assignments to her subordinates. At conferences, he was publicly critical of her work and suggested that she was not performing equal to her seven male counterparts in the region.

Janet sought advice from her previous boss, who encouraged her to persevere, assuring her that her positive and energetic approach and excellent efforts and performance would win Jim over. Janet persevered, but her situation continued to deteriorate and she began to doubt herself and her competence. Over the next year each of Janet's seven male colleagues received salary bonuses and expense-paid trips to professional conferences. Janet, whose sales productivity was comparable, was promised a bonus, which she never received, and was allotted no conference time. Jim often complimented his secretary's appearance in front of Janet, telling her, "You know how to look like a real woman." At the end of her second year in the region, Jim abruptly informed Janet that she would be terminated at the end of the year. Although Janet had received no formal performance evaluations, Jim told her that her work had been substandard and offered her a standard severance package, stating it was non-negotiable and generous, given her low productivity.

Although angered, Janet felt immobilized and unable to defend herself. She entered treatment for help, complaining of depression and an uncharacteristic lack of assertiveness, energy, and self-confidence. In the context of her initial evaluation, her therapist learned that Janet had recently terminated a relationship with a man she felt she loved. In addition, Janet acknowledged that she had become pregnant by this man a year earlier and had terminated the pregnancy secretly. Since then, she had suffered from intense guilt and a sense of worthlessness that had left her feeling she deserved the poor treatment she was receiving at work. She also revealed that although she had enjoyed and focused her full energy on her job, she had never planned a full-time career. The beloved fiancé she had planned to marry after college was killed in a car accident prior to the wedding. Janet's mother had been unable to help her with this trauma because of the mother's own preoccupation with the loss of her husband (Janet's father) 1 year previously.

It was at this point that Janet adopted her father's style of workaholic behavior and daily drinking. She avoided any real intimacy with men and was frightened by the possibility of having a child and marrying her boyfriend. Her therapist recommended medication, cessation of alcohol, consultation with an attorney, and continued therapy, initially to focus on her immediate work situation but ultimately focusing on the significant events in her past history. With her attorney's assistance, Janet was able to obtain an excellent termination package that included good recommendations, a 1-year severance payout, and the assistance of an outsourcing agency. In addition, she learned that Jim had received sharp criticism for his management of her. Her old boss was recruited to a new company and was willing to assist her with a placement. Despite the positive outcome, Janet was unable to move forward. With continued treatment, she was able to recognize and deal with the unresolved grief of the earlier loss of her fiancé and achieve a less critical perception of her subsequent relationships and her response to her recent pregnancy. After 4 months, she was able to pursue and obtain a job in another pharmaceutical company and allow herself more leisure time to create a satisfactory personal life and more intimate relationships with men.

SUMMARY

Sexual harassment and other forms of workplace and academic sex discrimination present significant challenges to an individual's internal and external stability. Despite their initial presentation as primarily legal or management issues, they belong on a clinical continuum with other gender-based abuses, such as a rape, domestic violence, childhood sexual abuse, and sexual exploitation in professional relationships. Untreated, these events can cause psychiatric illness and long-lasting negative changes in the internal perception of self, others, and the world. They severely hinder a woman's enjoyment of her abilities and deprive the workplace of her valuable and much-needed talent. Appropriate clinical interventions can provide the patient with an opportunity to assess the seriousness of the immediate work crisis, ventilate and process feelings, monitor and contain symptomatology, prevent maladaptive coping, develop an effective plan of action, protect against further negative consequences, grieve losses and recover, and reinvest in life. The treatment model that has just been described provides a sequential but flexible framework for the accomplishment of these tasks.

References

Adams, J. (1997). Sexual harassment and Black women: An historical perspective. In W. O'Donohue (Ed.), *Sexual harassment: Theory, research and treatment* (pp. 213–225). Boston: Allyn and Bacon.

American Psychiatric Association. (1994). *Diagnostic & statistical manual of mental disorders* (4th ed.). Washington DC: Author.

Avina, C., & O'Donohue, W. (2002). Sexual harassment and PTSD: Is sexual harassment diagnosable trauma? *Journal of Traumatic Stress, 15*(1) 69–75.

Barak, A. (1997). Cross cultural perspectives on sexual harassment. In W. O'Donohue (Ed.), *Sexual harassment: Theory, research and treatment* (pp. 263–293). Boston: Allyn and Bacon.

Barnett, O. W., & LaViolette, A. D. (1993). *It could happen to anyone. Why battered women stay.* Newbury Park, CA: Sage.

Bell, E. L. (1992). Myths, stereotypes, and realities of black women: A personal reflection. *Journal of Applied Behavioral Science, 28*(3), 363–376.

Benedek, E. P. (1996). Forensic aspects of sexual harassment: Serving as an expert witness, providing courtroom testimony, and preparing legal reports. In D. K. Shrier (Ed.), *Sexual harassment in the workplace and academia* (pp. 113–132). Washington, DC: American Psychiatric Press.

Benson, K. A. (1984). Comments on Crocker's: "An analysis of university definitions of sexual harassment." *Signs, 9,* 516–519.

Bernard, J. (1988). The inferiority curriculum. *Psychology of Women Quarterly, 12*(3), 261–268.

Berstein, A. E., & Lenhart, S. A. (1993). *The psychodynamic treatment of women.* Washington, DC: American Psychiatric Press.

Binder, R. L. (1992). Sexual harassment: Issues for forensic psychiatrists. *Bulletin of the American Academy of Psychiatry and the Law, 20*(4), 409–418.

Blumberg, R. H. (1979). Paradigm for predicting the positions of women: Policy implications and problems. In J. Lipman-Blumen & J. Bernard (Eds.), *Sex roles and social policy* (pp. 113–142). London: Sage.

Bond, M. (1991). Division 27 sexual harassment survey: Definitions, impact, and environmental context. In M. A. Paludi & R. B. Barickman (Eds.), *Academic and workplace sexual harassment: A resource manual* (pp. 189–198). Albany: State University of New York Press.

Bondurant, B., & White, J. (1996). Men who sexually harass: An embedded perspective. In D. Schrier (Ed.), *Sexual harassment in the workplace and academia* (pp. 59–79). Washington, DC: American Psychiatric Press.

Bowes-Sperry, L., & Tata, J. (1999). A multiperspective framework of sexual harassment: Reviewing two decades of research. In G. Powell (Ed.), *Gender and work* (pp. 263–281). Thousand Oaks: Sage.

Bratton, E. (1987). The eye of the beholder: An interdisciplinary examination of law and social research on sexual harassment. *New Mexico Law Review, 17*(1), 91–114.

Broderick v. Ruder. (D.D.C. 1988). 685 F. Supp. 1269.

Bularzik, M. (1978). Street harassment at the workplace: Historical notes. Reprinted in pamphlet from *Radical American*. Somerville, MA: New England Free Press.

Burgess, A. W., & Holmstrom, L. L. (1974). Rape trauma syndrome. *American Journal of Psychiatry, 131,* 981–986.

Burlington Industries, Inc. v. Ellerth and Faragher v. Boca Raton. (1998).

Burrell, G., & Hearn, J. (1989). The sexuality of organization. In G. Burell, J. Hearn, D. L. Sheppard, & P. Tancred-Sheriff (Eds.), *The sexuality of organization* (pp. 1–29). Newbury Park, CA: Sage.

Carmen, E. H., & Rieker, P. P. (1989). A psychological model of the victim-to-patient process. *Psychiatric Clinics of North America, 31,* 431–443.

Carmen, E. H., Russo, N. F., & Miller, J. B. (1981). Inequality and women's mental health: An overview. *American Journal of Psychiatry, 138,* 1319–1330.

Charney, D. A., & Russell, R. C. (1994). An overview of sexual harassment. *American Journal of Psychiatry, 151,* 10–17.

Clark, L., & Lewis, D. (1977). *The price of coercive sexuality.* Toronto: Women's Press.

Cleveland, J., & McNamara, K. (1996). In M. Stockdale (Ed.), *Sexual harassment in the workplace* (pp. 217–240). Thousand Oaks, CA: Sage.

Cooper, C. L., & Lewis, S. (1999). Gender and the changing nature of work. In G. Powell (Ed.), *Handbook of gender and work* (pp. 37–47). Thousand Oaks, CA: Sage.

Courtois, C. A. (1988). *Healing the incest wound: Adult survivors in therapy.* New York: W. W. Norton.

Crull, P. (1981). *Effects of sexual harassment on the job.* New York: Working Women's Institute.

Crull, P. (1982). Stress effects of sexual harassment on the job: Implications for counseling. *American Journal of Orthopsychiatry, 52,* 539–544.

Crull, P. (1991). Women's explanations of their harasser's motivations. In M. A. Paludi & R. B. Barickman (Eds.), *Academic and workplace sexual harassment: A resource manual* (pp. 199–205). Albany: State University of New York Press.

Culbertson, A. L., Rosenfeld, P., & Booth-Kewley, S. (1992). *Assessment of sexual harassment in the Navy: Results of the 1989 Navy-wide survey* (TR-92-11). San Diego, CA: Navy Personnel Research and Development Center.

Dansky, B. S., & Kilpatrick, P. G. (1997). The effects of sexual harassment. In W. O'Donohue (Ed.), *Sexual harassment theory, research and treatment* (pp. 152–172). Boston: Allyn and Bacon.

DiTomaso, N. (1989). Sexuality in the workplace: Discrimination and harassment. In J. Hearn, D. L. Sheppard, & P. Tancred-Sheriff (Eds.), *The sexuality of organization* (pp. 71–90). London: Sage.

Dziech, B. W., & Weiner, L. (1984). *The lecherous professor: Sexual harassment on campus.* Boston, MA: Beacon Press.

Ellison v. Brady. (9th Cir. 1991). 924 F.2d 872.

Equal Employment Opportunity Commission (1980, revised 1991). *Guidelines on discrimination because of sex* (sexual harassment, 29 C.F.R. 1604.11.)

Esacove, A. W. (1998). A diminishing of self: Women's experiences of unwanted sexual attention. *Healthcare for Women International, 19,* 181–192.

Evans, K. M., & Herr, E. L. (1991). The influence of racism and sexism in the career development of African American women. *Journal of Multicultural Counseling and Development, 19*(4), 130–135.

Fain, T. C., & Anderson, D. L. (1987). Sexual harassment: Organizational context and diffuse status. *Sex Roles, 17,* 291–311.

Figley, C. R. (Ed.) (1985). *Trauma and its wake: The study and treatment of post traumatic stress disorder.* New York: Brunner Mazel.

Figley, C. R. (Ed.). (1986). *Trauma and its wake, Volume 2: Traumatic stress theory, research, and intervention.* New York: Brunner Mazel.

Fitzgerald, L. F. (1990). Sexual harassment: The definition and measurement of a construct. In M. Paludi (Ed.), *Ivory power: Sexual harassment on campus* (pp. 21–44). Albany: State University of New York Press.

Fitzgerald, L. F. (1993). Sexual harassment: Violence against women in the workplace. *American Psychology, 48,* 1070–1076.

Fitzgerald, L. F., Gelfand, M. J., & Drasgow, F. (1994). Sexual harassment: Theoretical and psychometric advances. Paper presented at the 9th Annual Conference of the Society of Industrial and Organizational Psychology, Nashville, TN.

Fitzgerald, L. F., & Schullman, S. L. (1993). Sexual harassment: A research analysis and agenda for the 1990s. Special issue: Sexual harassment in the workplace. *Journal of Vocational Behavior, 42*(1), 5–27.

Fitzgerald, L. F., Schullman, S. L., Bailey, N., Richards, M., Swecker, J., Gold, Y., Omerad, I., & Weitzman, I. (1988). The incidence and dimensions of sexual harassment in academia and the workplace. *Journal of Vocational Behavior, 32*(2), 152–175.

Fitzgerald, L. F., Swan, S., & Mugley, V. J. (1997). But was it really sexual harassment? Legal behavioral & psychological definitions of the workplace victimization of women. In W. O'Donohue (Ed.) *Sexual harassment* (pp. 5–28). Needham Heights, MA: Viacom.

Foner, P. (1947). *History of the labor movement in the United States: Vol. I.* New York: International.

Forell, C. (1993). Sexual and racial harassment: Whose perspective should control? *Trial, 29*(3), 70–74.

Foreman, B. O. (1980). Psychotherapy with rape victims. *Psychotherapy: Theory, Research & Practice, 17,* 304–311.

Franklin v. Gwinnett County School District. (U.S. Feb. 26, 1992). 112 S. CT, 60 U.S.L.W. 4167.

Furr, S. (2002). Men and women in cross-gender careers. In L. Daimant & J. A. Lee (Eds.), *The psychology of sex, gender, and jobs: Issues and solutions.* Westport, CT: Praeger.

Gabbard, G. O. (Ed.). (1989). Sexual exploitation in professional relationships. Washington DC: American Psychiatric Press.

Genovich-Richards, J. (1992). A poignant absence: Sexual harassment in the health care literature. *Medical Care Review, 49*(2), 133–159.

Gilligan, C. (1982). *In a different voice: Psychological theory and women's development.* Cambridge, MA: Harvard University Press.

Goodman, L. A., Koss, M. P., Fitzgerald, L. F., Russo, N. F., & Keita, G. P. (1993). Male violence against women: Current research and future directions. *American Psychologist, 48*(10), 1054–1058.

Gosselin H. L. (1984). Sexual harassment on the job: Psychological, social and economic repercussions. *Canada's Mental Health, 32*(3), 21–24.

Gruber, J. E., & Bjorn, L. (1982). Blue-collar blues: The sexual harassment of women autoworkers. *Work and Occupations, 9,* 271–298.

Gruber, J. E., & Bjorn, L. (1986). Women's responses to sexual harassment: An analysis of sociocultural, organizational, and personal resource models. *Social Science Quarterly, 67,* 814–826.

Gutek, B. A. (1985). *Sex and the workplace.* San Francisco, CA: Jossey-Bass (Jossey-Bass Management Series).

Gutek, B. A. (1993). Sexual harassment: Rights and responsibilities. *Employee Responsibilities and Rights Journal, 6*(4), 325–340.

Gutek, B. A., & Cohen, A. G. (1987). Sex ratios, sex-role spillover, and sex at work: A comparison of men's and women's experiences. *Human Relations, 40,* 97–115.

Gutek, B. A., & Dunwoody, V. (1987). Understanding sex in the workplace. In A. H. Stromberg, L. Larwood, & B. A. Gutek (Eds.), *Women and work: An annual review* (Vol. 2, pp. 249–269). Newbury Park, CA: Sage.

Gutek, B. A., & Koss, M. P. (1993a). Effects of sexual harassment on women and organizations. *Occupational Medicine, 8*(4), 807–819.

Gutek, B. A., & Koss, M. P. (1993b). Changed women and changed organizations: Consequences and coping with sexual harassment. *Journal of Vocational Behavior, 42,* 28–48.

Gutek, B. A., & Koss, M. P. (1996). How women deal with sexual harassment and how organizations respond to reporting. In D. Schrier (Ed.), *Sexual harassment in the workplace and academia* (pp. 39–59). Washington, DC: American Psychiatric Press.

Gutek, B. A., & Morash, B. (1982). Sex-ratios, sex role spillover, and sexual harassment of women at work. *Journal of Social Issues, 38,* 55–74.

Hamilton, J. A. (1989). Emotional consequences of victimization and discrimination in "special populations" of women. *Psychiatric Clinics of North America, 12,* 35–51.

Hamilton, J. A., Alagna, S. W., King, L. S., & Lloyd, C. (1987). The emotional consequences of gender-based abuse in the workplace: New counseling programs for sex discrimination. In M. Braude (Ed.), *Women, power and therapy* (pp. 155–182). New York: Haworth.

Hamilton, J. A., & Jensvold, M. (1992). Personality, psychopathology and depressions in women. In L. S. Brown & M. Ballou (Eds.), *Theories of personality and psychopathology: Feminist reappraisals* (pp. 116–143). New York: Guilford Press.

Harris v. Forklift Systems, Inc. (1993). 1145 S Ct. 367, 63 Fair Empl. Prac. Cas.

Hartman, H. (1981). Capitalism, patriarchy and job segregation by sex. In L. Sargent (Ed.), *Women and Revolution* (pp. 1–41). Boston: South End Press.

Harvey, M., & Koss, M. P. (1987). *The rape victim: Clinical & community approaches to treatment.* Lexington, MA Green Press

Haslett, B., Geis, F. H., & Carter, M. R. (1992). *The organizational woman: Power and paradox.* Norwood, NJ: Ablex.

Herman, J. L. (1993). *Trauma and recovery: The aftermath of violence—From domestic abuse to political terror.* New York: Basic Books.

Herman, J. L. (with L. Hirschman) (1981). *Father daughter incest.* Cambridge, MA: Harvard University Press.

Herman, J. L., & Schatzow, E. (1993). Recovery and verification of memories of childhood sexual trauma. *Psychoanalytic Psychology, 4,* 1–14.

Hobfoil, L. E. (1991). Traumatic stress: A theory based on rapid resource loss. *Anxiety Research, 4,* 187–197.

Hogbacka, R., Kandolin, I., Haavio-Mannila, E., & Kauppin-Toropainen, K. (1987). *Sexual harassment in the workplace: Result of a survey of Finns.* Ministry of Social Affairs and Health, Equality Publications, Series E: Abstracts 1. Helsinki, Finland: Valtion Painatuskeskus.

Hollander, A., Sherer, A., Newman, R., Prystowsky, R., Shreier, D., Sofair, J., & Naficy, M. J. (1993). *Guide to clinical assessment of patients with sexual harassment and/or discrimination complaints.* New Jersey Psychiatric Association Committee on Women. Bridgewater, NJ: New Jersey Psychiatric Association.

Holmes, T. H. (1978). Life, situations, emotions and disease. *Psychosomatics, 19,* 747–754.

Horowitz, M. J. (1986). *Stress response syndromes.* New York: Jason Aronson.

Hughes, J. O. & Sandler, B. R. (1986). *In case of sexual harassment: A guide for women students.* Washington, DC: Project on the Status and Education of Women, Association of American Colleges.

Jacobs, J. A., (1999). The sex segregation of occupations: Prospects for the 21st century. In G. Powell (Ed.), *Handbook of gender and work* (pp. 125–144). Thousand Oaks, CA: Sage Publications.

Janoff-Bulman, R., & Frieze, I. H. (1983). A theoretical perspective for understanding reactions to victimization. *Journal of Social Issues, 39,* 1–17.

Jensen v. Evaleth Taconite. (D. Minn. 1993). 824 F. Supp. 847, 876.

Jensen, I. W., & Gutek, B. A. (1982). *Journal of Social Issues, 38,* 121–136.

Jensvold, M. F. (1996). The potential for misuse and abuse of psychiatry in workplace sexual harassment. In D. K. Shrier (Ed.), *Sexual harassment in the workplace and academia: Psychiatric issues.* Washington, DC: American Psychiatric Press.

Kanter, R. M. (1977). *Men and women of the corporation.* New York: Basic Books.

Kilpatrick, D. G., Veronen, L. J., & Resick, P. A. (1981). Effects of a rape experience. *Journal of Social Issues, 37*(4), 105–122.

Klein, F. (1988, July/August). *The 1988 working women sexual harassment report executive report.* Cambridge, MA. Klein Associates.

Klein, F. (1989). Sexual harassment in Massachusetts trial courts and the legal profession: Implications from the gender bias study. *Boston Bar Journal,* 17–19.

Klein, F. (1993). Unpublished report. Cambridge, MA: Klein Associates.

Kluft, R. P. (1989). Treatment of victims of sexual abuse. *Psychiatric Clinics of North America, 12,* 385–408.

Knapp, D. E., Faley, R. H., Ekeberg, W. C., & Dubois, C. H. (1997). Determinants of target responses to sexual harassment: A conceptual framework. *Academy of Management Review, 29*(3), 687–729.

Koss, M. P. (1990). Changed lives: The psychological impact of sexual harassment. In M. A. Paludi (Ed.), *Ivory power: Sexual harassment on campus* (pp. 73–92). Albany: State University of New York Press.

Koss, M. P., Gidycz, C. A., & Wisniewski, N. (1987). The scope of rape: Incidence and prevalence of sexual aggression and victimization in a national sample of higher education students. *Journal of Consulting and Clinical Psychology, 55,* 162–170.

Koss, M. P., Goodman, L. A., Browne, A., Fitzgerald, L. F., Keita, G., & Russo, N. F. (1994). *No safe haven: Male violence against women at home, at work, and in the community.* Washington, DC: American Psychological Association.

Krystal, H. (1998). *Integration and self healing: Affect, trauma, alexithymia.* Hillsdale, NJ: Analytic Press.

Lach D. H., & Gwartney-Gibbs, P. A. (1993). Sociological perspectives on sexual harassment and workplace dispute recognition. *Journal of Vocational Behavior, 42*(1), 102–115.

Lapointe, J. B. (1990). Industrial organizational psychology: A view from the field. In K. R. Murphy & F. E. Saal (Eds.), *Psychology in organizations: Integrating science and practice* (pp. 7–22). Hillsdale, NJ: Erlbaum.

Lazarus, R. S., & Folkman, S. (1984). *Stress, appraisal, & coping.* New York: Springer.

Lee, J. A. (2002). Role conflicts: Family life, gender, and work. In L. Daimant & J. A. Lee (Eds.), *The psychology of sex, gender, and jobs: Issues and solutions.* Westport, CT: Praeger.

Lee, J. A. (1997). Balancing elder care responsibilities and work: Two empirical studies. *Journal of Occupational Health Psychology, 2,* 220–228.

Lenhart, S. A. (1996). *The psychological impact of sexual harassment and gender discrimination in the workplace.* New York: Guilford Press.

Lenhart, S. A., & Evans, C. H. (1991). Sexual harassment and gender discrimination: A primer for women physicians. *Journal of American Medical Women's Association, 48,* 155–159.

Lenhart, S. A., & Schrier, D. K. (1996). Potential costs and benefits of sexual harassment litigation. *Psychiatric Annals, 26*(3), 132–138.

Lerner, G. (1972). *Black women in White America: A documentary history.* New York: Vintage Books.

Loy, P. H., & Stewart, L. P. (1984). The extent and effects of sexual harassment of working women. *Sociological Focus, 17,* 31–43.

MacKinnon, C. A. (1979). *Sexual harassment of working women: A case of sex discrimination.* New Haven, CT: Yale University Press.

Marmar, C .R. (1991). Brief dynamic psychotherapy of posttraumatic stress disorder. *Psychiatric Annals, 21,* 405–419.

Marmar, C. R., Foy, D., Kagan, B., & Pynoos, R. (1993). An integrated approach for treating posttraumatic stress. In J. M. Oldham, M. B. Riba, & A. Tasman (Eds.), *American Psychiatric Press Review of Psychiatry, Vol. 12* (pp. 238–272). Washington, DC: American Psychiatric Press.

McFarlane, A. C. (1994). Individual psychotherapy for post-traumatic stress disorder. *Psychiatric Clinics of North America, 17,* 393–408.

McKinney, K., & Maroules, N. (1991). Sexual harassment. In E. Grauerholz & M. A. Koralewski (Eds.), *Sexual coercion: A source book on its nature, causes, and prevention* (pp. 29–45). Lexington, MA: Lexington.

Meritor Savings Bank v. Vinson. (1986). 477 U.S. 57.

Miller, J. B. (1976). *Toward a new psychology of women.* Boston: Beacon Press.

Miller, J. B. (1983). *The construction of women's sense of self* (Work in Progress No. 4, pp. 1–7). Wellesley, MA: The Stone Center for Developmental Services and Studies, Wellesley College.

Miller, J. B. (1984). *The construction of women's sense of self* (Work in Progress No. 12, pp. 1–9). Wellesley, MA: The Stone Center for Developmental Services and Studies, Wellesley College.

Moscarello, R. (1992). Victims of violence: Aspects of the victim-to-patient process in women. *Canadian Journal of Psychiatry, 37,* 497–501.

Nadelson, C. C. (1989). Professional issues for women. *Psychiatric Clinics of North America, 12*(1), 25–33.

Nicarthy, G., Gottlieb, N., & Coffman, S. (1993). *You don't have to take it! A woman's guide to confronting emotional abuse at work.* Seattle, WA: Seal Press.

Nieva, V. F. (1982). Equity for women at work: Models of change. In B. A. Gutek (Ed.), *Sex role stereotyping and affirmative action policy* (pp. 185–227). Los Angeles: Institute of Industrial Relations, University of California.

Notman, J. T., & Nadelson, C. C. (1980). Psychodynamic and life stage considerations in response to rape. In S. L. McCombie (Ed.), *The rape crisis intervention handbook: A guide for victim care* (pp. 131–142). New York: Plenum.

Oncale v. Sundowner Offshore Service. (1998).

Paetzold, R., & O'Leary-Kelly, A. (1996). The implications of U.S. Supreme Court and circuit court decisions for hostile environment sexual harassment cases. In

M. Stockdale (Ed.), *Sexual harassment in the workplace* (pp. 85–105). Thousand Oaks, CA: Sage.

Pagelow, M .D. (1992). Adult victims of domestic violence. *Journal of Interpersonal Violence, 7,* 87–120.

Paludi, M. A. (Ed.). (1990). *Ivory power: Sexual harassment on campus.* Albany: State University of New York Press.

Paludi, M. A., & Barickman, R. B. (1991). *Academic and workplace sexual harassment: A resource manual.* Albany: State University of New York Press.

Pendergrass, V. E., Kimmel, E., Joesting, J., Péterson, J., & Bush, E. (1976). Sex discrimination counseling. *American Psychology, 31,* 36–46.

Powell, G. N. (1999a). Introduction: Examining the intersection of gender and work. In G. N. Powell (Ed.), *Handbook of gender and work* (pp. 9–20). Thousand Oaks, CA: Sage.

Powell, G. N. (1999b). Reflections on the glass ceiling: Recent trends and future prospects. In G. Powell (Ed.), *Handbook of gender and work* (pp. 325–346). Thousand Oaks, CA: Sage.

Pryor, J. B. (1987). Sexual harassment proclivities in men. *Sex Roles, 17,* 269–290.

Pryor, J. B. (1992). *The social psychology of sexual harassment: Person and situation factors which give rise to sexual harassment.* Proceedings of the First National Congress on Sex and Power in the Workplace. Bellevue, WA.

Pryor, J. B. (1994, August). *The phenomenology of sexual harassment.* Paper presented at the Meeting of the American Psychological Association. Los Angeles, CA.

Pryor, J. B., LaVite, C. M., & Stoller, L. M. (1993). A social psychological analysis of sexual harassment: The person/situation interaction. *Journal of Vocational Behavior, 42,* 68–83.

Pryor, J., & Whelan, N. (1997). A typology of sexual harassment: Characteristics of harassers and the social circumstances under which sexual harassment occurs. In W. O'Donohue (Ed.), *Sexual harassment: Theory, research and treatment* (pp. 213–225). Boston: Allyn and Bacon.

Quina, K., & Carlson, N. L. (1989). *Rape, incest, and sexual harassment: A guide for helping survivors.* New York: Praeger.

Rabinowitz, V. C. (1990). Coping with sexual harassment. In M. A. Paludi (Ed.), *Ivory power: Sexual harassment on campus* (pp. 103–118). Albany: State University of New York Press.

Ragins, B. R., & Scandura, T. A. (1992). *Antecedents and consequences of sexual harassment.* Paper presented at the Society for Industrial/Organizational Psychology Conference. Montreal, Canada.

Ragins, B. R., & Sundstrom, E. (1989). Gender and power in organizations: A longitudinal perspective. *Psychological Bulletin, 19*(2), *105*(1), 51–58.

Raskin, J. G., & Struening, E. L. (1976). Life events, stress and illness. *Science, 194,* 1013–1020.

Renshaw, D. C., (1989). Treatment of sexual exploitation, rape, & incest. *Psychiatric Clinics of North America, 12,* 257–277.

Richman, J. A., Rospenda, K. M., Nawyn, S. J., Flaherty, J. A., Fenrich, M., Drum, L., & Johnson, T. P. (1999). Sexual harassment and generalized work place abuse among university employees: Prevalence and mental health correlates. *American Journal of Public Health, 89*(3), 358–363.

Riger, S. (1991). Gender dilemmas in sexual harassment policies and procedures. *American Psychology, 46,* 497–505.

Roeske, N. C., & Pleck, J. (1983). Towards the new psychology of women and men: III. Patterns of sex discrimination in education and employment. *Journal of Psychiatric Education, 7*(1), 23–31.

Robinson v. Jacksonville Shipyards. (MD. Fla. 1991). 760 F. Supp. 1486.

Rose, D. S. (1986), "Worse than death": Psychodynamics of rape victims and the need for psychotherapy. *American Journal of Psychiatry, 143,* 817–824.

Roos, P. A., & Gatta, M. L. (1999). The gender gap in earnings: Trends, explanations & prospects. In G. Powell (Ed.), *Handbook of gender and work* (pp. 95–124). Thousand Oaks, CA: Sage.

Roth, E. (1993). The civil rights history of "sex." *Ms, 3*(5), 84–85.

Rowe, M. P. (1977). *The Saturn rings phenomena: Microinequities and unequal opportunity in the American economy.* Proceeding of the WSF Conference on Women's Leadership and Authority. University of California, Santa Cruz.

Rowe, M. P. (1981). Dealing with sexual harassment. *Harvard Business Review, 59,* 42–46.

Rowe, M. P. (1990). Barriers to equality: The power of subtle discrimination to maintain unequal opportunity. *Employee Responsibilities and Rights Journal, 3,* 153–163.

Rowe, M. P. (1994). Personal communication.

Roy, P. (1974). Sex in the factory: Informal heterosexual relations between supervisors and work groups. In C. Bryant (Ed.), *Deviant behavior: Occupational and organizational bases.* Chicago: Rand-McNally.

Rush, R. R. (1993). A systemic commitment to women in the academy: Barriers, harassment prevent "being all we can be." *Journalism Educator, 48*(1), 71–79.

Russell, D. E. H. (1984). *Sexual exploitation: Rape, child sexual abuse, and workplace harassment.* Beverly Hills, CA: Sage.

Saal, F. (1996). Men's misperceptions of women's interpersonal behaviors and sexual harassment. In M. Stockdale (Ed.), *Sexual harassment in the workplace* (pp. 67–85). Thousand Oaks, CA: Sage.

Salisbury, J., Ginorio, A. B., Remick, H., & Stringer, D. M. (1986, Summer). Counseling victims of sexual harassment. *Psychotherapy, Theory, Research, Practice, Training, 23*(2), 316–324.

Sandroff, R. (1988, December). Sexual harassment in the Fortune 500. *Working Woman Magazine, 13,* 69–73.

Sanford, W. (Ed.). (1981). *Fighting sexual harassment: An advocacy handbook.* Boston: Allyson Publication/The Alliance Against Sexual Coercion.

Schafran, L. H. (1996). Sexual harassment cases in the courts, or therapy goes to war: Supporting a sexual harassment victim during litigation. In. D. K. Shrier (Ed.), *Sexual harassment in the workplace and academia* (pp. 133–152). Washington, DC: American Psychiatric Press.

Schneider, B. E. (1991). Put up and shut up: Workplace sexual assaults. *Gender and Society, 5,* 533–548.

Schneider, K. T., Swan, S., & Fitzgerald, L. F. (1997). Job related and psychological effects of sexual harassment in the workplace: Empirical evidence from two organizations. *Journal of Applied Psychology, 82*(3), 401–415.

Shrier, D. (1992). Sexual harassment and discrimination in the workplace: Therapeutic interventions and resources. *Family Violence and Sexual Assault Bulletin, 8,* 15–16.

Shrier, D. K. (Ed.). (1996). *Sexual harassment: Psychiatric issues.* Washington, DC: American Psychiatric Press.

Shrier D. K., & Hamilton, J. A. (1996) Therapeutic interventions and resources. In D. K. Shrier (Ed.) *Sexual harassment in the workplace and academia: Psychiatric issues* (pp. 95–112). Washington, DC: American Psychiatric Press.

Schwartz, R. A., & Prout, M. F. (1991). Integrative aproaches in the treatment of posttraumatic stress disorder. *Psychotherapy, 28,* 364–373.

Shengold, L. (1979). Child abuse and deprivation: Soul murder. *Journal of the American Psychoanalytical Association, 27,* 553–559.

Shotland, L. (1992). A theory of the causes of courtship rape: Part 2. *Journal of Social Issuses, 48,* 127–143.

Shullman, S., & Fitzgerald, L. (1985). *The development and validation of an objectively scored measure of sexual harassment.* Paper presented at the American Psychological Association. Los Angeles, CA.

Silverman, D. C., & Apfel, R. J. (1983) Caring for victims of rape. In C. C. Nadelson & D. B. Marcotte (Eds.), *Treatment interventions in human sexuality.* New York: Plenum.

Simon, R. I. (1996). The credible forensic psychiatric evaluation in sexual harassment litigation. *Psychiatric Annals, 26*(3), 139–148.

Stockdale, M. S. (Ed.). (1996). *Sexual harassment in the workplace.* Thousand Oaks, CA: Sage.

Stroh, L. A., & Reilly, A. H. (1997). Rekindling organizational loyalty: The impact of career mobility. *Journal of Career Development, 24*(1), 39–54.

Surrey, J. L. (1983). *Self-in-relation: A theory of women's development* (Working Paper No. 83-13). Wellesley, MA: Stone Center for Developmental Services and Studies, Wellesley College.

Sutherland, S. M, & Davidson, J. R. T. (1989). Pharmacotherapy for post-traumatic stress disorder. *Psychiatric Clinics of North America, 12,* 409–424.

Swim, J. K., Aiken, K. J., Hall, W. S., & Hunter, B. A. (1995). Sexism and racism: Old fashioned and modern prejudices. *Journal of Personality and Social Psychology, 68,* 199–214.

Tangri, S. S., Burt, M. R., & Johnson, L. B. (1982). Sexual harassment at work: Three explanatory models. *Journal of Social Issues, 38,* 33–54.

Taylor, S. E. (1983). Adjustment to threatening events: A theory of cognitive adaptation. *American Psychological, 38,* 1161–1173.

Terpstra, D. E., & Baker, D. D. (1986). Psychological and demographic correlates of perceptions of sexual harassment. *Genetic, Social and General Psychology Monographs, 112*(4), 459–478.

Terpstra, D. E., & Baker, D. D. (1987). A hierarchy of sexual harassment. *Journal of Psychology, 121,* 599–605.

Terpstra, D. E., & Baker, D. D. (1991). Sexual harassment at work: The psychosocial issues. In M. J. Davidson & J. Earnshaw (Eds.), *Vulnerable workers: Psychosocial and legal issues* (pp. 179–201). New York: John Wiley & Sons.

Thacker, R. A., & Gohman, S. F., (1996). Emotional and psychological consequences of sexual harassment: A descriptive study. *Journal of Psychology, 130*(4), 429–446.

Till, F. (1980). *Sexual harassment: A report on the sexual harassment of students.* Washington, DC: National Advisory Council on Women's Educational Programs.

Tomb, D. A. (Ed.). (1994). Post-traumatic stress disorder. *Psychiatric Clinics of North America, 17* (entire issue).

Touhey, J. E. (1974). Effects of addition of women professionals on ratings of occupational prestige and desirability. *Journal of Personality and Social Psychology, 29,* 86–89.

U.S. Department of labor, Bureau of Labor Statistics. (1998a). *Employment and Earnings, 45*(1), p. 163, table 2.

U.S. Department of Labor, Bureau of Labor Statistics. (1998b). *Employment and Earnings, 45*(9), p. 7, table A-2, p. 27, table A.

U.S. Merit Systems Protection Board. (1981). *Sexual harassment in the federal workplace: Is it a problem?* Washington, DC: U.S. Government Printing Office.

U.S. Merit Systems Protection Board. (1987). Sexual harassment in the federal government: An update. Washington, DC: U.S. Government Printing Office.

Van der Kolk, B. A., (1987). *Psychological trauma.* Washington, DC: American Psychiatric Press.

Van der Kolk, B. A., McFarlane, A. C., & Weisaeth, L. (Eds.). (1996). *Traumatic stress: The effects of overwhelming experience on mind, body and society.* New York: Guilford Press.

Van Roosmalen, E., & McDaniel, S. A. (1968). Sexual harassment in academia: A hazard to women's health. *Women and Health, 28*(2), 33–51.

Waldo, C. R., Berndahl, J. L., & Fitzgerald, L. E. (1998). Are men sexually harassed? If so, by whom? *Law and Human Behavior, 26*(2), 59–79.

Wilborn, S. H. (1991). Vulnerable workers in the United States: A psychological and legal perspective. In M. J. Davidson & J. Earnshaw (Eds.), *Vulnerable workers: Psychosocial and legal issues* (pp. 45–65). New York: John Wiley & Sons.

Wilson, J. P., & Raphael, B. (Eds.). (1993). *International handbook of traumatic stress syndromes.* New York: Plenum.

Women's Legal Defense Fund. (1988). *Sex discrimination in the workplace: A legal handbook.* Washington, DC: Women's Legal Defense Fund.

Wood, J. T (1992). Telling our stories: Narratives as a basis for theorizing sexual harassment. *Journal of Applied Communication Research, 20*(4), 349–362.

Yalom, I. (1975). *The theory and practice of group psychotherapy* (2nd ed.). New York: Basic Books.

Zalk, S. R. (1990). Men in the academy: A psychological profile of harassment. In M. A. Paludi (Ed.), *Ivory power: Sexual harassment on campus* (pp. 141–175). Albany: State University of New York Press.

Index